Lucille Beresford

In Excelsis
for School and Chapel

[SEVENTEENTH EDITION]

NEW YORK
THE CENTURY CO
1922

PREFACE.

HE selections in this book are mainly from "In Excelsis" (which is already in use in a large number of representative churches), with the addition of many beautiful Christmas and Easter carols and hymns for young children. It is based upon the conviction that the children and young people of the church can and should be taught to sing the noblest compositions which are used in the great congregation, and that substantially the same hymns and tunes should be employed in all the services of the church. Many of the melodies are exceedingly simple, and they are generally well within the compass of children's voices. The tunes are all from the best composers.

THE CENTURY CO.

New York City, January, 1900.

Contents

Index of First Lines.

ALPHABETICAL INDEX OF TUNES.

ix

x

Opening Sentences.

R. Farrant (1530 [?]—1580).

1 The *Lord* is in His | ho-ly | temple ‖ let all the *earth* keep | si-· lence be- | fore — | Him.—*Hab. ii. 20.*

2 O worship the *Lord* in the | beauty · of | holiness ‖ *fear* be- | fore Him | all the | earth.—*Ps. xcvi. 9.*

W. Russell (1777—1813).

3 Let the words of my mouth, and the medi*ta*tion | of my | heart ‖ be acceptable in Thy sight, O Lord my | strength and | my re- | deemer.—*Ps. xix. 14.*

4 O send out Thy light and Thy *truth* that | they may | lead me ‖ and bring me unto Thy *holy* | hill and | to Thy | dwelling.—*Ps. xliii. 3.*

5 This is the *day* which the | Lord hath | made ‖ we will re*joice* | and be | glad in | it. —*Ps. cxviii. 24.*

6 I was glad when they *said* | un-to | me ‖ Let us *go* into the | house — | of the | Lord.—*Ps. cxxii. 1.*
Pray for the *peace* | of Je- | rusalem ‖ *they* shall | prosper · that | love — | Thee.—*Ps. cxxii. 2.*

R. Langdon (1729—1803).

7 I will arise and *go* | to my | Father ‖ *and* | will say | un-to | Him ‖ Father, I have sinned against *heaven* and be- | fore — | Thee ‖ and am no more wor*thy* to be | call-ed | Thy — | son.— *Luke xv. 18, 19.*

8 From the rising of the sun even unto the going *down* | of the | same ‖ My *name* shall be | great a- | mong the | Gentiles ‖ and in every place incense shall be offered unto My *Name* and a | pure — | offering ‖ for My Name shall be great among the hea*then* | saith the | Lord of | hosts. — *Mal. i. 11.*

The Ten Commandments.

GOD spake all these words, saying, I am the Lord thy God, which have brought thee out of the land of Egypt, out of the house of bondage.

I.—Thou shalt have no other gods before Me.

II.—Thou shalt not make unto thee any graven image, or any likeness of any thing that is in heaven above, or that is in the earth beneath, or that is in the water under the earth: thou shalt not bow down thyself to them, nor serve them: for I the Lord thy God am a jealous God, visiting the iniquity of the fathers upon the children unto the third and fourth generation of them that hate Me ; and showing mercy unto thousands of them that love Me, and keep My commandments.

III. —Thou shalt not take the Name of the Lord thy God in vain ; for the Lord will not hold him guiltless that taketh His Name in vain.

IV.—Remember the Sabbath-day, to keep it holy. Six days shalt thou labor, and do all thy work: but the seventh day is the Sabbath of the Lord thy God ; in it thou shalt not do any work, thou, nor thy son, nor thy daughter, thy man-servant, nor thy maid-servant, nor thy cattle, nor thy stranger that is within thy gates ; for in six days the Lord made heaven and earth, the sea, and all that in them is, and rested the seventh day : wherefore the Lord blessed the Sabbath-day, and hallowed it.

V.—Honor thy father and thy mother: that thy days may be long upon the land which the Lord thy God giveth thee.

VI.—Thou shalt not kill.

VII.—Thou shalt not commit adultery.

VIII.—Thou shalt not steal.

IX.—Thou shalt not bear false witness against thy neighbor.

X.—Thou shalt not covet thy neighbor's house, thou shalt not covet thy neighbor's wife, nor his man-servant, nor his maid-servant, nor his ox, nor his ass, nor any thing that is thy neighbor's.

HEAR also what our Lord Jesus Christ saith: Thou shalt love the Lord thy God with all thy heart, and with all thy soul, and with all thy mind. This is the first and great commandment. And the second is like unto it: Thou shalt love thy neighbor as thyself. On these two commandments hang all the law and the prophets.

The Apostles' Creed.

I BELIEVE in GOD THE FATHER Almighty, Maker of heaven and earth :

And in JESUS CHRIST His only Son our Lord ; who was conceived by the Holy Ghost ; born of the Virgin Mary ; suffered under Pontius Pilate ; was crucified, dead, and buried ; He descended into hell ; the third day He rose again from the dead ; He ascended into heaven ; and sitteth on the right hand of God the Father Almighty ; from thence he shall come to judge the quick and the dead.

I believe in the HOLY GHOST ; the holy Catholic Church ; the Communion of Saints ; the Forgiveness of sins ; the Resurrection of the body ; and the Life everlasting. Amen.

Responses to the Commandments.

Ancient Chant

1—9 Lord, have *mercy up* - on us, and incline our *hearts* to............... keep this law.

10 Lord, have *mercy up* - on us, and write all these Thy laws in our }

hearts (*p*) we be - - - - - } seech...... Thee

C. F. GOUNOD (1818—1893).

After 9 Commandments.

Lord, have mer - cy up - on us, and in - cline our hearts to keep this law.

After the 10th Commandment.

Piu lento.

us, and write all these Thy laws in our hearts, we be - seech Thee.

p

The Lord's Prayer.

GREGORIAN.

1. { Our Father which art in *heaven*, | Hallowed | be Thy | name;
   { Thy kingdom come; Thy will be *done* on | earth · as it | is in | heaven;

2. { Give *us* this | day our | dai-ly | bread;
   { And forgive us our *debts*, as | we for- | give our | debtors;

3. { And lead us not into tempta*tion*, but de- | liv-er | us from | evil;
   { For Thine is the kingdom, and the power, and the glo*ry*, for- | ev-er. | A- — | men.

xiii

In Excelsis

For School and Chapel.

Glory to God in the highest.

I

SYNESIUS, Born cir. 375.
Tr. A. W. CHATFIELD, 1876.   "IN EXCELSIS GLORIA."   A. L. PEACE, 1890.

1. Glo - ry to God in the high - est Shall be our song to - day:
2. Glo - ry to God in the high - est Shall be our song to - day;
3. Glo - ry to God in the high - est Shall be our song to - day.

The song that woke the glo - rious morn, When Da - vid's great - er Son was born,
And while we with the an - gels sing, Gifts with the wise men let us bring
O, may we an un - bro - ken band A - round the throne of Je - sus stand,

Sung by a heav'n - ly host, and we Would join th'an - gel - ic com - pa - ny. A - men.
Un - to the Babe of Beth - le - hem, And of - fer our young hearts to Him.
And there with an - gels and the throng Of His re - deemed ones join the song.

1 E

Lord, we come before Thee now.

W. HAMMOND, 1745.   "ST. BEES."   J. B. DYKES, 1874.

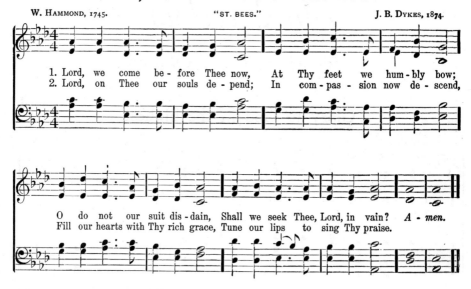

1. Lord, we come be-fore Thee now, At Thy feet we hum-bly bow;
2. Lord, on Thee our souls de-pend; In com-pas-sion now de-scend,

O do not our suit dis-dain, Shall we seek Thee, Lord, in vain? *A - men.*
Fill our hearts with Thy rich grace, Tune our lips to sing Thy praise.

3 In Thine own appointed way,
Now we seek Thee, here we stay;
Lord, we know not how to go,
Till a blessing Thou bestow.

4 Send some message from Thy word,
That may joy and peace afford;
Let Thy Spirit now impart
Full salvation to each heart.

5 Comfort those who weep and mourn,
Let the time of life return;
Those that are cast down lift up,
Strong in faith, and love, and hope.

6 Grant that those who seek may find
Thee a God sincere and kind;
Heal the sick, the captive free,
Let us all rejoice in Thee.

3

Come, Thou almighty King.

C. WESLEY, 1757.   "ITALIAN HYMN."   F. DE GIARDINI, 1769.

1. Come, Thou al-might-y King, Help us Thy name to sing, Help us to praise! Fa-ther all-
2. Come, Thou In-car-nate Word, Gird on Thy might-y sword, Our pray'r at-tend! Come, and Thy
3. Come, Ho-ly Com-fort-er, Thy sa-cred wit-ness bear, In this glad hour! Thou, who al-
4. To the great One in Three The highest prais-es be, Hence ev-er-more; His sovereign

Come, Thou almighty King.—*Concluded.*

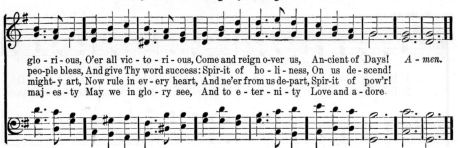

glo - ri - ous, O'er all vic - to - ri - ous, Come and reign o-ver us, An-cient of Days! A - men.
peo-ple bless, And give Thy word success: Spir-it of ho - li - ness, On us de - scend!
might-y art, Now rule in ev - ery heart, And ne'er from us de-part, Spir-it of pow'r!
maj - es - ty May we in glo - ry see, And to e - ter - ni - ty Love and a - dore.

Father, again in Jesus' name we meet.

4

L. E. G. WHITMORE, 1824.   "FELIX."   F. MENDELSSOHN (1809—1847).

1. Fa - ther, a - gain in Je - sus' name we meet, And bow in pen - i - tence be-
2. Oh, we would bless Thee for Thy cease-less care, And all Thy work from day to

neath Thy feet; A - gain to Thee our fee - ble voic - es raise, To sue for
day de - clare! Is not our life with hour - ly mer - cies crowned? Does not Thy

mer - cy, and to sing Thy praise. A - men.
arm en - cir - cle us a - round?

3 Alas! unworthy of Thy boundless love,
Too oft with careless feet from Thee we rove
But now, encouraged by Thy voice, we come,
Returning sinners, to a Father's home.

4 Oh, by that name which in all fulness dwells,
Oh, by that love which every love excels,
Oh, by that blood so freely shed for sin,
Open blest mercy's gate, and take us in!

5

Holy, holy, holy!

R. Heber, 1827.   "NICAEA."   J. B. Dykes, 1861.

1. Ho - ly, ho - ly, ho - ly! Lord God Al - might - y! Ear - ly in the
2. Ho - ly, ho - ly, ho - ly! all the saints a - dore Thee, Cast-ing down their

morn - ing our song shall rise to Thee; Ho - ly, ho - ly, ho - ly!
gold-en crowns a - round the glass - y sea, Cher - u - bim and ser - a - phim

mer - ci - ful and might - y! God in Three Per - sons, bless-ed Trin-i - ty! A - men.
fall-ing down be - fore Thee, Which wert and art and ev - er-more shalt be.

3 Holy, holy, holy! though the darkness hide Thee,
   Though the eye of sinful man Thy glory may not see,
   Only Thou art holy; there is none beside Thee,
   Perfect in power, in love and purity.

4 Holy, holy, holy! Lord God Almighty!
   All Thy works shall praise Thy name, in earth, and sky, and sea;
   Holy, holy, holy! merciful and mighty!
   God in Three Persons, blessèd Trinity!

Round the Lord in glory seated.

R. MANT, 1837. "FABEN." J. H. WILCOX, 1849.

1. Round the Lord in glo - ry seat - ed Cher - u - bim and ser - a - phim
2. Heav'n is still with glo - ry ring - ing, Earth takes up the an - gels' cry,
3. "Lord, Thy glo - ry fills the heav - en, Earth is with its ful - ness stored;

Filled His tem - ple and re - peat - ed Each to each th'al - ter - nate hymn:
"Ho - ly, ho - ly, ho - ly," sing - ing, "Lord of hosts, the Lord Most High!"
Un - to Thee be glo - ry giv - en, Ho - ly, ho - ly, ho - ly Lord!"

"Lord, Thy glo - ry fills the heav - en, Earth is with its ful - ness stored;
With His ser - aph train be - fore Him, With His ho - ly Church be - low,
Thus Thy glo - rious Name con - fess - ing, We a - dopt Thine an - gels' cry,

Un - to Thee be glo - ry giv - en, Ho - ly, ho - ly, ho - ly Lord!" A - men.
Thus con-spire we to a - dore Him, Bid we thus our an - them flow:
"Ho - ly, ho - ly, ho - ly!" bless - ing Thee, the Lord of hosts Most High.

7

Sing to the Lord a joyful song.

J. S. B. MONSELL, 1862. "JORDAN." J. BARNBY, 1872.

1. Sing to the Lord a joy-ful song, Lift up your hearts, your voic-es raise;
2. For life and love, for rest and food, For dai-ly help and night-ly care,
3. For strength to those who on Him wait, His truth to prove, His will to do,
4. For life be-low, with all its bliss, And for that life, more pure and high,

To us His gra-cious gifts be-long, To Him our songs of love and praise.
Sing to the Lord, for He is good, And praise His name, for it is fair.
Praise ye our God, for He is great; Trust in His name, for it is true.
That in-ner life which o-ver this Shall ev-er shine, and nev-er die,

Voices in Unison. *In harmony.*

For He is Lord of heav'n and earth, Whom an-gels serve, and saints a-dore,
For He is Lord, &c.
For He is Lord, &c.
Sing to the Lord, &c.

Voices in Unison. *In harmony.*

The Fa-ther, Son, and Ho-ly Ghost, To whom be praise for ev-er-more. A-men.

Crown Him with many crowns.

M. BRIDGES, 1848.   "DIADEMATA."   G. J. ELVEY, 1868.

1. Crown Him with ma - ny crowns, The Lamb up - on His throne;
2. Crown Him the Lord of love; Be - hold His hands and side,
3. Crown Him the Lord of peace, Whose pow'r a scep - tre sways
4. Crown Him the Lord of years, The po - ten - tate of time,

Hark! how the heav'n-ly an - them drowns All mu - sic but its own;
Rich wounds, yet vis - i - ble a - bove In beau - ty glo - ri - fied:
From pole to pole, that wars may cease, And all be pray'r and praise.
Cre - a - tor of the roll - ing spheres, In ef - fa - bly sub - lime.

A - wake, my soul, and sing Of Him who died for thee,
No an - gel in the sky Can ful - ly bear that sight,
His reign shall know no end, And round His pierc - ed feet
All hail, Re - deem - er, hail! For Thou hast died for me;

And hail Him as thy matchless King Thro' all e - ter - ni - ty. A - men.
But downward bends His wond'ring eye At mys - ter - ies so bright.
Fair flow'rs of Par - a - dise ex - tend Their fragrance ev - er sweet.
Thy praise shall nev - er, nev - er fail Throughout e - ter - ni - ty.

9

God Almighty, in Thy temple.

R. H. BAYNES, 1880. "ETON COLLEGE." J. BARNBY, 1885.

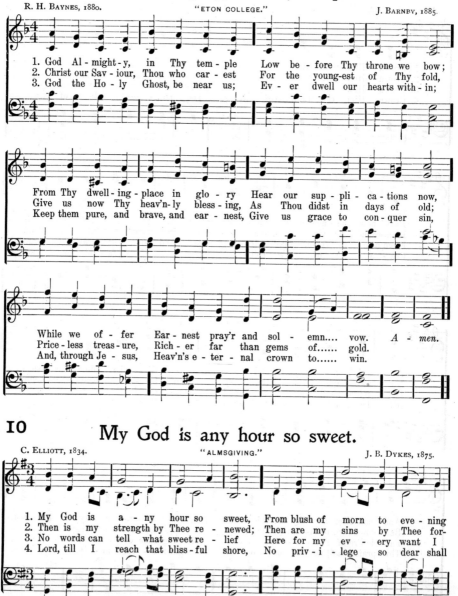

1. God Al - might - y, in Thy tem - ple Low be - fore Thy throne we bow;
2. Christ our Sav - iour, Thou who car - est For the young - est of Thy fold,
3. God the Ho - ly Ghost, be near us; Ev - er dwell our hearts with - in;

From Thy dwell - ing - place in glo - ry Hear our sup - pli - ca - tions now,
Give us now Thy heav'n - ly bless - ing, As Thou didst in days of old;
Keep them pure, and brave, and ear - nest, Give us grace to con - quer sin,

While we of - fer Ear - nest pray'r and sol - emn.... vow. A - men.
Price - less treas - ure, Rich - er far than gems of...... gold.
And, through Je - sus, Heav'n's e - ter - nal crown to...... win.

10

My God is any hour so sweet.

C. ELLIOTT, 1834. "ALMSGIVING." J. B. DYKES, 1875.

1. My God is a - ny hour so sweet, From blush of morn to eve - ning
2. Then is my strength by Thee re - newed; Then are my sins by Thee for -
3. No words can tell what sweet re - lief Here for my ev - ery want I
4. Lord, till I reach that bliss - ful shore, No priv - i - lege so dear shall

My God is any hour so sweet.—*Concluded.*

star,   As that which calls me   to..... Thy feet,   The hour of pray'r? A - men.
giv'n;   Then dost Thou cheer my   sol - i - tude   With hopes of heav'n.
find,   What strength for war - fare, balm for grief, What peace of mind.
be   As thus my in - most soul   to pour   In pray'r to Thee.

Lord, dismiss us with Thy blessing.

II

J. FAWCETT, 1773.   "ST. RAPHAEL."   E. J. HOPKINS, (1818—).

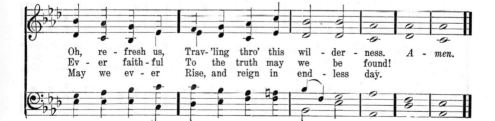

1. Lord, dis - miss us   with Thy bless - ing,   Fill our hearts with joy   and   peace;
2. Thanks we give and   ad - o - ra - tion   For Thy Gos - pel's joy ful - sound;
3. So, when-e'er the   sig - nal's giv - en   Us from earth to   call a - way,

Let us each, Thy love pos - sess - ing,   Tri - umph in   re - deem - ing grace;
May the fruits of Thy   sal - va - tion   In our hearts and lives   a - bound;
Borne on an - gels' wings to   heav - en,   Glad the sum - mons to   o - bey,

Oh,   re - fresh us,   Trav-'ling thro' this   wil - der - ness.   A - men.
Ev - er   faith - ful   To the truth may   we   be   found!
May   we   ev - er   Rise, and reign in   end - less   day.

12 Saviour, again to Thy dear name.

J. Ellerton, 1866. "BENEDICTION." (ELLERS.) E. J. Hopkins, 1867.

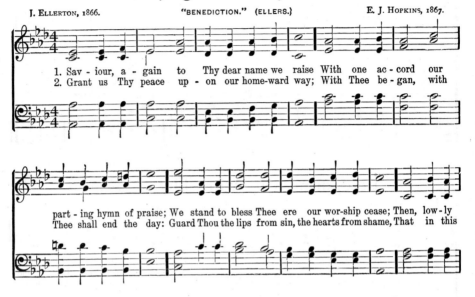

1. Sav - iour, a - gain to Thy dear name we raise With one ac - cord our
2. Grant us Thy peace up - on our home-ward way; With Thee be - gan, with

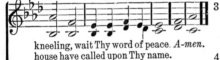

part - ing hymn of praise; We stand to bless Thee ere our wor-ship cease; Then, low-ly
Thee shall end the day: Guard Thou the lips from sin, the hearts from shame, That in this

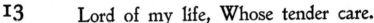

kneeling, wait Thy word of peace. A-men.
house have called upon Thy name.

3 Grant us Thy peace, Lord, through the coming night;
Turn Thou for us its darknesss into light;
From harm and danger keep Thy children free,
For dark and light are both alike to Thee.

4 Grant us Thy peace throughout our earthly life,
Our balm in sorrow, and our stay in strife;
Then, when Thy voice shall bid our conflict cease,
Call us, O Lord, to Thine eternal peace.

13 Lord of my life, Whose tender care.

Chelsea, 1838. "WESSEX." E. J. Hopkins, (1818—).

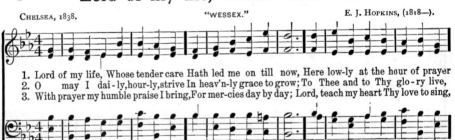

1. Lord of my life, Whose tender care Hath led me on till now, Here low-ly at the hour of prayer
2. O may I dai-ly,hour-ly,strive In heav'n-ly grace to grow; To Thee and to Thy glo-ry live,
3. With prayer my humble praise I bring,For mer-cies day by day; Lord, teach my heart Thy love to sing,

Lord of My Life, Whose tender care.—*Concluded.*

Be-fore Thy throne I bow; I bless Thy gracious hand, and pray Forgiveness for an-oth-er day. *A-men.*
Dead else to all below; Tread in the path my Saviour trod, Though thorny, yet the path to God!
Lord, teach me how to pray! All that I have, I am, to Thee I of-fer thro' e - ter-ni - ty.

Sweet Saviour, bless us ere we go. 14

F. W. FABER, 1852.   "ST. MATTHIAS."   W. H. MONK, 1861.

1. Sweet Sav - iour, bless us ere we go; Thy word in - to our minds in - stil;
2. The day is gone, its hours have run, And Thou hast tak - en count of all,
3. For all we love, the poor, the sad, The sin - ful, un - to Thee we call;
4. Sweet Sav - iour, bless us; night is come; Thro' night and dark - ness near us be;

And make our luke - warm hearts to glow With low - ly love and fer - vent will.
The scan - ty tri - umphs grace hath won, The bro - ken vow, the fre - quent fall.
O let Thy mer - cy make us glad; Thou art our Sav - iour, and our all.
Good an - gels watch a - bout our home, And we are one day near - er Thee.

Thro' life's long day and death's dark night, O gen - tle Je - sus, be our light. *A-men.*

15

Still, still with Thee.

Mrs. H. B. Stowe, 1855, Ab.　　　　　"WINDSOR."　　　　　J. Barnby, (1838—1896).

1. Still, still with Thee, when pur - ple morn - ing break - eth, When the bird
2. A - lone with Thee, a - mid the mys - tic shad - ows, The sol - emn

wak - eth, and the shad-ows flee; Fair - er than morn - ing, love-lier than the
hush of na - ture new - ly born; A - lone with Thee, in breathless ad - o -

the sweet
the calm

day - light, Dawns the sweet con - scious-ness, I am with Thee! *A-men.*
ra - tion, In the calm dew and fresh-ness of the morn.

the sweet
the calm

3 When sinks the soul, subdued by toil, to slumber,
　Its closing eye looks up to Thee in prayer;
　Sweet the repose beneath Thy wings o'ershading,
　But sweeter still, to wake and find Thee there.

4 So shall it be at last, in that bright morning,
　When the soul waketh, and life's shadows flee;
　Oh, in that hour, fairer than daylight dawning,
　Shall rise the glorious thought, I am with Thee!

When morning gilds the skies.

German, 1828. Tr. E. Caswall, 1854. "LAUDES DOMINI." J. Barnby, 1868.

1. When morn - ing gilds the skies, My heart a - wak - ing cries
2. When sleep her balm de - nies, My si - lent spir - it sighs,
3. Does sad - ness fill my mind, A sol - ace here I find,
4. The night be - comes as day, When from the heart we say,

May Je - sus Christ be praised! A - like at work and pray'r,
May Je - sus Christ be praised! When e - vil thoughts mo - lest,
May Je - sus Christ be praised! Or fades my earth - ly bliss,
May Je - sus Christ be praised! The pow'rs of dark - ness fear,

To Je - sus I re - pair; May Je - sus Christ be praised! A - men.
With this I shield my breast, May Je - sus Christ be praised!
My com - fort still is this, May Je - sus Christ be praised!
When this sweet chant they hear, May Je - sus Christ be praised!

5 In heaven's eternal bliss
 The loveliest strain is this,
  May Jesus Christ be praised!
 Let earth, and sea, and sky
 From depth to height reply,
  May Jesus Christ be praised!

6 Be this, while life is mine,
 My canticle divine,
  May Jesus Christ be praised!
 Be this the eternal song
 Through ages all along,
  May Jesus Christ be praised!

17

Every morning mercies new.

G. PHILLIMORE, 1863.　　　"KELSO."　　　E. J. HOPKINS, 1872.

1. Ev - 'ry morn - ing mer - cies new　Fall as fresh as morn - ing dew;
2. Still the great - ness of Thy love　Dai - ly doth our sins re - move;

Ev - 'ry morn - ing let us pay　Trib - ute with the ear - ly day;
Dai - ly, far as east from west,　Lifts the bur - den from the breast;

For Thy mer - cies, Lord, are sure,　Thy com - pas - sion doth en - dure.　A - men.
Gives unbought, to those who pray,　Strength to stand in e - vil day.

3　Let our prayers each morn prevail,
　　That these gifts may never fail;
　　And, as we confess the sin
　　And the tempter's power within,
　　Feed us with the Bread of Life,
　　Fit us for our daily strife.

4　As the morning light returns,
　　As the sun with splendor burns,
　　Teach us still to turn to Thee,
　　Ever blessèd Trinity,
　　With our hands our hearts to raise,
　　In unfailing prayer and praise.

Now, when the dusky shades of night.

Anon.   "MORNING PRAISE."   J. Stainer, 1872.

1. Now, when the dusk - y shades of night, re - treat - ing Be - fore the
2. To Thee, whose word, the fount of life un - seal - ing, When hill and
3. Look from the height of heav'n and send to cheer us Thy light and

sun's red ban - ner, swift - ly flee; Now when the ter - rors of the dark are
dale in thick-est dark - ness lay, A - woke bright rays a - cross the dim earth
truth, and guide us on - ward still; Still let Thy mer - cy, as of old, be

fleet - ing, O Lord, we lift our thank - ful hearts to Thee. A - men.
steal - ing, And bade the eve and morn com - plete the day.
near us, And lead us safe - ly to Thy ho - ly hill.

4 So, when the morn of endless light is waking,
    And shades of evil from its splendors flee,
    Safe may we rise, this earth's dark vale forsaking,
    Through all the long bright day to dwell with Thee.

5 Be this by Thee, O God thrice holy, granted,
    O Father, Son, and Spirit, ever blest;
    Whose glory by the heaven and earth is chanted,
    Whose name by men and angels is confest.

19

New every morning is the love.

J. KEBLE, 1827.　　　"MELCOMBE."　　　S. WEBBE (1740—1816).

1. New ev - ery morn-ing is the love Our wak'ning and up - ris - ing prove;
2. New mer - cies, each re - turn-ing day, Hov - er a - round us while we pray;

Thro' sleep and darkness safe - ly brought, Re-stor'd to life, and pow'r and tho't. A - men.
New per - ils past, new sins for - giv'n, New tho'ts of God, new hopes of heav'n.

3 If on our daily course our mind
Be set to hallow all we find,
New treasures still, of countless price,
God will provide for sacrifice.

4 Old friends, old scenes, will lovelier be,
As more of heaven in each we see;
Some softening gleam of love and prayer
Shall dawn on every cross and care.

5 The trivial round, the common task,
Will furnish all we ought to ask—
Room to deny ourselves, a road
To bring us daily nearer God.

6 Only, O Lord, in Thy dear love,
Fit us for perfect rest above,
And help us this and every day,
To live more nearly as we pray.

20

My soul, awake! thy rest forsake.

J. E. LIVOCK, 1880.　　　"BRACONDALE."　　　J. BOOTH (1852—).

1. My soul, a - wake! thy rest for - sake, And greet the morn - ing light;
2. With cour - age drest, strong-heart - ed, blest, Ful - fil thy work a - broad;
3. A - mid the strife of dai - ly life, A - mid its noon - tide heat,
4. In lib - er - ty of ho - ly glee, Ac - cept thy child - hood's part,

My soul, awake! thy rest forsake.—*Concluded.*

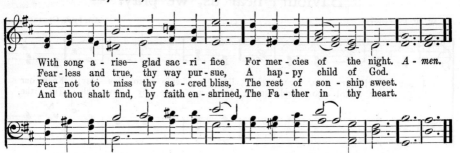

With song a - rise— glad sac - ri - fice For mer - cies of the night. *A - men.*
Fear - less and true, thy way pur - sue, A hap - py child of God.
Fear not to miss thy sa - cred bliss, The rest of son - ship sweet.
And thou shalt find, by faith en - shrined, The Fa - ther in thy heart.

5 Oh, blessèd rest! With such a guest
   Life's duty grows divine,
  Dross becomes gold, and, as of old,
   The water turns to wine.

6 Eternal praise to Thee we raise,
   Who deign'st with men to dwell;
  Great Word of God, Jehovah! Lord!
   Adored Emmanuel!

Come, my soul, thou must be waking. 2I

F. R. L. von Canitz, 1699.
Tr. H. J. Buckoll, 1848.
       "STAINER."
             J. Stainer, 1872.

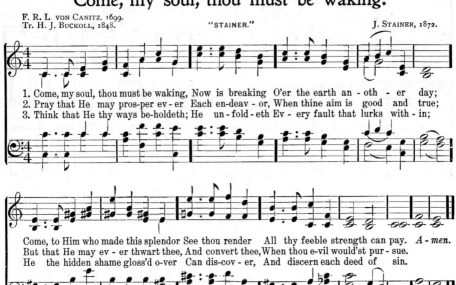

1. Come, my soul, thou must be waking, Now is breaking O'er the earth an - oth - er day;
2. Pray that He may pros-per ev - er Each en-deav - or, When thine aim is good and true;
3. Think that He thy ways be-holdeth; He un-fold-eth Ev - ery fault that lurks with - in;

Come, to Him who made this splendor See thou render All thy feeble strength can pay. *A - men.*
But that He may ev - er thwart thee, And convert thee, When thou e-vil would'st pur - sue.
He the hidden shame gloss'd o - ver Can dis-cov - er, And discern each deed of sin.

4 Mayest thou on life's last morrow,
  Free from sorrow,
   Pass away in slumber sweet;
  And, released from death's dark sadness,
  Rise in gladness,
   That far brighter Sun to greet.

5 Only God's free gifts abuse not,
  Light refuse not,
   But His Spirit's voice obey;
  Thou with Him shalt dwell, beholding
  Light enfolding
   All things in unclouded day.

2 E

22

Saviour! hear us, we pray.

W. W. Ellsworth.   "LUCY."   Arr. by A. Cortada.

1. Sav - iour! hear us, we pray, Keep us safe thro' this day; Keep our
2. Be our Guard - ian and Guide; May we walk by Thy side Till the

lives free from sin, And our hearts pure with - in. Je - sus, Lord! hear our pray'r, May we
evening shades fall O - ver us— o - ver all.

Refrain.

rest in Thy care, Je - sus, Lord! hear our pray'r, May we rest in Thy care. *A - men.*

23

Father of love and power.

G. Rawson, (1807—).   "FIAT LUX."   J. B. Dykes.

1. Fa - ther of love and pow'r, Guard Thou our eve-ning hour, Shield with Thy might! For all Thy
2. Je - sus, Em - man - u - el, Come in Thy love to dwell In hearts con - trite; For ma - ny
3. Spir - it of truth and love, Life - giv-ing, ho - ly Dove, Shed forth Thy light; Heal ev - ery

Father of love and power.—*Concluded.*

care this day Our grateful thanks we pay, And to our Fa-ther pray: Bless us to-night. *A-men.*
sins we grieve, But we Thy grace re-ceive, And on Thy word believe: Bless us to-night.
sinners' smart, Still every throbbing heart, And Thine own peace impart: Bless us to-night.

God, that madest earth and heaven. 24

R. HEBER, 1827, and
R. WHATELEY, 1855.

"HARRIETTELLE."

H. G. B. HUNT.

1. God, that mad-est earth and heav-en, Dark-ness and light, Who the day for
2. Guard us wak-ing, guard us sleep-ing, And, when we die, May we in Thy

toil hast giv-en, For rest the night, May Thine an-gel-guards de-fend us, Slumber sweet Thy
mighty keeping, All peace-ful lie. When the last dread call shall wake us, Do not Thou, our

mer-cy send us, Ho-ly dreams and hopes at-tend us, This live-long night. A - - men.
God, for-sake us, But to reign in glo-ry take us With Thee on high.

25

Softly now the light of day.

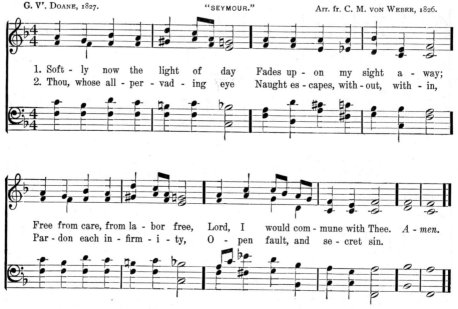

G. V^t, Doane, 1827.   "SEYMOUR."   Arr. fr. C. M. von Weber, 1826.

1. Soft - ly now the light of day Fades up - on my sight a - way;
2. Thou, whose all - per - vad - ing eye Naught es - capes, with - out, with - in,

Free from care, from la - bor free, Lord, I would com - mune with Thee. A - *men.*
Par - don each in - firm - i - ty, O - pen fault, and se - cret sin.

3 Soon, for me, the light of day
    Shall for ever pass away;
  Then, from sin and sorrow free,
    Take me, Lord, to dwell with Thee.

4 Thou who, sinless, yet hast known
    All of man's infirmity,
  Then, from Thine eternal throne,
    Jesus, look with pitying eye.

26

The sun is sinking fast.

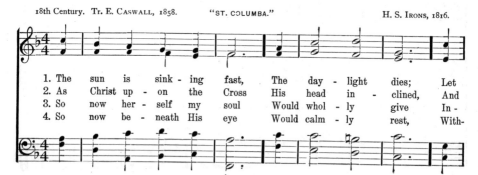

18th Century. Tr. E. Caswall, 1858.   "ST. COLUMBA."   H. S. Irons, 1816.

1. The sun is sink - ing fast, The day - light dies; Let
2. As Christ up - on the Cross His head in - clined, And
3. So now her - self my soul Would whol - ly give In -
4. So now be - neath His eye Would calm - ly rest, With-

The sun is sinking fast.—*Concluded.*

love a - wake, and pay Her eve - ning sac - ri - fice. A - men.
to His Fa - ther's hands His part - ing soul re - signed.
to His sa - cred charge, In whom all spir - its live;
out a wish or thought A - bid - ing in the breast,

5 Save that His will be done,
   Whate'er betide—
   Dead to herself, and dead
   In Him to all beside.

6 Thus would I live: yet now
   Not I, but He,

In all His power and love,
Henceforth alive in me.

7 One sacred Trinity,
   One Lord divine,
   May I be ever His,
   And He for ever mine.

Holy Father, cheer our way. 27

R. H. Robinson, 1869.   "VESPERI LUX."   J. B. Dykes (1823—1876).

1. Ho - ly Fa - ther, cheer our way With Thy love's per - pet - ual ray;
2. Ho - ly Sav - iour, calm our fears, When earth's brightness dis - ap - pears;
3. Ho - ly Spir - it, be Thou nigh When in mor - tal pains we lie;
4. Ho - ly, bless - ed Trin - i - ty, Dark - ness is not dark to Thee;

Grant us ev - 'ry clos - ing day Light at eve - ning - time. A - men.
Grant us in our lat - er years Light at eve - ning - time.
Grant us, as we come to die, Light at eve - ning - time.
Those Thou keep-est al - ways see Light at eve - ning - time.

28

The radiant morn hath passed away.

G. Thring, 1864.   "WOODTHORPE."   J. Adcock.

1. The ra - diant morn hath pass'd a - way, And spent too soon her
2. Our life is but a fad - ing dawn; Its glo - rious noon how
3. O by Thy soul - in - spir - ing grace, Up - lift our hearts to

gold - en store; The shad-ows of de - part - ing day Creep on once more. A-men.
quick - ly past! Lead us, O Christ, when all is gone, Safe home at last!
realms on high; Help us to look to that bright place Be - yond the sky;

4 Where light and life and joy and peace
    In undivided empire reign,
And thronging angels never cease
    Their deathless strain;—

5 Where saints are cloth'd in spotless white,
    And evening shadows never fall;
Where Thou, eternal Light of light,
    Art Lord of all'

SECOND TUNE.

"RADIANT MORN."   C. F. Gounod, 1872.

1. The ra - diant morn hath pass'd a - way And spent too soon her gold - en store;

The radiant morn hath passed away.—*Concluded.*

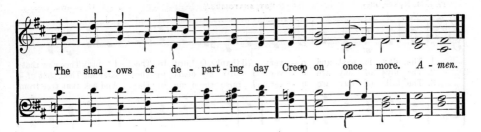

The shad-ows of de-part-ing day Creep on once more. A - men.

Our day of praise is done.

29

J. ELLERTON, 1867.   "SCHUMANN." (HEATH.)   Arr. fr. R. SCHUMANN (1810—1856).

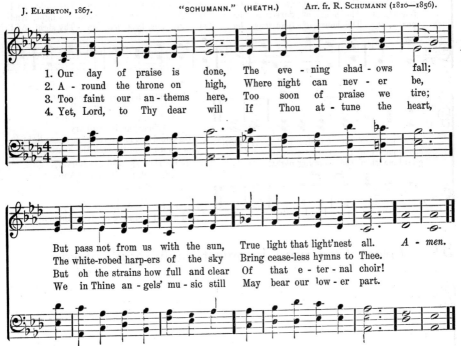

1. Our day of praise is done, The eve-ning shad-ows fall;
2. A-round the throne on high, Where night can nev-er be,
3. Too faint our an-thems here, Too soon of praise we tire;
4. Yet, Lord, to Thy dear will If Thou at-tune the heart,

But pass not from us with the sun, True light that light'nest all. A - men.
The white-robed harp-ers of the sky Bring cease-less hymns to Thee.
But oh the strains how full and clear Of that e-ter-nal choir!
We in Thine an-gels' mu-sic still May bear our low-er part.

5 'T is Thine each soul to calm,
　　Each wayward thought reclaim
And make our life a daily psalm
　　Of glory to Thy name.

6 A little while, and then
　　Shall come the glorious end;
And songs of angels and of men
　　In perfect praise shall blend.

30

The day is past and over.

ANATOLIUS, 800.
Tr. J. M. NEALE, 1853.

"ST. ANATOLIUS."

A. H. BROWN, 1862.

1. The day is past and o - ver; All thanks, O Lord, to Thee! I pray Thee now that
2. The joys of day are o - ver. I lift my heart to Thee, And ask Thee, that of -
3. The toils of day are o - ver. I raise the hymn to Thee, And ask that free from

sin - less The hours of dark may be. O Je - sus, keep me in Thy sight And
fence-less The hours of dark may be. O Je - sus, make their dark-ness light, And
per - il The hours of fear may be. O Je - sus, keep me in Thy sight, And

save me thro' the com-ing night! A - men.
save me thro' the com-ing night!
guard me thro' the com-ing night!

4 Lighten mine eyes, O Saviour,
　Or sleep in death shall I,
And he, my wakeful tempter,
　Triumphantly shall cry
"He could not make their darkness light,
Nor guard them through the hours of night."

5 Be Thou my soul's preserver,
　O God, for Thou dost know
How many are the perils
　Through which I have to go.
Lover of men, oh, hear my call,
And guard and save me from them all!

31

Great God who knowest each man's need.

E. TENNYSON.

"ABENDS."

H. S. OAKELEY, 1873.

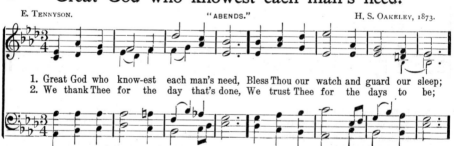

1. Great God who know-est each man's need, Bless Thou our watch and guard our sleep;
2. We thank Thee for the day that's done, We trust Thee for the days to be;

Great God who knowest each man's need.—*Concluded.*

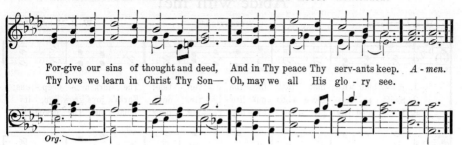

For-give our sins of thought and deed, And in Thy peace Thy serv-ants keep. A - men.
Thy love we learn in Christ Thy Son— Oh, may we all His glo - ry see.

Org.

Sun of my soul, Thou Saviour dear. 32

J. KEBLE, 1820.　　　　　　"HURSLEY."　　　　　P. RITTER, 1792.
　　　　　　　　　　　　　　　　　　Arr. by W. H. MONK, 1861.

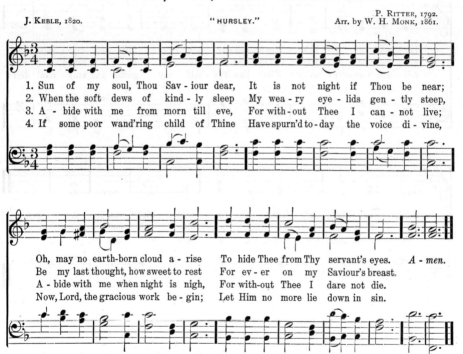

1. Sun of my soul, Thou Sav - iour dear, It is not night if Thou be near;
2. When the soft dews of kind - ly sleep My wea - ry eye - lids gen - tly steep,
3. A - bide with me from morn till eve, For with-out Thee I can - not live;
4. If some poor wand'ring child of Thine Have spurn'd to-day the voice di - vine,

Oh, may no earth-born cloud a - rise To hide Thee from Thy servant's eyes. A - men.
Be my last thought, how sweet to rest For ev - er on my Saviour's breast.
A - bide with me when night is nigh, For with-out Thee I dare not die.
Now, Lord, the gracious work be - gin; Let Him no more lie down in sin.

5 Watch by the sick; enrich the poor
　With blessings from Thy boundless store;
　Be every mourner's sleep to-night,
　Like infant's slumbers, pure and light.

6 Come near and bless us when we wake,
　Ere through the world our way we take,
　Till in the ocean of Thy love
　We lose ourselves in heaven above

33

Abide with me!

H. F. LYTE, 1847.   "EVENTIDE."   W. H. MONK, 1861.

1. A - bide with me: fast falls the e - ven - tide; The dark-ness deep - ens;
2. Swift to its close ebbs out life's lit - tle day; Earth's joys grow dim, its
3. I need Thy pres - ence ev - ery pass-ing hour: What but Thy grace can

Lord, with me a - bide: When oth - er help - ers fail, and com - forts flee,
glo - ries pass a - way; Change and de - cay in all a - round I see:
foil the tempt-er's pow'r? Who like Thy - self my guide and stay can be?

Help of the help - less, oh, a - bide with me. A - men.
O Thou who chang - est not, a - bide with me!
Through cloud and sun - shine, oh, a - bide with me!

4 I fear no foe, with Thee at hand to bless;
  Ills have no weight, and tears no bitterness;
  Where is death's sting? where, grave, thy victory?
  I triumph still, if Thou abide with me.

5 Hold Thou Thy cross before my closing eyes;
  Shine through the gloom, and point me to the skies.
  Heaven's morning breaks, and earth's vain shadows flee—
  In life, in death, O Lord, abide with me!

Now God be with us.

Bohemian Brethren, 1530.
Tr. C. Winkworth, 1858. Abr.   "NIGHTFALL."   J. Barnby, 1872.

1. Now God be with us, for the night is clos - ing; The light and
2. Let e - vil thoughts and spir - its flee be - fore us; Till morn - ing
3. Let ho - ly thoughts be ours when sleep o'er-takes us; Our ear - liest

dark - ness are of His dis - pos - ing, And 'neath His shad - ow
com - eth, watch, O Mas - ter, o'er us; In soul and bod - y
thoughts be Thine when morn- ing wakes us. All sick and mourn - ers

Slower.

here to rest we yield us, For He will shield... us. A - men.
Thou from harm de - fend us, Thine an - gels send..... us.
we to Thee com- mend them, Do Thou be - friend... them.

4 We have no refuge, none on earth to aid us
But Thee, O Father, who Thine own hast made us.
Keep us in life; forgive our sins; deliver
Us now and ever.

5 Praise be to Thee through Jesus our salvation,
God, Three in One, the ruler of creation,
High throned, o'er all Thine eye of mercy casting,
Lord everlasting.

35

The day is gently sinking to a close.

C. WORDSWORTH, 1863.   "NACHTLIED."   H. SMART, 1872.

1. The day is gen-tly sink-ing to a close,.... Faint-er and yet more faint the
2. Our changeful lives are ebb-ing to an end;.... On-ward to dark-ness and to
3. Thou, Who in dark-ness walk-ing didst ap-pear.... Up-on the waves, and Thy dis-
4. The wea-ry world is mould'ring to de-cay,.... Its glo-ries wane, its pa-geants

sun-light glows. O bright-ness of...... Thy Fa-ther's glo-ry, Thou E-ter-nal
death we tend; O conqueror of...... the grave, be Thou our guide, Be Thou our
ci-ples cheer, Come, Lord, in lone-some days, when storms as-sail, And earth-ly
fade a-way; In that last sun-set when the stars shall fall, May we a-

light of light, be with us now: Where Thou art pres-ent, dark-ness can-not
light in death's dark e-ven-tide: Then in our mor-tal hour will be no
hopes and hu-man suc-cors fail: When all is dark may we be-hold Thee
rise a-wak-ened by Thy call, With Thee, O Lord, for ev-er to a-

be,...... Mid-night is glo-rious noon, O Lord, with Thee. A-men.
gloom,.. No sting in death, no ter-ror in the tomb.
nigh.... And hear Thy voice, "Fear not, for it is I."
bide..... In that blest day which has no e-ven-tide.

The shadows of the evening hours.

A. A. Procter, 1858. Abr. "ST. LEONARD." H. Hiles, 1867.

1. The shad-ows of the eve-ning hours Fall from the dark-'ning sky;
2. The sor-rows of Thy serv-ants, Lord, Oh, do not Thou de-spise,
3. Slow-ly the rays of day-light fade: So fade with-in our heart
4. Let peace, O Lord, Thy peace, O God, Up-on our souls de-scend;

Up-on the fra-grance of the flow'rs The dews of eve-ning lie.
But let the in-cense of our pray'rs Be-fore Thy mer-cy rise.
The hopes in earth-ly love and joy, That one by one de-part.
From mid-night fears, and per-ils, Thou Our trem-bling hearts de-fend.

Be-fore Thy throne, O Lord of heav'n, We kneel at close of day;
The bright-ness of the com-ing night Up-on the dark-ness rolls;
Slow-ly the bright stars, one by one, With-in the heav-ens shine:
Give us a res-pite from our toil; Calm and sub-due our woes;

Look on Thy chil-dren from on high, And hear us while we pray. A - men.
With hopes of fu-ture glo-ry chase The shad-ows from our souls.
Give us, O Lord, fresh hopes in heav'n, And trust in things di-vine.
Thro' the long day we la-bor, Lord, Oh, give us now re-pose.

37

Now the day is over.

Rev. Sabine Baring-Gould, 1865.   "LYNDHURST."   Anon.

1. Now the day is o - ver, Night is draw-ing nigh, Shad-ows of the eve - ning Steal a - cross the sky. Now the dark-ness gath - ers, Stars be - gin to peep; Birds, and beasts, and flow - ers Soon will be a - sleep. A - men.

2. Je - sus, give the wea - ry Calm and sweet re - pose; With Thy ten-d'rest bless - ing May mine eye - lids close. Grant to lit - tle chil - dren Vi - sions bright of Thee; Guard the sail - ors, toss - ing On the deep blue sea.

3. Com - fort ev - ery suf - f'rer Watch-ing late in pain; Those who plan some e - vil From their sin re - strain. Thro' the long night watch - es May Thine an - gels spread Their white wings a - bove me, Watch-ing round my bed.

4. When the morn-ing wak - ens, Then may I a - rise Pure, and fresh, and sin - less In Thy ho - ly eyes. Glo - ry to the Fa - ther, Glo - ry to the Son, And to Thee, blest Spir - it, Whilst all a - ges run.

SECOND TUNE.

"TWILIGHT."   J. Barnby, 1868.

1. Now the day is o - ver, Night is draw - ing nigh;......

Now the day is over.—*Concluded.*

Shad-ows of the eve-ning Steal a-cross the sky. A-men.

eve-ning steal a - cross the sky;

Thro' the day Thy love has spared us. 38

"GUNTHER." J. BARNBY, 1872.

1. Thro' the day Thy love has spared us, Now we lay us down to rest;.....
2. Pil - grims here on earth, and stran - gers, Dwell-ing in the midst of foes,.....

Thro' the si - lent watch-es guard us, Let no foe our peace mo - lest;
Us and ours pre-serve from dan - gers; In Thine arms may we re - pose,

Je - sus, Thou our guar-dian be, Sweet it is to trust in Thee. A - men.
And, when life's short day is past, Rest with Thee in heav'n at last.

39 Fading, still fading, the last beam is shining.

ANON, 1830.   "SALVATION."   ANON.

1. Fad - ing, still fad - ing, the last beam is shining; Fa - ther in Heav - en, the day is de - clining. Safe - ty and in - no - cence fly with the light, Tempt - a - tion and dan - ger walk forth with the night. From the fall of the shade till the morning bells chime Shield me from dan - ger, save me from crime.

2. Fa - ther in Heav - en, oh, hear when we call; Hear, for Christ's sake, who is Sav - iour of all. Fee - ble and faint - ing, we trust in Thy might; In doubt - ing and dark - ness, Thy love be our light. Let us sleep on Thy breast when the night - ta - per burns, Wake in Thy arms when morn - ing re - turns.

Refrain.

Fa - ther, have mer - cy, Fa - ther, have mer - cy, Fa - ther, have mer - cy, thro' Je - sus Christ our Lord. A - men.

Day is dying in the west.

MARY A. LATHBURY, 1880.　　　"CHAUTAUQUA."　　　W. F. SHERWIN, 1877.

1. Day is dy - ing in the west; Heav'n is touch - ing earth with rest;
2. Lord of life, be - neath the dome Of the U - ni - verse, Thy home,

Wait and wor - ship while the night Sets her eve - ning lamps a - light
Gath - er us who seek Thy face To the fold of Thy em - brace,

Refrain.

Thro' all the sky....... } Ho - ly, ho - ly, ho - ly
For Thou art nigh...... }

Lord God of Hosts!... Heav'n and earth are full of Thee!

cres.

Heav'n and earth are prais - ing Thee, O Lord most high!... A - men.

3 E

41

Jesus, we love to meet on this Thy holy Day.

Mrs. E. R. Parson, 1836. "BEECHCROFT." T. G. Reed, 1880?

1. Je - sus, we love to meet on this Thy ho - ly Day;...
2. We dare not tri - fle now on this Thy ho - ly Day;...
3. We list - en to Thy Word on this Thy ho - ly Day;...

We wor - ship 'round Thy seat on this Thy ho - ly Day.
In si - lent awe we bow on this Thy ho - ly Day.
Bless all that we have heard on this Thy ho - ly Day.

Thou ten - der, heav'n - ly Friend, to Thee our pray'rs as - cend,
Check ev - ery wan - d'ring thought, and let us all be taught
Go with us when we part, and to each youth - ful heart

Jesus, we love to meet on this Thy holy Day.—*Concluded.*

O'er our young spir - its bend, on this Thy ho - ly Day. A - men.
To serve Thee as we ought, on this Thy ho - ly Day.
Thy sav - ing grace im - part on this Thy ho - ly Day.

Lord, this day Thy children meet.

42

W. W. How, 1854.   "HARDACRE."   G. A. Hardacre, 1867.

1. Lord, this day Thy chil - dren meet   In Thy courts with will - ing feet;
2. Not a - lone the day of rest   With Thy wor - ship shall be blest:
3. Help us un - to Thee to pray,   Hal - low - ing our hap - py day;
4. All our pleas-ures here be - low,   Sav - iour, from Thy mer - cy flow:
5. Make, O Lord, our child-hood shine   With all low - ly grace, like Thine:

Un - to Thee this day they raise   Grate-ful hearts in hymns of praise. A - men.
In our pleas-ure and our glee,   Lord, we would re - mem - ber Thee.
From Thy pres-ence thus to win   Hearts all pure, and free from sin.
But if earth has joys like this,   What shall be our heav'n-ly bliss!
Then thro' all e - ter - ni - ty   We shall live in heav'n with Thee.

43

The dawn of God's dear Sabbath.

A. C. Cross, 1866. "ST. GEORGE'S, BOLTON." J. Walch, 1875.

1. The dawn of God's dear Sab - bath Breaks o'er the earth a - gain,
2. Lord, we would bring for of - f'ring, Though marr'd with earth - ly soil,
3. And we would bring our bur - den Of sin - ful thought and deed,
4. And with that sor - row min - gling, A stead - fast faith, and sure,

As some sweet sum - mer morn - ing Af - ter a night of pain;
A week of ear - nest la - bor, Of stead - y, faith - ful toil;
In Thy pure pres - ence kneel - ing, From bond - age to be freed;
And love so deep and fer - vent, That tries to make it pure;

It comes as cool - ing show - ers To some ex - haust - ed land,
Fair fruits of self - de - ni - al, Of strong, deep love to Thee,
Our heart's most bit - ter sor - row For all Thy work un - done—
In His dear pres - ence find - ing The par - don that we need,

As shade of clus - ter'd palm - trees 'Mid wea - ry wastes of sand. A - men.
Fos - ter'd by Thine own Spir - it, In our hu - mil - i - ty.
So ma - ny tal - ents wast - ed! So few bright lau - rels won!
And then the peace so last - ing— Ce - les - tial peace in - deed.

The dawn of God's dear Sabbath.—*Concluded.*

5 So be it, Lord, for ever.
　　Oh, may we evermore,
　In Jesus' holy presence
　　His blessèd name adore.
　Upon His peaceful Sabbath,
　　Within His temple-walls—
　Type of the stainless worship
　　In Zion's golden halls.

6 So that, in joy and gladness,
　　We reach that home at last,
　When life's short week of sorrow
　　And sin and strife is past;
　When angel-hands have gathered
　　The fair, ripe fruit for Thee,
　O Father, Lord, Redeemer!
　　Most Holy Trinity!

Again returns the day of holy rest.　44

W. MASON, 1796.　　　　　"PAX DEI."　　　　　J. B. DYKES, 1868.

1. A - gain re - turns the day of ho - ly rest..... Which, when He
2. Let us de - vote this con - se - crat - ed day...... To learn His
3. Fa - ther of heav'n, in whom our hopes con - fide,..... Whose pow'r de -

made the world, Je - ho - vah blessed; When, like His own, He bade our
will, and all we learn o - bey; So shall He hear, when fer - vent -
fends us, and whose pre - cepts guide, In life our guard - ian and in

la - bors cease, And all be pi - e - ty, and all be peace. A - men.
ly we raise Our sup - pli - ca - tions and our songs of praise.
death our Friend, Glo - ry su-preme be Thine till time shall end.

45 O day of rest and gladness.

C. WORDSWORTH, 1858. "DAY OF REST." J. W. ELLIOTT (1833—).

1. O day of rest and glad - ness, O day of joy and light,
2. On thee, at the cre - a - tion, The light first had its birth;
3. To - day on wea - ry na - tions The heav'n - ly man - na falls;
4. New grac - es ev - er gain - ing From this our day of rest;

O balm of care and sad - ness, Most beau - ti - ful, most bright,
On thee for our sal - va - tion Christ rose from depths of earth;
To ho - ly con - vo - ca - tions The sil - ver trump - et calls,
We reach the rest re - main - ing To spir - its of the blest.

On thee the high and low - ly, Through a - ges joined in tune,
On thee our Lord vic - to - rious, The Spir - it sent from heav'n;
Where Gos - pel - light is glow - ing, With pure and ra - diant beams
To Ho - ly Ghost be prais - es, To Fa - ther, and to Son;

Unison. Harmony.

Sing ho - ly, ho - ly, ho - ly! To the great God Tri - une. A - men.
And thus on thee most glo - rious A tri - ple light was giv'n.
And liv - ing wa - ter flow - ing With soul - re - fresh-ing streams.
The Church her voice up - rais - es To Thee, blest Three in One.

This is the day of light.

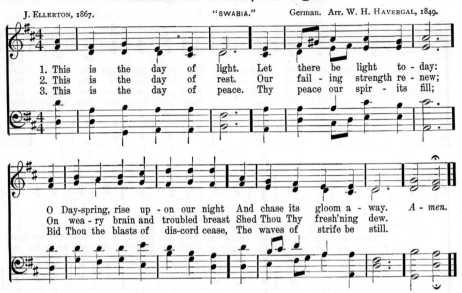

J. ELLERTON, 1867. "SWABIA." German. Arr. W. H. HAVERGAL, 1849.

1. This is the day of light. Let there be light to-day:
2. This is the day of rest. Our fail-ing strength re-new;
3. This is the day of peace. Thy peace our spir-its fill;

O Day-spring, rise up-on our night And chase its gloom a-way. A - men.
On wea-ry brain and troubled breast Shed Thou Thy fresh'ning dew.
Bid Thou the blasts of dis-cord cease, The waves of strife be still.

4 This is the day of prayer.
   Let earth to heaven draw near;
   Lift up our hearts to seek Thee there;
   Come down to meet us here.

5 This is the first of days.
   Send forth Thy quickening breath,
   And wake dead souls to love and praise,
   O vanquisher of death!

SECOND TUNE.

"DOMENICA." H. S. OAKELEY, 1874.

This is the day of light. Let there be light to-day:

O Day-spring, rise up-on our night And chase its gloom a-way. A - men.

47

Again the morn of gladness.

J. ELLERTON, 1886. Abr. "ROSWELL." A. COTTMAN (c. 1842—1879).

1. A - gain the morn of glad - ness, The morn of light is here; And
2. A - gain, O lov - ing Sav - iour, The chil - dren of Thy grace Pre-
3. The Church on earth re - joic - es To join with these to - day; In
4. Tell out, sweet bells, His prais - es; Sing, chil - dren, sing His name! Still

earth it - self looks fair - er, And heav'n it - self more near. The bells, like an - gel
pare them-selves to seek Thee With - in Thy chos - en place. Our song shall rise to
ev - ery tongue and na - tion She calls her sons to pray; A - cross the northern
loud - er and still fur - ther His might - y deeds pro-claim, Till all whom He re-

voic - es, Speak peace to ev - ery breast; And all the land lies qui - et To
greet Thee, If Thou our hearts wilt raise; If Thou our lips wilt o - pen, Our
snow - fields, Be - neath the In - dian palms, She makes the same pure of - f'ring, And
deem - ed Shall own Him Lord and King, Till ev - ery knee shall wor - ship And

Refrain.

His chil - dren

keep the day of rest.......
mouth shall show Thy praise....
sings the same sweet psalms...
ev - ery tongue shall sing......
} Glo - ry be to Je - sus! Let all His chil-dren

all.......... His

Let all........ His

Again the morn of gladness.—*Concluded.*

say:

chil - dren say:

say: He rose a - gain, He rose a - gain, On this glad day! A - men

chil - dren say:

Holy, holy, holy Lord. 48

C. Wordsworth, 1862.　　　　　"ST. ATHANASIUS."　　　　　E. J. Hopkins, 1872.

1. Ho - ly, ho - ly, ho - ly Lord, God of hosts, e - ter - nal King, By the heaven and
2. Since by Thee were all things made, And in Thee do all things live, Be to Thee all
3. Thousands, tens of thousands stand, Spir - its blest be - fore Thy throne, Speed-ing thence at
4. Cher - u - bim and ser - a - phim Veil their fac - es with their wings; Eyes of an - gels

earth a - dored! An - gels and arch - an - gels sing, Chant - ing ev - er - last - ing - ly
hon - or paid, Praise to Thee let all things give, Sing - ing ev - er - last - ing - ly
Thy com - mand; And, when Thy be - hests are done, Sing - ing ev - er - last - ing - ly
are too dim To be - hold the King of kings, While they sing e - ter - nal - ly

To the bless - ed Trin - i - ty. A - men.
To the bless - ed Trin - i - ty.
To the bless - ed Trin - i - ty.
To the bless - ed Trin - i - ty.

5 Thee, apostles, prophets, Thee,
　Thee, the noble martyr band,
Praise with solemn jubilee,
　Thee, the Church in every land,
Singing everlastingly
To the blessèd Trinity.

6 Alleluia, Lord, to Thee,
　Father, Son, and Holy Ghost,
Three in One, and One in Three!
　Join we with the heavenly host,
Singing everlastingly
To the blessèd Trinity.

49

Hark! hark! the organ loudly peals.

G. Thring, (1823—). "LAUS DEO." J. W. Elliott (1833—).

1. Hark! hark! the organ loudly peals, Our thankful hearts in-vit - ing To sing our great Cre - a - tor's praise, Both rich and poor u - nit - ing!

2. Hark! hark! the organ loudly peals, Our thankful hearts in-vit - ing To sing the praise of Christ our King, Both rich and poor u - nit - ing!

Hark! hark! the organ loudly peals.—*Concluded.*

Ye heav'ns and earth, re - joice!   And ev - ery heart and voice   Your joy-ous strains up -
Who left His throne on high,   And low - ly came to die,   That we from earth might

raise,   In notes of end-less praise,   Be-fore His throne for ev-er, for ev - er. A - men.
rise   To realms beyond the skies,   And live with Him for ev-er, for ev - er.

Hark! hark! the organ loudly peals,
 Our thankful hearts inviting
To sing the Holy Spirit's praise,
 Both rich and poor uniting!
  Who bids us flee from sin,
  And makes us pure within,
  Till, warmed with heavenly love,
  We yearn to sing above
 Glad songs of praise for ever!

4 Hark! hark! the organ loudly peals,
 Our thankful hearts inviting
To high upraise our songs of praise,
 Both rich and poor uniting!
  To God the Father, Son,
  And Spirit, Three in One,
  Till soaring higher and higher,
  We join the heavenly choir
 Before His Throne for ever!

50

God is Love, by Him upholden.

J. S. B. MONSELL, 1856. "REGENT SQUARE." H. SMART, 1867.

1. God is Love, by Him up - hold - en Hang the glo - rious orbs of light,
2. And the teem - ing earth re - joic - es In that mes - sage from a - bove,

In their lan - guage, glad and gold - en, Speak-ing to us day and night
With ten thou - sand thou- sand voic - es Tell - ing back, from hill and grove

Their great sto - ry, their great sto - ry, God is Love, and God is Might. A - men.
Her glad sto - ry, her glad sto - ry, God is Might, and God is Love.

3 With these anthems of creation,
 Mingling in harmonious strife, .
Christian songs of Christ's salvation,
 To the world with blessings rife,
 ‖: Tell their story, :‖
God is Love, and God is Life.

4 Through the precious Love He sought us,
 Wandering from His holy ways,
With that precious Life He bought us;
 Then let all our future days
 ‖: Tell the story, :‖
Love is Life—our lives be Praise.

Angel-voices, ever singing.

F. POTT, 1861.　　　"ANGEL-VOICES."　　　A. S. SULLIVAN, 1872.

1. An - gel - voic - es, ev - er sing - ing Round Thy throne of light—
2. Thou, who art be - yond the far - thest Mor - tal eye can scan,
3. Yes, we know Thy love re - joic - es O'er each work of Thine;

An - gel harps, for ev - er ring - ing, Rest not day nor night; Thou-sands
Can it be that Thou re - gard - est Songs of sin - ful man? Can we
Thou didst ears and hands and voic - es For Thy praise com - bine; Po - et's

on - ly live to bless Thee, And con - fess Thee, Lord of might. A - men.
feel that Thou art near us, And wilt hear us? Yea, we can.
art and mu - sic's measure For Thy pleas - ure Didst de - sign.

4 In Thy house, great God, we offer
　　Of Thine own to Thee;
And for Thine acceptance proffer,
　　All unworthily,
Hearts and minds, and hands and voices,
In our choicest
　　Melody.

5 Honor, glory, might, and merit,
　　Thine shall ever be,
Father, Son, and Holy Spirit,
　　Blessèd Trinity!
Of the best that Thou hast given,
Earth and heaven
　　Render Thee!

52 Let us with a gladsome mind.

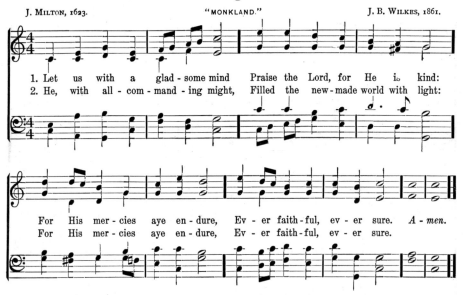

J. MILTON, 1623.　　　　　"MONKLAND."　　　　　J. B. WILKES, 1861.

1. Let us with a glad - some mind　Praise the Lord, for He is kind:
2. He, with all - com - mand - ing might,　Filled the new - made world with light:

For His mer - cies aye en - dure,　Ev - er faith - ful, ev - er sure. A - men.
For His mer - cies aye en - dure,　Ev - er faith - ful, ev - er sure.

3 He His chosen race did bless
　In the wasteful wilderness:
　For His mercies aye endure
　Ever faithful, ever sure.

4 He hath, with a piteous eye,
　Looked upon our misery:
　For His mercies aye endure,
　Ever faithful, ever sure.

5 All things living He doth feed,
　His full hand supplies their need:
　For His mercies aye endure,
　Ever faithful, ever sure.

6 Let us therefore warble forth
　His high majesty and worth:
　For His mercies aye endure,
　Ever faithful, ever sure.

53　O Lord, how good, how great art Thou.

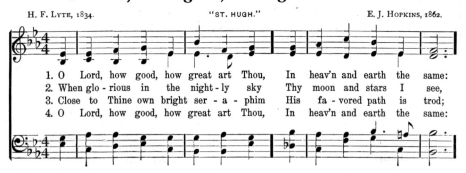

H. F. LYTE, 1834.　　　　　"ST. HUGH."　　　　　E. J. HOPKINS, 1862.

1. O Lord, how good, how great art Thou,　In heav'n and earth the same:
2. When glo - rious in the night - ly sky　Thy moon and stars I see,
3. Close to Thine own bright ser - a - phim　His fa - vored path is trod;
4. O Lord, how good, how great art Thou,　In heav'n and earth the same:

O Lord, how good, how great art Thou.—*Concluded.*

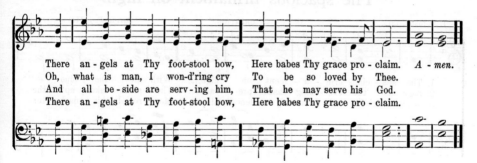

There an - gels at Thy foot-stool bow, Here babes Thy grace pro - claim. *A - men.*
Oh, what is man, I won-d'ring cry To be so loved by Thee.
And all be - side are serv-ing him, That he may serve his God.
There an - gels at Thy foot-stool bow, Here babes Thy grace pro - claim.

Lord of all being, throned afar. 54

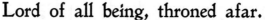

O. W. Holmes, 1848.   "BOWEN."   Fr. F. J. Haydn (1732—1809).

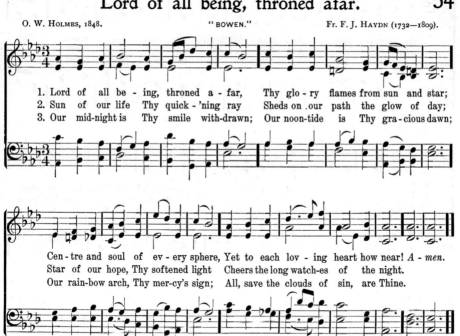

1. Lord of all be - ing, throned a - far, Thy glo - ry flames from sun and star;
2. Sun of our life Thy quick - 'ning ray Sheds on .our path the glow of day;
3. Our mid-night is Thy smile with-drawn; Our noon-tide is Thy gra - cious dawn;

Cen - tre and soul of ev - ery sphere, Yet to each lov - ing heart how near! *A - men.*
Star of our hope, Thy softened light Cheers the long watch-es of the night.
Our rain-bow arch, Thy mer-cy's sign; All, save the clouds of sin, are Thine.

4 Lord of all life, below, above,
  Whose light is truth, whose warmth is love,
  Before Thy ever-blazing throne
  We ask no lustre of our own.

5 Grant us Thy truth to make us free,
  And kindling hearts that burn for Thee,
  Till all Thy living altars claim
  One holy light, one heavenly flame.

55

The spacious firmament on high.

J. ADDISON, 1712. "CREATION." Arr. fr. F. J. HAYDN, 1798.

1. The spa - cious firm - a - ment on high,... With all the blue e -
2. Soon as the eve - ning shades pre - vail,.... The moon takes up the
3. What though in sol - emn si - lence all...... Move round this dark ter -

the - real sky.... And span - gled heav'ns, a shin - ing frame, Their
won - drous tale,... And night - ly to the list - 'ning earth Re -
res - trial ball;... What though no re - al voice nor sound A -

great o - rig - in - al pro - claim. The unwea-ried sun from day to day,
peats the sto - ry of her birth; Whilst all the stars that round her burn,
midst their ra - diant orbs be found; In rea - son's ear they all re - joice,

Does his...... Cre - a - tor's power dis - play, And pub - lish - es...... to
And all...... the plan - ets in...... their turn, Con - firm the ti - dings
And ut - ter forth a glo - rious voice; For - ev - er sing - ing,

Ped.

The spacious firmament on high.—*Concluded.*

ev - ery land   The work... of an...... al - might - y hand.   *A - men.*
as   they roll,   And spread the truth... from pole to   pole.
as   they shine, "The hand... that made... us is   di - vine."

Praise, my soul, the King of heaven.   56

H. F. LYTE, 1834.   "BENEDIC ANIMA."   J. GOSS, 1867.

1. Praise, my soul, the King of heav - en,   To His feet thy trib - ute bring;
2. Praise Him for His grace and fa - vor,   To our fa - thers in dis - tress;
3. Fa - ther - like, He tends and spares us; Well our fee - ble frame He knows;
4. An - gels, help us to a - dore Him;   Ye be - hold Him face to face;

Ran - som'd, heal'd, re - stor'd, for - giv - en, Who, like me, His praise should sing?
Praise Him, still the same for ev - er,   Slow to chide, and swift to bless,
In His hands He gen - tly bears us,   Res - cues us from all our foes;
Sun and moon, bow down be - fore Him;   Dwell - ers all in time and space,

Praise Him, praise Him, praise Him, praise Him, Praise the Ev - er - last - ing King. *A - men.*
Praise Him, praise Him, praise Him, praise Him, Glo - rious in His faith - ful - ness.
Praise Him, praise Him, praise Him, praise Him, Wide - ly as His mer - cy goes.
Praise Him, praise Him, praise Him, praise Him, Praise with us the God of grace.

4 E

57

Souls of men, why will ye scatter.

F. W. Faber, 1854. "BETHANY." (SMART). H. Smart, 1867.

1. Souls of men, why will ye scat - ter Like a crowd of fright-ened sheep?
2. It is God: His love looks might - y, But is might-ier than it seems.
3. For the love of God is broad - er Than the meas - ures of man's mind,
4. There is plen - ti - ful re - demp-tion In the blood that has been shed;

Fool - ish hearts, why will ye wan - der From a love so true and deep?
'T is our Fa - ther, and His fond - ness Goes far out be - yond our dreams.
And the heart of the E - ter - nal Is most won - der - ful - ly kind.
There is joy for all the mem - bers In the sor - rows of the Head.

Was there ev - er kind - est shep - herd Half so gen - tle, half so sweet,
There's a wide - ness in God's mer - cy, Like the wide - ness of the sea;
But we make His love too nar - row By false lim - its of our own,
If our love were but more sim - ple, We should take Him at His word;

As the Sav - iour who would have us Come and gath - er at His feet? A - men.
There's a kind - ness in His jus - tice, Which is more than lib - er - ty.
And we mag - ni - fy His strict - ness With a zeal He will not own.
And our lives would be all sun - shine In the sweet - ness of our Lord.

SECOND TUNE.

"ILSLEY."

F. W. FABER, 1854.

F. G. ILSLEY, 1887.

1. Souls of men, why will ye scat-ter Like a crowd of fright-en'd sheep?
2. It is God: His love looks might-y, But is might-ier than it seems.
3. For the love of God is broad-er Than the meas-ures of man's mind,
4. There is plen-ti-ful re-demp-tion In the blood that has been shed;

Fool-ish hearts, why will ye wan-der From a love so true and deep?
'Tis our Fa-ther, and His fond-ness Goes far out be-yond our dreams.
And the heart of the E-ter-nal Is most won-der-ful-ly kind.
There is joy for all the mem-bers In the sor-rows of the Head.

Was there ev-er kind-est shep-herd Half so gen-tle, half so sweet,
There's a wide-ness in God's mer-cy, Like the wide-ness of the sea;
But we make His love too nar-row By false lim-its of our own,
If our love were but more sim-ple, We should take Him at His word;

As the Sav-iour who would have us Come and gath-er at His feet? A-men.
There's a kind-ness in His jus-tice, Which is more than lib-er-ty.
And we mag-ni-fy His strict-ness With a zeal He will not own.
And our lives would be all sun-shine In the sweet-ness of our Lord.

58

God our Father, Thee we praise.

"EPSOM COLLEGE."

S. J. ROWTON.

1. God our Fa - ther, Thee we praise, Guard - ian of our help - less days;
2. God our Sav - iour, Thee we bless For Thy life of right - eous - ness;

Thou hast made us by Thy pow'r, Thou hast kept us to this hour;
For Thy fear - ful death of shame, Youth - ful voic - es bless Thy name.

Thou hast giv'n Thy Son to die, Sent Thy Spir - it from on high. A-men.
Should our tongues no prais - es bring, Stones would find a voice to sing.

3 God the Spirit, Thee we praise
For Thy sanctifying grace;
For the new and tender heart
Thou hast promised to impart;
For the Word inspired by Thee,
That reveals eternity.

4 Great Eternal, Three in One,
Hear, O hear us from Thy throne!
We are children of a day,
Like the flowers, we pass away;
Yet Thy power can bid us rise
To adorn a paradise.

Come, let us all unite and sing.

C. R. HURDITCH, 1859.   "UNITY."   S. P. WARREN, 1886.

With spirit.

1. Come, let us all u - nite and sing, "God is love." Let
2. O tell the earth's re - mot - est bound "God is love!" In
3. What though our heart and flesh should fail: God is love; Thro'
4. In heav - en we shall sing a - gain, "God is love," Yes,

heav'n and earth their prais - es bring: "God...... is love;" Let
Christ is full re - demp - tion found: God...... is love, His
Christ we shall o'er death pre - vail: God...... is love. In
this shall be our no - blest strain, "God...... is love." While

ev - ery soul from sin a - wake, Each in his heart sweet mu - sic make,
blood can cleanse our sins a - way; His Spir - it turns our night to day,
Jor - dan's swell we need not fear, For Je - sus will be with us there
end - less a - ges roll a - long, In con - cert with the heav'n - ly throng,

And sweet - ly sing for Je - sus' sake, "God...... is love." A - men.
And leads our soul with joy to say, "God...... is love."
Our souls a - bove the waves to bear: God...... is love.
This still shall be our sweet - est song, "God...... is love."

60

Songs of praise the angels sang.

J. Montgomery, 1819. Abr.   "THANKSGIVING.   W. B Gilbert, 1865.

1. { Songs of praise the an-gels sang, Heav'n with al-le-lu-ias rang }
   { When Je-ho-vah's work be-gun, When He spake and it was done. } Songs of

2. { Heav'n and earth must pass a-way; Songs of praise shall crown that day: }
   { God will make new heav'ns and earth; Songs of praise shall hail their birth. } And can

praise a-woke the morn When the Prince of Peace was born; Songs of praise a-rose when He
man a-lone be dumb, Till that glo-rious king-dom come? No; the church de-lights to raise

Cap-tive led cap-tiv-i-ty. A-men.
Psalms, and hymns, and songs of praise.

3 Saints below, with heart and voice,
Still in songs of praise rejoice,
Learning here, by faith and love,
Songs of praise to sing above.
Borne upon their latest breath,
Songs of praise shall conquer death;
Then amidst eternal joy,
Songs of praise their powers employ.

61

O God, our help in ages past.

I. Watts, 1719. Abr.   "ST. ANNE."   W. Croft, 1708.

1. O God, our help in a-ges past, Our hope for years to come,
2. Be-fore the hills in or-der stood, Or earth re-ceived her frame,
3. A thou-sand a-ges in Thy sight Are like an eve-ning gone;

O God, our help in ages past.—*Concluded.*

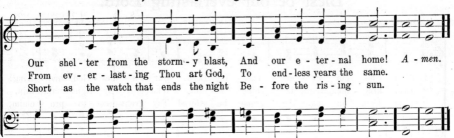

Our shel - ter from the storm - y blast, And our e - ter - nal home! A - men.
From ev - er - last - ing Thou art God, To end - less years the same.
Short as the watch that ends the night Be - fore the ris - ing sun.

4 Time, like an ever-rolling stream,
   Bears all its sons away;
They fly, forgotten, as a dream
   Dies at the opening day.

5 O God, our help in ages past,
   Our hope for years to come,
Be Thou our guard while life shall last,
   And our eternal home.

We thank Thee, Lord, for this fair earth. 62

G. E. L. Cotton, 1856.   "MAINZER."   Jos. Mainzer (1801—1851).

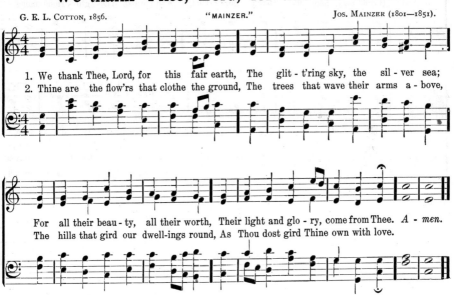

1. We thank Thee, Lord, for this fair earth, The glit - t'ring sky, the sil - ver sea;
2. Thine are the flow'rs that clothe the ground, The trees that wave their arms a - bove,

For all their beau - ty, all their worth, Their light and glo - ry, come from Thee. A - men.
The hills that gird our dwell-ings round, As Thou dost gird Thine own with love.

3 Yet teach us still how far more fair,
   More glorious, Father, in Thy sight,
Is one pure deed, one holy prayer,
   One heart that owns Thy Spirit's might.

4 So while we gaze with thoughtful eye
   On all the gifts Thy love has given,
Help us in Thee to live and die,
   By Thee to rise from earth to heaven.

63

Blest be our everlasting Lord.

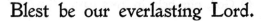

C. WESLEY, 1762. "CHRISTIAN MARTYR." J. BLOCKLEY, 1860.
Arr. by A. S. SULLIVAN.

1. Blest be our ev - er - last - ing Lord, Our Fa - ther, God, and King!
2. The king - dom, Lord, is Thine a - lone, Who dost Thy right main - tain,
3. Thou hast on us the grace be - stowed Thy great - ness to pro - claim;

Thy sov - 'reign good-ness we re - cord, Thy glo - rious pow'r we sing.
And, high on Thine e - ter - nal throne, O'er men and an - gels reign.
And there - fore now we thank our God, And praise Thy glo - rious name.

By Thee the vic - to - ry is giv'n; The maj - es - ty di - vine,
Rich - es, as seem - eth good to Thee, Thou dost, and hon - or give;
Thy glo - rious name and na - ture's pow'rs Thou dost to us make known;

And strength, and might, and earth and heav'n, And all there - in, are Thine. A - men.
And kings their pow'r and dig - ni - ty Out of Thy hand re - ceive.
And all the De - i - ty is ours, Thro' Thy in - car - nate Son.

There is no name so sweet on earth.

G. W. BETHUNE, 1858. "THE BLESSED NAME." J. BARNBY (1838—1896).

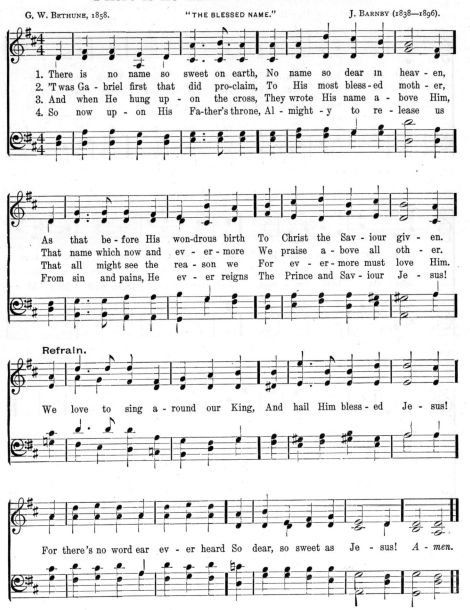

1. There is no name so sweet on earth, No name so dear in heav - en,
2. 'Twas Ga - briel first that did pro-claim, To His most bless - ed moth - er,
3. And when He hung up - on the cross, They wrote His name a - bove Him,
4. So now up - on His Fa-ther's throne, Al - might - y to re - lease us

As that be - fore His won-drous birth To Christ the Sav - iour giv - en.
That name which now and ev - er - more We praise a - bove all oth - er.
That all might see the rea - son we For ev - er - more must love Him.
From sin and pains, He ev - er reigns The Prince and Sav - iour Je - sus!

Refrain.

We love to sing a - round our King, And hail Him bless - ed Je - sus!

For there's no word ear ev - er heard So dear, so sweet as Je - sus! A - men.

65

What star is this, with beams so bright.

C. COFFIN, 1736.　Tr. J. CHANDLER, 1837.　"STAR."　E. G. MONK (1819—).

1. What star is.... this,... with beams so bright, Which shame the
   sun's less ra - diant light? It shines t'an - nounce a new - born
   King, Glad ti - dings of our God to bring. A - men.

2. 'T is now ful - fill'd... what God de - creed, "From Ja - cob
   shall a star pro - ceed;" And lo, the east - ern sa - ges
   stand, To read...... in heaven the Lord's com - mand.

3. While out - ward signs.. the star dis - plays, An in - ward
   light the Lord con - veys, And urg - es them, with force be -
   nign, To seek...... the giv - er of the sign.

4 True love can brook no dull delay,
　Nor toil nor dangers stop their way;
　Home, kindred, fatherland, and all,
　They leave at once, at God's high call.

5 O Jesus, while the Star of grace
　Invites us now to seek Thy face,
　May we no more that grace repel,
　Or quench that light which shines so well.

Oh come, oh come, Emmanuel.

Anon. (Latin, c. 12th Cent.)
Tr. J. M. Neale, 1851.

"CAREY'S."

H. Carey, 1723.

1. Oh come, oh come, Em-man-u-el, And ran-som cap-tive
2. Oh come, Thou Rod of Jes-se, free Thine own from Sa-tan's

Is - ra - el, That mourns in lone-ly ex-ile here Un-til the
tyr - an-ny; From depths of hell Thy peo-ple save, And give them

Son of God ap-pear. Re-joice! Re-joice! Em-man-u-el Shall come to
vic-t'ry o'er the grave. Re-joice! Re-joice! Em-man-u-el Shall come to

thee, O Is - ra - el. A - men.
thee, O Is - ra - el.

3 Oh come, Thou Day-Spring, come and cheer
  Our spirits by Thine advent here;
  Disperse the gloomy clouds of night,
  And death's dark shadows put to flight.
      Rejoice! Rejoice! Emmanuel
      Shall come to thee, O Israel.

4 Oh come, Thou Key of David, come,
  And open wide our heavenly home;
  Make safe the way that leads on high,
  And close the path to misery.
      Rejoice! Rejoice! Emmanuel
      Shall come to thee, O Israel.

67

Thou didst leave Thy throne.

EMILY E. S. ELLIOTT, 1864.   "VENI, DOMINE JESU."   J. BARNBY (1838—1896).

1. Thou didst leave Thy... throne and Thy king-ly crown When Thou cam-est to
2. Heav-en's arch-es..... rang when the an-gels sang, Pro - claim-ing Thy
3. Thou...... cam-est, O Lord, with the liv-ing word, That should set Thy...
4. When Heav'n's arch-es shall ring, and her choirs shall sing, At Thy com-ing to

earth for... me; But in Beth-le - hem's home there was found no...... room
roy - al de-gree; But in low-ly...... birth didst Thou come to...... earth,
peo - ple... free; But with mock-ing.... scorn, and with crown of...... thorn,
vic - to - ry, Let Thy voice call me home, say-ing, "Yet there is room,

Refrain.

For Thy ho - ly na-tiv-i-ty.
And in great hu-mil-i-ty.
They bore Thee to...... Cal-va-ry.
There is room at My side for Thee."

Oh, come to my heart, Lord
For 4th. verse.
And my heart shall re - joice, Lord

pp   *rit.*

Je - sus, There is room in my heart for Thee! A - men.
Je - sus, When Thou com-est and call-est for me.

Angels, from the realms of glory.

J. Montgomery, 1819.   "WILDERSMOUTH."   E. J. Hopkins, 1879.

1. An - gels, from the realms of glo - ry, Wing your flight o'er all the earth;
2. Shep-herds, in the field a - bid - ing, Watch-ing o'er your flocks by night,

Ye, who sang cre - a - tion's sto - ry, Now pro - claim Mes - si - ah's birth;
God with man is now re - sid - ing, Yon - der shines the in - fant - light;

Come and wor - ship, Wor - ship Christ, the new - born King. A - - men.
Come and wor - ship, Wor - ship Christ, the new - born King.

3 Sages, leave your contemplations,
   Brighter visions beam afar;
Seek the great Desire of nations,
   Ye have seen His natal star;
   Come and worship,
   Worship Christ, the new-born King.

4 Saints before the altar bending,
   Watching long in hope and fear,
Suddenly the Lord, descending,
   In His temple shall appear;
   Come and worship,
   Worship Christ, the new-born King.

69

In the field with their flocks abiding.

F. W. FARRAR, 1871.   "IN THE FIELD."   JOHN FARMER, 1871.

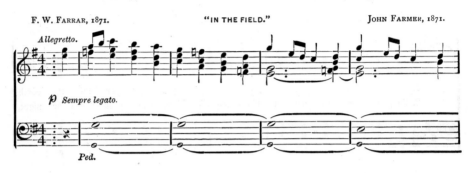

1. In   the   field   with their   flocks   a - bid - ing,
2. "To........ you   in   the   cit - y   of   Da - vid
3. And   the   shep - herds..... came   to   the   man - ger,

In the field with their flocks.—*Continued*.

They lay on the dew - y ground; And glim - 'ring un - der the
A Sav - iour is born to - day;" And sud - den a host of the
And gazed on the Ho - ly Child; And calm - ly o'er that rude

star - light, The sheep lay white a - round; When the light of the Lord stream'd
heav'nly ones Flash'd forth to join the lay. O, nev - er hath sweet - er
cra - dle The Vir - gin Moth - er smiled; And the sky, in the star - lit

o'er........ them, And lo ! from the heav'n a - bove An
mes - - sage Thrill'd home to the souls of men, And the
si - - lence, Seem'd full of the an - gel lay : "To

In the field with their flocks.—*Concluded.*

an - gel leaned from the Glo - ry, And sang his song of love:
heav'ns them - selves had nev - er heard A glad - der choir till then,
you in the cit - y of Da - vid A Sav - iour is born to - day."

He sang, that first sweet Christ - mas, The song that shall nev - er cease:
For they sang that Christ-mas car - ol That nev - er on earth shall cease:
On they sang—and I ween that nev - er The car - ol on earth shall cease:

"Glo - ry to God in the high - est, On earth good - will and peace."

f

Oh come, all ye faithful.

ANON. (Latin, 17th Cent.)
Tr. F. OAKELEY, 1841.

"PORTUGUESE HYMN."

J. READING, 1692.

1. Oh come, all ye faith-ful, Joy-ful and tri-umph-ant, Oh come ye, oh
2. God of God, Light of Light, Lo! He ab-
3. Sing, choirs of An-gels, Sing in ex-ult-a-tion, Sing, all ye
4. Yea, Lord, we greet Thee, Born this hap-py morn-ing, Je-sus, to

come ye to Beth - le - hem; Come and be - hold Him Born the King of
hors not the Vir - gin's womb; Ver - y God, Be - got - ten, not cre-
ci - ti-zens of heav'n a - bove: Glo - ry to God In the
Thee be glo - ry giv'n; Word of the Fa - ther, Now in flesh ap-

After each verse.

An - gels;
at - ed;   Oh come, let us a - dore Him, Oh come, let us a - dore Him,
high - est;
pear - ing;

Oh come, let us a - dore Him, Christ, the Lord. A - men.

While shepherds watched their flocks by night.

71

N. Tate, 1702.   "NOEL."   Arr. by A. S. Sullivan (1842—).

1. While shep-herds watch'd their flocks by night, All seat-ed on the ground,
2. "To you, in Da-vid's town, this day Is born of Da-vid's line
3. Thus spake the ser-aph; and forth-with Ap-pear'd a shin-ing throng

The an-gel of the Lord came down, And glo-ry shone a-round.
The Sav-iour, who is Christ the Lord; And this shall be the sign:
Of an-gels, prais-ing God, who thus Ad-dress'd their joy-ful song:

"Fear not," said he, for might-y dread Had seized their trou-bled mind;
The heav'n-ly Babe you there shall find To hu-man view dis-play'd,
"All glo-ry be to God on high, And to the earth be peace;

"Glad ti-dings of great joy I bring To you and all man-kind. A-men.
All mean-ly wrapt in swath-ing bands, And in a man-ger laid."
Good-will henceforth from heav'n to men Be-gin, and nev-er cease."

It came upon the midnight clear.

E. H. Sears. 1850.   "CAROL."   R. Storrs Willis, 1849.

1. It came up-on the mid-night clear, That glo-rious song of old,
2. Still through the clo-ven skies they come, With peace-ful wings un-furled,
3. O ye, be-neath life's crush-ing load, Whose forms are bend-ing low,
4. For lo! the days are hast-'ning on, By proph-et-bards fore-told,

From an-gels bend-ing near the earth To touch their harps of gold;
And still their heav'n-ly mu-sic floats O'er all the wea-ry world;
Who toil a-long the climb-ing way With pain-ful steps and slow,
When with the ev-er-cir-cling years Comes round the age of gold;

Peace on the earth, good-will to men, From heav'n's all-gra-cious King;
A-bove its sad and low-ly plains They bend on heav'n-ly wing,
Look now! for glad and gold-en hours Come swift-ly on the wing;
When peace shall o-ver all the earth Its an-cient splen-dors fling,

The world in sol-emn still-ness lay To hear the an-gels sing. A-men.
And ev-er o'er its Ba-bel sounds The bless-ed an-gels sing.
O rest be-side the wea-ry road, And hear the an-gels sing.
And the whole world send back the song Which now the an-gels sing.

73

Holy night! peaceful night!

J. Mohr, 1818.

"HOLY NIGHT."

J. Barnby, 1868.

1. Ho - ly night! peace-ful night! Through the dark-ness beams a light, Ho - ly night!
2. Si - lent night! ho - liest night! Dark - ness flies, and all is light! Si - lent night!
3. Si - lent night! ho - liest night! Guid - ing Star, O lend thy light! Si - lent night!
4. Si - lent night! ho - liest night! Won - drous Star, O lend thy light! Si - lent night!

peace - ful night! Through the dark - ness beams a light, Through the dark - ness
ho - liest night! Dark - ness flies, and all is light! Dark - ness flies, and
ho - liest night! Guid - ing Star, O lend thy light! Guid - ing Star, O
ho - liest night! Won - drous Star, O lend thy light! Won - drous Star, O

beams a light, Yon - der, where they sweet vig - ils keep O'er the Babe who, in
all is light! Shep - herds hear the an - gels sing: "Al - le - lu - ia!
lend thy light! See the east - ern wise men bring Gifts of hom - age
lend thy light! With the an - gels let us sing Al - le - lu - ia!

Rallentando.

si - lent sleep, Rests in heav-en-ly peace, Rests in heav-en-ly peace. *A - men.*
hail the King! Je - sus the Sav-iour is here! Je - sus the Sav-iour is here!"
to our King! Je - sus the Sav-iour is here! Je - sus the Sav-iour is here!
to our King! Je - sus the Sav-iour is here! Je - sus the Sav-iour is here!

Hark! what mean those holy voices.

J. CAWOOD, 1819.   "BETHANY." (SMART).   H. SMART, 1867.

1. Hark! what mean those ho - ly voic - es, Sweet - ly sound - ing through the skies?
2. "Peace on earth, good - will from heav - en, Reach - ing far as man is found,
3. "Hast - en, mor - tals, to a - dore Him; Learn His name, and taste His joy;

Lo! th'an - gel - ic host re - joic - es, Heav'n - ly al - le - lu - ias rise.
Souls re - deemed, and sins for - giv - en, Loud our gold - en harps shall sound.
Till in heav'n ye sing be - fore Him, 'Glo - ry be to God most High!'"

List - en to the won - drous sto - ry Which they chant in hymns of joy:
Christ is born, the great A - noint - ed: Heav'n and earth His glo - ry sing;
Let us learn the won - drous sto - ry Of our great Re - deem - er's birth;

"Glo - ry in the high - est, glo - ry! Glo - ry be to God most high! A - men.
Glad re - ceive whom God ap - point - ed For your Proph - et, Priest, and King.
Spread the bright - ness of His glo - ry Till it cov - er all the earth.

75

O little town of Bethlehem.

P. Brooks, 1868.   "BETHLEHEM."*   J. Barnby (1838—1896).

1. O lit - tle town of Beth - le - hem, How still we see thee lie!......
2. For Christ is born of Ma - ry, And gath - ered all a - bove,....

A - bove thy deep and dream - less sleep The si - lent stars go by;
While mor - tals sleep, the an - gels keep Their watch of won - d'ring love.

Yet in thy dark streets shin - eth The ev - er - last - ing light;
O morn - ing stars, to - geth - er Pro - claim the ho - ly birth!

The hopes and fears of all the years Are met in thee to - night. A - men.
And prais - es sing to God the King And peace to men on earth.

O little town of Bethlehem—*Concluded.*

3 How silently, how silently,
  The wondrous gift is given!
So God imparts to human hearts
  The blessings of His heaven.
No ear may hear His coming,
  But in this world of sin,
Where meek souls will receive Him still,
  The dear Christ enters in.

4 O holy Child of Bethlehem!
  Descend to us, we pray;
Cast out our sin, and enter in;
  Be born in us to-day.
We hear the Christmas angels
  The great glad tidings tell;
O come to us, abide with us,
  Our Lord Emmanuel!

SECOND TUNE.

"ST. LOUIS."

L. H. REDNER, 1868.

1. O lit - tle town of Beth - le - hem, How still we see thee lie!

A - bove thy deep and dream-less sleep The si - lent stars go by;

Yet in thy dark streets shin - eth The ev - er - last - ing light;

The hopes and fears of all the years Are met in thee to - night. A - men.

76

Like silver lamps in a distant shrine.

W. C. Dix (1837—).   "ST. STEPHEN THE MARTYR."   C. Steggal (1826—).

1. Like sil - ver lamps in a dis - tant shrine, The stars are spark - ling bright;
4. The stars of heav'n still shine as at first They gleam'd on this wonder-ful night;
5. Faith sees no lon - ger the sta - ble - floor, The pave-ment of sap - phire is there;

The bells of the cit - y of God ring..... out, For the
The bells of the cit - y of God peal..... out, And the
The clear light of heav - en streams out to the world: And the

Son... of Ma - ry was born to-night; The gloom is past, and the
an - gels' song still rings in.... the height; And love still turns where the
an - gels of God.... are crowding the air; And heav'n and earth, through the

morn at last Is...... com - ing with... o - rient light.   *A - men.*
God - head burns, Hid.... in Flesh from.. flesh - ly sight.
spot - less birth, Are at peace... on this night so fair.

Like silver lamps in a distant shrine.—*Concluded.*

2. Nev - er fell mel - o - dies half so sweet As those which are fill - ing the skies;
3. Now a new Pow'r has come on the earth, A match for the ar - mies of hell:

And nev - er a pal - ace shone half so...... fair As the
A Child.... is born..... who shall con - quer the foe, And......

man - ger - bed where our Sav - iour lies; No night in the year is
all...... the spir - its of....... wick - ed - ness quell; For Ma - ry's Son is the

half so dear As this which has end - ed our sighs.
Might - y One Whom the proph - ets of God fore - tell.

77

Once in royal David's city.

C. F. ALEXANDER, 1848.   "IRBY."   H. J. GAUNTLETT (1805—1876).

1. Once in roy - al Da - vid's cit - y Stood a low - ly cat - tle shed,
2. He came down to earth from heav - en, Who is God and Lord of all,
3. For He is our child-hood's pat - tern; Day by day like us He grew;

Where a moth - er laid her Ba - by In a man - ger for His bed:
And His shel - ter was a sta - ble, And His cra - dle was a stall:
He was lit - tle, weak, and help - less, Tears and smiles like us He knew:

Ma - ry was that moth-er mild, Je - sus Christ her lit - tle Child. A men.
With the poor, and mean, and low - ly, Lived on earth our Sav - iour holy.
And He feel-eth for our sad-ness, And He shar - eth in our glad- ness.

4 And our eyes at last shall see Him,
    Through His own redeeming love;
For that Child so dear and gentle
  Is our Lord in heaven above:
And He leads His children on
  To the place where He is gone.

5 Not in that poor lowly stable,
    With the oxen standing by,
We shall see Him, but in heaven,
  Set at God's right hand on high:
When like stars His children crowned,
  All in white shall wait around.

Calm on the listening ear of night.

E. H. SEARS, 1834.   "CALM."   E. J. HOPKINS (1818—).

1. Calm on the list - 'ning ear of night Come heav'n's me - lo - dious strains,
2. The an - swering hills of Pal - es - tine Send back the glad re - ply;
3. "Glo - ry to God!" the sound - ing skies Loud with their an - thems ring,

Where wild Ju - de - a stretch - es far Her sil - ver - man - tled plains.
And greet, from all their ho - ly heights, The day - spring from on high.
"Peace to the earth, good - will to men, From heav'n's e - ter - nal King!"

Ce - les - tial choirs from courts a - bove Shed sa - cred glo - ries there;
O'er the blue depths of Gal - i - lee There comes a ho - lier calm,
Light on Thy hills, Je - ru - sa - lem! The Sav - iour now is born:

And an - gels, with their sparkling lyres, Make mu - sic on the air. *A - men.*
And Sha - ron waves, in sol - emn praise, Her si - lent groves of palm.
More bright on Bethlehem's joy - ous plains Breaks the first Christmas morn.

79
Now join we all with holy mirth.

H. Blunt. "HOLY MIRTH." J. Stainer, 1886.

1. Now join we all with ho - ly mirth, To cel - e - brate the Saviour's birth,
2. And from the heav - ens all a - round, Broke forth such strange, ce - les - tial sound,
3. Fear not, O shep-herds! naught but bliss Can come of heav'n - ly throng like this;
4. "For un - to you this Child is born, His swaddling clothes hold not in scorn,

For He has come from heav'n to earth, In hum - ble guise and low - ly;
Th' en - tranc- ed shep- herds on the ground Stand spell-bound, in - ly dream- ing;
The an - gel's gra - cious mes - sage is With sweet-est ac - cents blend - ed:
Nor Vir - gin Moth - er, so for - lorn, His na - ture He is veil - ing;

The heav'ns the bright-est plan - et lent, That e'er had graced the firm - a - ment,
If such di - vine, me - lo - dious hymn, Of cher - u - bim and ser - a - phim,
"All glo - ry be to God on high! And peace on earth, for which a sigh
The Won - der - ful— the Coun - sel - or, The might - y God Him - self is there,

Ped.

And wise men from the east were sent To greet this babe so ho - - ly. *A - men.*
These har-mon - ies that round them swim, Are real, or on - ly seem - - ing.
Hath long been raised, e'en now is nigh, Em - man - uel hath de - scend - ed."
Has come your deep-est woes to share—A Sav - iour, all - a - vail - - ing!"

Now join we all with holy mirth.—*Concluded.*

5 Then with the shepherds we will go—
   Come young and old, come high and low,
   We'll troop to Bethlehem and shew
     Our homage by confessing;
   We'll cast away our nature's sin,
   And seek Thy pardoning grace to win,
   We knock, O Jesus! take us in,
     To join Thy flock we're pressing.

6 Thus in our ears, life's path along,
   Shall linger still the angels' song,
   Its theme of comfort, simple, strong,
     Till heaven's bright day is dawning;
   Nor will we fail with honors meet,
   With thankful hearts and carols sweet,
   As each year runs its course, to greet
     Thine advent, Christmas morning!

Who is He, in yonder stall? 80

B. R. HANBY.   "LOWLINESS."   B. R. HANBY.

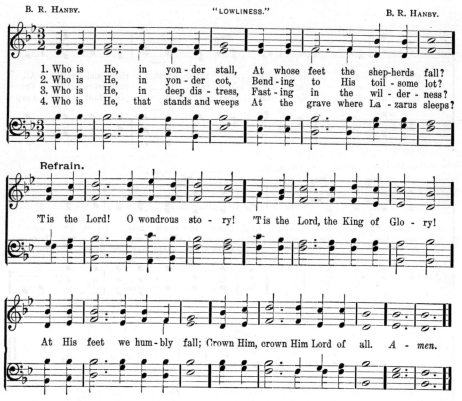

1. Who is He, in yon-der stall, At whose feet the shep-herds fall?
2. Who is He, in yon-der cot, Bend-ing to His toil-some lot?
3. Who is He, in deep dis-tress, Fast-ing in the wil-der-ness?
4. Who is He, that stands and weeps At the grave where La-zarus sleeps?

Refrain.

'Tis the Lord! O wondrous sto-ry! 'Tis the Lord, the King of Glo-ry!

At His feet we hum-bly fall; Crown Him, crown Him Lord of all. A - men.

5 Lo! at midnight, who is He
  Prays in dark Gethsemane?

6 Who is He, in Calvary's throes,
  Asks for blessings on His foes?

7 Who is He that from the grave
  Comes to heal and help and save?

8 Who is He that on yon throne
  Rules the world of light alone?

81

There came three kings, ere break of day.

ANON. 16th Century.   "EPIPHANY."   R. F. SMITH.

1. There came three kings, ere.... break of day, All on E -
2. The star shone bright - ly...... o - ver - head, The air was
3. An old man knelt at a man - ger low, A Babe lay

piph - a - ny; Their gifts they bare, both... rich and rare, All,
calm and still, O'er Beth - lehem's fields its..... rays were shed, The
in the stall; The star - light play'd on the In - fant brow, Deep

all, Lord Christ, for Thee; Gold, frank - in - cense and... myrrh are there,
dew lay on the hill; We see no throne, no..... pal - ace fair,
si - lence lay o'er all; A maid - en bent o'er the Babe in prayer,

Where is the King? O where? O where? O where is the King? O where?
Where is the King? O where? O where? O where is the King? O where?
There is the King! O there! O there! O there is the King! O there!

There came a little Child to earth.

E. E. S. Elliott, 1856.   "BETHLEHEM'S HILL."   H. Walton.

1. There came a lit - tle Child to earth Long a - go;.... And the an - gels of God pro-claimed His birth, High and low...... Out.... on the night, so... calm and still, Their song was heard; For they knew that the Child on Beth-le-hem's hill Was... Christ the Lord. *A - men.*

2. Far a - way in a good - ly land, Fair and bright, Chil - dren... with crowns of glo - ry stand, Robed in white,... In...... white more pure than the spot - less snow; And their tongues u - nite... In the psalm which the an - gels sang long a - go On..... that still night.

3. They sing how the Lord of that world so fair A.... child was born, And, that they might a crown of glo - ry wear, Wore a crown of thorn,... And in mor - tal weakness, in... want and pain, Came forth to die,.... That the chil - dren of earth might for ev - er reign With.. Him on high.

4. He has put on His King-ly ap - par - el now, In that good - ly land; And He leads to where fountains of wa - ter flow That chos - en band;... And for ev - er-more, in their robes most fair And... un - de - filed,... Those... ran - som'd children His praise de - clare Who was once a child.

83

Ring the bells, the Christmas bells.

M. C. SEWARD. "CHIME." A. H. BROWN, 1865.

1. Ring the bells, the Christmas bells; Chime out the won-drous sto - ry; First in song on
2. Wise men hastened from the East To bring their rich - est treas - ure— Gold, and myrrh, and

an - gel tongues It came from realms of glo - ry; Peace on earth, good - will to men,
frank-in-cense, And jew - els with - out meas - ure. Him they sought, al-though a King,

An - gel - ic voic - es ring-ing— Christ the Lord to earth has come, His glo-rious mes-sage bring-ing.
They found in birth-place low - ly, There with - in a man-ger lay The babe so pure and ho - ly.

Refrain.

Ring the mer-ry Christmas bells; Chime out the wondrous sto - ry; Glo-ry be to God on high,

For ev - er - more be glo - ry. A - men.

3 Earthly crowns were not for Him;
  He came God's love revealing;
On the cross He died for us,
  His blood forgiveness sealing;
'Tis the Saviour promised long,
  Ring out your loudest praises;
Every heart this happy day
  Its grateful anthem raises.

We three kings of Orient are.

J. H. HOPKINS, 1862. "THE MORNING STAR." E. W. KELLOGG, 1862.

1. We three kings of O - ri - ent are; Bear - ing gifts we trav - erse a - far
2. Born a King on Beth - le - hem plain, Gold I bring to crown Him a - gain,
3. Frank-in - cense to of - fer have I; In - cense owns a De - i - ty nigh;
4. Myrrh is mine; its bit - ter per-fume Breathes a life of gath - er - ing gloom:
5. Glo - rious now be - hold Him a - rise, King and God and Sac - ri - fice:

Field and foun - tain, moor and moun - tain, Fol - low - ing yon - der star.
King for ev - er, ceas - ing nev - er O - ver us all to reign.
Pray'r and prais - ing all men rais - ing, Wor - ship Him God on high.
Sor - rowing, sigh - ing, bleed - ing, dy - ing, Sealed in the stone - cold tomb.
Heav'n sings Al - le - lu - ia; Al - le - lu - ia the earth re - plies.

Refrain.

O star of won - der, star of night, Star with roy - al beau - ty bright,

West-ward lead - ing, still pro-ceed - ing, Guide us to thy per - fect light. A - men.

85

There's a song in the air.

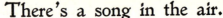

J. G. HOLLAND, 1872.   "HOLLAND."   THEODORE F. SEWARD, 1899.

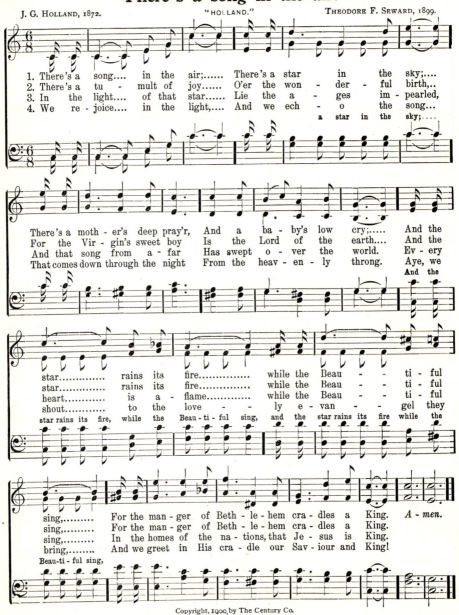

1. There's a song.... in the air;..... There's a star in the sky;....
2. There's a tu - mult of joy...... O'er the won - der - ful birth,..
3. In the light.... of that star...... Lie the a - ges im - pearled,
4. We re - joice.... in the light,.... And we ech - o the song...

a star in the sky;....

There's a moth - er's deep pray'r, And a ba - by's low cry;..... And the
For the Vir - gin's sweet boy Is the Lord of the earth.... And the
And that song from a - far Has swept o - ver the world. Ev - ery
That comes down through the night From the heav - en - ly throng. Aye, we

And the

star............ rains its fire............... while the Beau - - ti - ful
star............ rains its fire............... while the Beau - - ti - ful
heart............ is a - flame............... while the Beau - - ti - ful
shout............ to the love - - ly e - van - - gel they

star rains its fire, while the Beau - ti - ful sing, and the star rains its fire while the

sing,......... For the man - ger of Beth - le - hem cra - dles a King.   A - men.
sing,........ For the man - ger of Beth - le - hem cra - dles a King.
sing,........ In the homes of the na - tions, that Je - sus is King.
bring,........ And we greet in His cra - dle our Sav - iour and King!

Beau - ti - ful sing,

Good news on Christmas morning.

M. M. DODGE.   "CENTURY."   FRANCES J. HATTON, 1884.

1. Good news on Christmas morn-ing, Good news, O chil-dren dear! For Christ once born in
3. Good news on Christmas morn-ing, Good news, O chil-dren glad! Rare gifts are yours to

Beth - le - hem, Is liv - ing now, and here! 2. Good news on Christ-mas morn - ing,
give the Lord As ev - er wise men had. 4. Good news on Christ-mas morn - ing,

Good news, O chil-dren sweet! The way to find the Ho - ly Child Is
Good news, O chil-dren fair! Still doth the one good Shep-herd hold The

light - ed for your feet. 5. Thank God on Christmas morn-ing, Thank God, O chil-dren dear!
fee - blest in His care.

That Christ who came to Beth - le - hem, Is liv - ing now, and here. A - men.

87

God rest ye, merry gentlemen.

D. M. CRAIK.   "ST. PHILIPS."   L. H. REDNER, 1865.

1. God rest ye, mer-ry gen-tle-men, let noth-ing you dis - may, For Je - sus Christ, our
2. God rest ye, lit - tle chil - dren, let noth-ing you af - fright, For Je - sus Christ, your
3. God rest ye, all good Chris - tians, up - on this bless-ed morn, The Lord of all good

Sav - iour, was born on Christmas day; The dawn rose red o'er Beth - le - hem, the
Sav - iour, was born this hap-py night; A - long the hills of Beth - le - hem the
Chris-tians was of a wo-man born; Now all your sor-rows He doth heal, your

stars shone thro' the grey, When Je - sus Christ, our Sav - iour, was born on Christmas day;
white flocks sleeping lay, When Christ, the child of Nazareth, was born on Christmas day;
sins He takes a - way, For Je - sus Christ, our Sav - iour, was born on Christmas day;

When Je - sus Christ, our Sav - iour, was born on Christ-mas day. *A-men.*
When Christ, the child of Naz-a-reth, was born on Christ-mas day.
For Je - sus Christ, our Sav - iour, was born on Christ-mas day.

When Christ was born of Mary free.

"GLORIA."

A. H. Brown, 1865.

1. When Christ was born of Ma - ry free, In Beth - le-hem that fair cit - y,
2. these an - gels bright, To them appearing with great de - light,
3. The King is come to save man-kind, As in the Scripture truth we find,
4. for Thy great grace, Grant us in bliss to see Thy face,

An - gels sang there with mirth and glee, "In ex - cel - sis Glo - ri - a!"
Who said God's Son is born to - night. "In ex - cel - sis Glo - ri - a!"
There-fore this song we have in mind, "In ex - cel - sis Glo - ri - a!"
That we may sing to Thy sol - ace "In ex - cel - sis Glo - ri - a!"

Refrain.

In ex - cel - sis Glo - ri - a, In ex - cel - sis Glo - ri - a, In ex - cel - sis Glo - ri - a,

2d Verse.   4th Verse.

In ex - cel - sis Glo - ri - a.   Herds-men be-held, &c. Then, dear Lord, &c. A - men.

89

Hark! the herald angels sing.

C. WESLEY, 1739.   "MENDELSSOHN."   Arr. fr. MENDELSSOHN, 1840.

1. Hark! the her - ald an - gels sing, "Glo - ry to the new-born King; Peace on earth, and
2. Christ, by high - est heav'n a - dored; Christ, the ev - er - last - ing Lord; Late in time be -
3. Hail, the heav'n-born Prince of Peace! Hail, the Sun of Right-eousness! Light and life to

mer - cy mild, God and sin - ners rec - on - ciled!" Joy - ful all ye na - tions, rise,
hold Him come, Off - spring of the Vir - gin's womb: Veiled in flesh the God - head see;
all He brings, Ris'n with heal-ing in His wings. Mild He lays His glo - ry by,

Join the tri-umph of the skies; With th'an-gel - ic host pro-claim "Christ is born in
Hail th'In-car - nate De - i - ty, Pleased as man with men to dwell; Je - sus, our Em-
Born that man no more may die, Born to raise the sons of earth, Born to give them

Beth-le-hem."
man - u - el! Hark! the her - ald an-gels sing, "Glo - ry to the new-born King." A - men.
sec-ond birth.

Ped.

Ring out the bells for Christmas.

Anon.   "BELLS."   J. S. B. HODGES.

1. Ring out the bells for Christmas, The hap-py, hap-py day! In win-ter wild, the ho-ly Child
2. On Bethlehem's qui-et hill-side, In a-ges long gone by, In an-gel notes the Glory floats,
3. Where'er His sweet lambs gather With-in His gen-tle fold, The Sav-iour dear is waiting near,
4. Then sing your gladsome car-ols, And hail the new-born Sun; For Christmas light is passing bright,

With-in the cra-dle lay. Oh, won-der-ful! the Sav-iour Is in a man-ger lone;
Glo-ry to God on high! Yet wakes the sun as joy-ous As when the Lord was born,
As in the days of old: In each young heart you see Him, In ev-ery guile-less face,
It smiles on ev-ery one. And feast Christ's little children, His poor, His or-phan call;

Refrain.

His pal-ace is a sta-ble, And Ma-ry's arm His throne.
And still He comes to greet you On ev-ery Christmas morn.
You see the Ho-ly Je-sus, Who grew in truth and grace.
For He who chose the man-ger, He lov-eth one and all.

Ring out the bells for Christmas,

The hap-py, hap-py day! Ring out the bells for Christmas, The hap-py, hap-py day!

91

Ring merrily! ring merrily!

From "Home Words." "PELHAM MANOR." J. W. Treadwell, 1893.

1. Ring mer - ri - ly! ring mer - ri - ly! O hap - py Christmas bells; And let us hear a -
2. Ring ten - der - ly! ring ten - der - ly! O ho - ly Christmas bells: For ev - er with your
3. Ring joy - ous - ly! ring joy - ous - ly! O bless-ed Christmas bells; And show us of the
4. Ring mer - ri - ly! ring mer - ri - ly! O dear old Christmas bells, And bring all ho - ly

gain the tales Your mu - sic ev - er tells, Your mu - sic ev - er tells:— How
earth - ly peal A heav'n-ly cho - rus swells, A heav'n-ly cho - rus swells; The
fu - ture good Your wel-come chime fore-tells, Your wel-come chime fore-tells. We
bless - ings down From where all mer - cy dwells, From where all mer - cy dwells. Ring

Chris-tian men in oth - er days Made feast with-in their halls, Hung mis - tle - toe and
an - gels, who were first to bring The wel-come news to men, Still join with us to
know't will be a min-gled lot Of pleas-ure, pain and strife; That thorns will clus - ter
out your gen-tle mes - sa - ges, As ye have done of old, To help the wea - ry

(Org.)

hol - ly wreaths A - round their old oak walls; How rich and poor knelt side by side, At
cel - e - brate The Sav-iour's birth a - gain; And some whom we have lov'd and lost Sing
round the flow'rs A - long our path of life; But ye shall sing to us of hope; Of
and the sad, The weaklings of the fold; And tell a - gain the cheer-ing tale Of

Ring merrily! ring merrily!—*Concluded.*

call of Christmas chimes; And how the bonds of Christian love Bound up "the good old times." A-men.
car - ols with us now, With all the old love in their hearts, And new light on their brow.
help, of love un - told; Re-mind-ing us of that bright star That tips our clouds with gold.
Him who bore our woe; And gave His own heart's life and love, For breaking hearts below.

Saw you never, in the twilight. 92

C. F. ALEXANDER, 1853. "THE WISE MEN." BERTHOLD TOURS (1838—).

1. Saw you nev-er, in the twilight, When the sun had left the skies, Up in heav'n the clear stars
2. Heard you nev-er of the sto - ry How they cross'd the desert wild, Jour-ney'd on by plain and
3. Know ye not that low-ly Ba - by Was the bright and morning Star? He Who came to light the

shin - ing Thro' the gloom, like sil - ver eyes? So of old the wise men, watching, Saw a lit - tle
mountain, Till they found the Ho - ly Child? How they open'd all their treasure, Kneeling to that
Gen-tiles, And the dark-en'd isles a - far? And we, too, may seek His cradle; There our hearts' best

stran-ger star, And they knew the King was giv - en, And they fol-low'd it from far. A - men.
in - fant King; Gave the gold and fragrant in-cense, Gave the myrrh in of - fer-ing?
treas-ures bring; Love, and faith, and true de - vo - tion, For our Sav-iour, God, and King.

93

See! amid the winter's snow.

E. CASWALL, 1858.   "AGNUS DEI."   C. P. MORRISON.

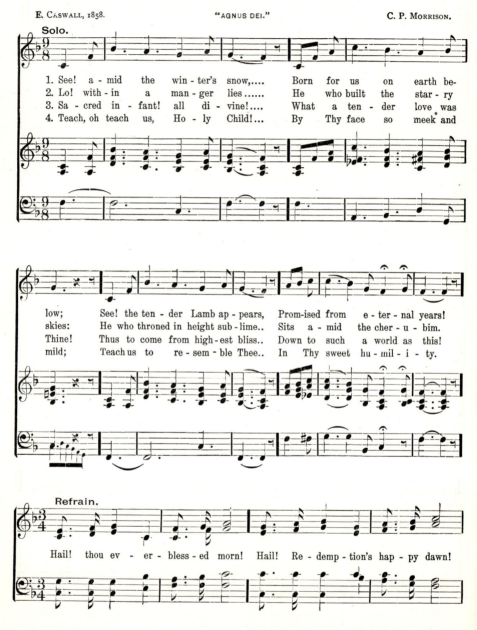

Solo.

1. See! a - mid the win - ter's snow,.... Born for us on earth be-
2. Lo! with - in a man - ger lies...... He who built the star - ry
3. Sa - cred in - fant! all di - vine!.... What a ten - der love was
4. Teach, oh teach us, Ho - ly Child!... By Thy face so meek and

low;   See! the ten - der Lamb ap - pears,   Prom-ised from e - ter - nal years!
skies: He who throned in height sub - lime..   Sits a - mid the cher - u - bim.
Thine!   Thus to come from high - est bliss..   Down to such a world as this!
mild;   Teach us to re - sem - ble Thee..   In Thy sweet hu - mil - i - ty.

Refrain.

Hail! thou ev - er - bless - ed morn! Hail! Re - demp - tion's hap - py dawn!

See! amid the winter's snow.—*Concluded.*

Sing thro' all Je - ru - sa - lem, Christ is born in Beth - le - hem! A - men.

A shining star.

94

L. A. COONLEY.   "OAK PARK."   W. A. BARTLETT, 1895.

1. A   shin - ing star Came from   a - far, Up - on   a snow - y   morn,
2. Sweet Christ - mas then Was given   to men   To bless the win - ter   wild,
3. All   hail   that morn When Christ was born! Wreathe hol - ly, pine and   bay,

An   an - gel near Sang, "Do   not fear, Be - hold! a child is   born,"
Since   in   a stall The Lord of all   Be - came   a lit - tle   child,
Let   chil - dren sing, Let   car - ols ring To bless our Christ-mas day,

An   an - gel near Sang, "Do   not fear, Be - hold a child is born." A - men.
Since   in   a stall The Lord of all   Be - came   a lit - tle child.
Let   chil - dren sing, Let   car - ols ring To bless our Christ-mas day.

95

Now let us sing the Angels' Song.

"THE ANGELS' SONG." A. RANDEGGER, 1870.

1. Now let us sing the An-gels' Song That rang so sweet and clear, When heav'n-ly light and mu-sic fell On earth-ly eye and

Now let us sing the Angels' Song.—*Concluded.*

ear,   To Him we sing, our Sav - iour King, Who al - ways deigns to

hear:...   "Glo - ry   to   God,... and peace   on   earth."   A - men.

2.

He came to tell the Father's love,
  His goodness, truth and grace;
To shew the brightness of His smile,
  The glory of His face;
With His own light, so full and bright,
  The shades of death to chase.
"Glory to God, and peace on earth."

3.

He came to bring the weary ones
  True peace and perfect rest;
To take away the guilt and sin
  Which darkened and distressed,
That great and small might hear His call,
  And all in Him be blessed.
"Glory to God, and peace on earth."

4.

He came to bring a glorious gift,
  Good-will to men;—and why?
Because He loved us, Jesus came
  For us to live and die:
Then, sweet and long, the Angels' Song,
  Again we raise on high:
"Glory to God, and peace on earth."

96

Ring out, O bells, in gladness!

AMY S. WOODS. "WOODS." CALEB SIMPER.

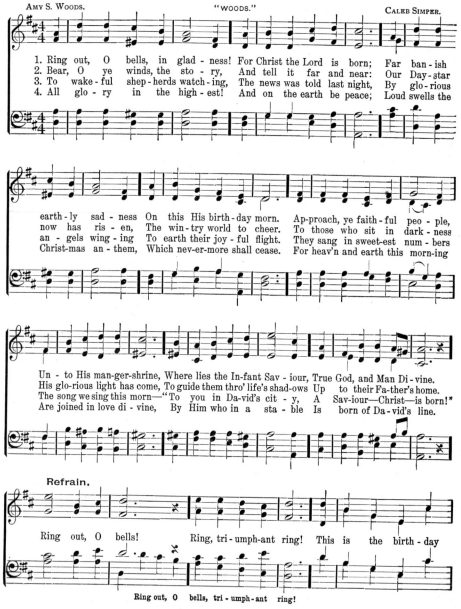

1. Ring out, O bells, in glad - ness! For Christ the Lord is born; Far ban - ish
2. Bear, O ye winds, the sto - ry, And tell it far and near: Our Day - star
3. To wake - ful shep - herds watch - ing, The news was told last night, By glo - rious
4. All glo - ry in the high - est! And on the earth be peace; Loud swells the

earth - ly sad - ness On this His birth - day morn. Ap-proach, ye faith - ful peo - ple,
now has ris - en, The win - try world to cheer. To those who sit in dark - ness
an - gels wing - ing To earth their joy - ful flight. They sang in sweet-est num - bers
Christ-mas an - them, Which nev-er-more shall cease. For heav'n and earth this morn - ing

Un - to His man-ger-shrine, Where lies the In-fant Sav - iour, True God, and Man Di - vine.
His glo-rious light has come, To guide them thro' life's shad-ows Up to their Fa-ther's home.
The song we sing this morn—"To you in Da-vid's cit - y, A Sav-iour—Christ—is born!"
Are joined in love di - vine, By Him who in a sta - ble Is born of Da-vid's line.

Refrain.

Ring out, O bells! Ring, tri - umph-ant ring! This is the birth - day

Ring out, O bells, tri - umph-ant ring!

Ring out, O bells.—*Concluded.*

of our King; O bells, tri-umph-ant ring! Ring out, O bells! [*Organ......*] O

bells, tri-umph-ant ring! Ring out, O bells! Ring, tri-umph-ant ring! *A-men.*

Ring out, O bells, tri-umph-ant ring!

All my heart this night rejoices. 97

P. GERHARDT, 1656.,
Tr. C. WINKWORTH, 1858.

"BONN."

J. G. EBELING (c. 1620—1676).

1. All my heart this night re - joic - es, As I hear, far and near, Sweet-est an-gel-voic - es;
2. Hark! a voice from yon-der man-ger, Soft and sweet, doth entreat, "Flee from woe and danger!
3. Come, then, let us hast-en yon - der! Here let all, great and small, Kneel in awe and won-der!
4. Heed-ful - ly my Lord I'll cher - ish, Live to Thee, and with Thee Dy-ing, shall not per - ish;

"Christ is born," their choirs are singing, Till the air ev-'ry-where Now with joy is ring - ing. *A - men.*
Breth-ren, come! from all that grieves you You are freed; all you need I will surely give you."
Love Him who with love is yearn-ing! Hail the Star that from far Bright with hope is burning!
But shall dwell with Thee for ev - er, Far on high, in the joy That can al - ter nev - er.

98

Who is this, so weak and helpless?

W. W. How, D.D. (1823—), 1867.   "EXALTATION."   Henry Leslie (1822—1896), 1887.

1. Who is this, so weak and help-less, Child of low-ly He-brew maid,
2. Who is this, a Man of sor-rows, Walk-ing sad-ly life's hard way,
3. Who is this that hang-eth dy-ing, While the rude world scoffs and scorns,

Rude-ly in a sta-ble shel-ter'd, Cold-ly in a man-ger laid?
Home-less, wea-ry, sigh-ing, weep-ing, O-ver sin and Sa-tan's sway?
Num-ber'd with the mal-e-fac-tors, Torn with nails and crown'd with thorns?

'Tis the Lord of all cre-a-tion, Who this won-drous path hath trod;
'Tis our God, our glo-rious Sav-iour, Who a-bove the star-ry sky
'Tis the God who ev-er liv-eth 'Mid the shin-ing ones on high,

He is God from ev-er-last-ing, And to ev-er-last-ing, God.   A-men.
Now for us a place pre-par-eth, Where no tear can dim the eye.
In the glo-rious gold-en cit-y Reign-ing ev-er-last-ing-ly.

From the eastern mountains.

"COLYTON."

W. H. MONK, 1881.

1. From the eas - tern moun - tains, Press-ing on they come, Wise men in their
2. Thou Who in a man - ger Once hast low - ly lain, Who dost now in
3. Gath - er in the out - casts, All who go a - stray, Throw Thy ra - diance

wis - dom, To His hum - ble home; Stirr'd by deep de - vo - tion, Hast - ing
glo - ry.... O'er all king-doms reign, Gath - er in the hea - then, Who in
o'er them, Guide them on their way; Those who nev - er knew Thee, Those who

from a - far, Ev - er journeying on - ward, Guid - ed by a star. A-men.
lands a - far Ne'er have seen the bright - ness Of Thy guid-ing star.
wan - der far, Guide them by the bright - ness Of Thy guid-ing star.

4 Onward through the darkness
　　Of the lonely night,
Shining still before them
　　With Thy kindly light.
Guide them, Jew and Gentile,
　　Homeward from afar,
Young and old together,
　　By Thy kindly star.

7 E

5 Until every nation,
　　Whether bond or free,
'Neath Thy starlit banner,
　　Jesus, follows Thee
O'er the distant mountains,
　　To that heavenly home,
Where no sin nor sorrow
　　Evermore shall come.

100
Brightest and best of the sons of the morning.

R. Heber, 1811.　　　　　"SANTA LAURA."　　　　　W. A. Barrett, 1865.

1. Bright-est and best of the sons of the morn-ing, Dawn on our
2. Cold on His cra-dle the dew-drops are shin-ing, Low lies His
3. Shall we not yield Him, in cost-ly de-vo-tion, O-dors of

darkness and lend us thine aid; Star of the east, the ho-ri-zon a-
head with the beasts of the stall; An-gels a-dore Him in slum-ber re-
E-dom, and of-f'rings di-vine? Gems of the moun-tain, and pearls of the

dorn-ing, Guide where our in-fant Re-deem-er is laid. A-men.
clin-ing, Mak-er and Mon-arch and Sav-iour of all.
o-cean, Myrrh from the for-est, and gold from the mine?

4 Vainly we offer each ample oblation,
　　Vainly with gifts would His favor secure;
　Richer by far is the heart's adoration,
　　Dearer to God are the prayers of the poor.

5 Brightest and best of the sons of the morning,
　　Dawn on our darkness and lend us thine aid;
　Star of the east, the horizon adorning,
　　Guide where our infant Redeemer is laid.

As with gladness men of old.

W. C. DIX, 1856.   "DIX."   Arr. fr. C. KÖCHER (1786—1872).

1. As with glad-ness men of old   Did the guid-ing star be-hold,
2. As with joy-ful steps they sped   To that low-ly man-ger-bed,
3. As they of-fered gifts most rare   At that man-ger rude and bare,

As with joy they hailed its light,   Lead-ing on-ward, beam-ing bright,
There to bend the knee be-fore   Him whom heav'n and earth a-dore,
So may we with ho-ly joy,   Pure and free from sin's al-loy,

So, most gra-cious Lord, may we   Ev-er-more be led to Thee.   A-men.
So may we with will-ing feet   Ev-er seek the mer-cy-seat.
All our cost-liest treas-ures bring,   Christ, to Thee our heav'n-ly King.

4 Holy Jesus, every day
  Keep us in the narrow way;
  And, when earthly things are past,
  Bring our ransomed souls at last
  Where they need no star to guide,
  Where no clouds Thy glory hide.

5 In the heavenly country bright,
  Need they no created light;
  Thou its light, its joy, its crown,
  Thou its Sun which goes not down;
  There for ever may we sing
  Alleluias to our King.

102

O Master, let me walk with Thee.

W. GLADDEN, 1880.   "MARYTON."   H. P. SMITH, 1874.

1. O Mas-ter, let me walk with Thee In low-ly paths of ser-vice free;
2. Help me the slow of heart to move By some clear, win-ning word of love;
3. Teach me Thy pa-tience; still with Thee In clos-er, dear-er com-pa-ny,
4. In hope that sends a shin-ing ray Far down the fu-ture's broad-'ning way,

Tell me Thy se-cret, help me bear The strain of toil, the fret of care. A-men.
Teach me the way-ward feet to stay, And guide them in the homeward way.
In work that keeps faith sweet and strong, In trust that tri-umphs o-ver wrong,
In peace that on-ly Thou canst give, With Thee, O Mas-ter, let me live.

103

Fairest Lord Jesus.

ANON. (German), 1677.
Tr. R. S. WILLIS, 1850.   "CRUSADERS' HYMN."   GERMAN.
Arr. by R. S. WILLIS, 1850.

1. Fair-est Lord Je-sus, Rul-er of all na-ture, O Thou of God and man the Son,
2. Fair are the mead-ows, Fair-er still the wood-lands, Robed in the blooming garb of spring;
3. Fair is the sun-shine, Fair-er still the moon-light, And all the twink-ling, star-ry host;

Thee will I cher-ish, Thee will I hon-or, Thou, my soul's glory, joy, and crown. A-men.
Je-sus is fair-er, Je-sus is pur-er, Who makes the wo-ful heart to sing.
Je-sus shines brighter, Je-sus shines pur-er Than all the an-gels heav'n can boast.

I heard the voice of Jesus say.

H. BONAR, 1846. "VOX DILECTI." J. B. DYKES, 1868

1. I heard the voice of Je - sus say, "Come un - to Me and rest;
2. I heard the voice of Je - sus say, "Be - hold, I free - ly give
3. I heard the voice of Je - sus say, "I am this dark world's light;

Lay down, thou wea - ry one, lay down Thy head up - on My breast."
The liv - ing wa - ter; thirst - y one, Stoop down and drink, and live."
Look un - to Me, thy morn shall rise, And all thy day be bright."

I came to Je - sus as I was, Wea - ry, and worn, and sad,
I came to Je - sus, and I drank Of that life - giv - ing stream;
I looked to Je - sus, and I found In Him my star, my sun;

I found in Him a rest - ing place, And He has made me glad. A - men.
My thirst was quench'd, my soul re - vived, And now I live in Him.
And in that light of life I'll walk Till trav - 'ling days are done.

105

Jesus, King of Glory.

E. HARLAND, 1863.　　　　　　　"AMBLESIDE."　　　　　　　A. LOWE, 1876.

1. Je - sus, King of Glo - ry, Thron'd a - bove the sky, Je - sus, ten - der Sav - iour,
2. For the lit - tle chil-dren, Who have come to Thee; For the glad, bright spir-its
3. For Thy faith - ful serv-ants Who have en - tered in; For Thy fear-less sol - diers
4. When the shad-ows lengthen, Show us, Lord, Thy way; Thro' the dark-ness lead us

Hear Thy chil-dren cry. Par - don our trans - gres - sions, Cleanse us from our sin;
Who Thy glo - ry see; For the lov'd ones rest - ing In Thy dear em - brace;
Who have conquer'd sin; For the count-less le - gions, Who have fol - low'd Thee,
To the heav'n-ly day. When our course is fin - ish'd, End - ed all the strife,

Refrain.

By Thy Spir - it help us Heav'n-ly life to win.
For the pure and ho - ly Who be - hold Thy face,
Heed-less of the dan - ger, On to vic - to - ry;
Grant us with the faith - ful, Palms and crowns of life.

Je - sus, King of Glo - ry,

Thron'd a - bove the sky, Je - sus, ten-der Sav - iour, Hear Thy chil-dren cry. *A-men.*

I hear a voice, 'tis soft and sweet.

R. F. Sample, 1888. "VOX SALVATORIS." Beardsley Van de Water, 1888.

1. I hear a voice, 'tis soft and sweet, It bids my sin - sick soul re-joice;
2. When wea - ry with my load of guilt, I'll not for - get that "Christ is all:"
3. My soul is trou - bled like the sea, The surg - ing bil - lows roll a - round:

The same was heard in Sa - lem's street, And in the moun - tain's cool re - treat,
For me His pre - cious blood was spilt; He sweet - ly says, "Come, if thou wilt;"
But he who calmed far Ga - li - lee Doth kind - ly say, "Peace be to thee;"

Refrain.

My Sav - iour's voice.
How glad the call! } Sweet - er than chim - ing bells, Soft - er than eve - ning
How blest the sound!

rall.

rills, The voice that tells of par - don— Par - don, peace, and heaven. A - men.

107

I need Thee every hour.

Annie S. Hawks, 1872:
Refrain added by R. Lowry.

"NEED."

R. Lowry, 1872.

1. I need Thee ev - ery hour, Most gra - cious Lord;
2. I need Thee ev - ery hour; Stay Thou near by;
3. I need Thee ev - ery hour, In joy or pain;
4. I need Thee ev - ery hour, Teach me Thy will,
5. I need Thee ev - ery hour, Most Ho - ly One;

No ten - der voice like Thine Can peace af - ford.
Temp - ta - tions lose their pow'r When Thou art nigh.
Come quick - ly, and a - bide, Or life is vain.
And Thy rich prom - is - es In me ful - fil.
O make me Thine in - deed, Thou bless - ed Son.

Refrain.

I need Thee, O I need Thee, Ev - ery hour I need Thee;

O bless me now, my Sav - iour,— I come to Thee. A - men.

Copyright (words and music) by R. Lowry.

For the beauty of the earth.

F. S. Pierpoint, 1864.   "HEATHLANDS."   H. Smart (1813—1879).

1. For the beau - ty of the earth, For the beau - ty of the skies,
2. For the won - der of each hour Of the day and of the night,
3. For the joy of hu - man love, Broth - er, sis - ter, par - ent, child,

For the love which from our birth O - ver and a - round us lies,
Hill and vale, and tree and flow'r, Sun and moon, and stars of light,
Friends on earth, and friends a - bove, For all gen - tle thoughts and mild:

Christ our God, to Thee we raise This our hymn of grate-ful praise. A - men.
Christ our God, to Thee we raise This our hymn of grate-ful praise.
Christ our God, to Thee we raise This our hymn of grate-ful praise.

4 For Thy Church, that evermore
  Lifteth holy hands above,
Offering up on every shore
  Her pure sacrifice of love:
Christ our God, to Thee we raise
This our hymn of grateful praise.

5 For Thyself, best Gift Divine!
  To our race so freely given,
For that great, great love of Thine,
  Peace on earth, and joy in heaven;
Christ our God, to Thee we raise
This our hymn of grateful praise.

109

Immortal love, for ever full.

J. G. WHITTIER, 1866. "FAITH." J. B. DYKES, 1867.

1. Im - mor - tal love, for ev - er full, For ev - er flow - ing free,
2. Our out - ward lips con - fess the name All oth - er names a - bove;
3. We may not climb the heav'n - ly steeps To bring the Lord Christ down;

For ev - er shared, for ev - er whole, A nev - er ebb - ing sea! A - men.
Love on - ly know - eth whence it came, And com - pre - hend - eth love.
In vain we search the low - est deeps, For Him no depths can drown.

4 But warm, sweet, tender, even yet
   A present help is He;
And faith has still its Olivet,
   And love its Galilee.

5 The healing of His seamless dress
   Is by our beds of pain;
We touch Him in life's throng and press,
   And we are whole again.

6 Through Him the first fond prayers are said
   Our lips of childhood frame,
The last low whispers of our dead
   Are burdened with His name.

7 O Lord, and Master of us all!
   Whate'er our name or sign,
We own Thy sway, we hear Thy call,
   We test our lives by Thine.

110

Majestic sweetness sits enthroned.

S. STENNETT, 1787. "ORTONVILLE." T. HASTINGS, 1837.

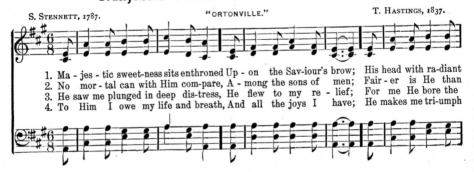

1. Ma - jes - tic sweet-ness sits enthroned Up - on the Sav-iour's brow; His head with ra-diant
2. No mor - tal can with Him com-pare, A - mong the sons of men; Fair - er is He than
3. He saw me plunged in deep dis-tress, He flew to my re - lief; For me He bore the
4. To Him I owe my life and breath, And all the joys I have; He makes me tri-umph

Majestic sweetness.—*Concluded.*

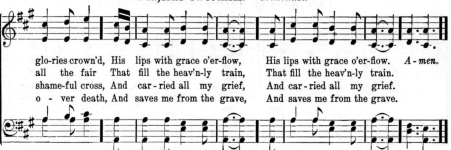

glo-ries crown'd, His lips with grace o'er-flow, His lips with grace o'er-flow. A - men.
all the fair That fill the heav'n-ly train, That fill the heav'n-ly train.
shame-ful cross, And car-ried all my grief, And car-ried all my grief.
o - ver death, And saves me from the grave, And saves me from the grave.

5 To heaven, the place of His abode,
   He brings my weary feet;
Shows me the glories of my God,
   And makes my joys complete.

6 Since from His bounty I receive
   Such proofs of love Divine,
Had I a thousand hearts to give,
   Lord, they should all be Thine.

Come, let us join our cheerful songs. III

Isaac Watts, 1707.   "AZMON."   Arr. from Carl G. Gläser, 1828, by Lowell Mason, 1839.

1. Come, let us join our cheer-ful songs With an-gels round the throne;
2. "Wor-thy the Lamb that died," they cry, "To be ex-alt-ed thus!"
3. Je-sus is wor-thy to re-ceive Hon-or and pow'r di-vine;

Ten thou-sand thou-sand are their tongues, But all their joys are one. A - men.
"Wor-thy the Lamb!" our lips rep-ly, "For He was slain for us."
And bless-ings more than we can give, Be, Lord, for ev-er Thine!

4 Let all that dwell above the sky,
   And air, and earth, and seas,
Conspire to lift Thy glories high,
   And speak Thine endless praise.

5 The whole creation join in one
   To bless the sacred name
Of Him that sits upon the throne,
   And to adore the Lamb.

112

All glory, laud, and honor.

THEODULPH, 820.
Tr. J. M. NEALE, 1854.

"ST. THEODULPH."

M. TESCHNER, 1615.

1. { All glo - ry, laud, and hon - or To Thee, Re - deem - er, King,
   { To whom the lips of chil - dren Made sweet ho - san - nas ring.

The 2nd and following verses.

2. Thou art the King of Is - - rael, Thou Da - vid's roy - al Son,
3. The com - pa - ny of an - gels Are prais - ing Thee on high;
4. The peo - ple of the He - brews With palms be - fore Thee went;
5. To Thee, be - fore Thy pas - sion, They sang their hymns of praise;
6. Thou didst ac - cept their prais - es; Ac - cept the pray'rs we bring,

Who in the Lord's name com - - est, The King and bless - ed one.
And mor - tal men, and all........ things Cre - at - ed, make re - ply.
Our praise and pray'rs and an - - thems Be - fore Thee we pre - sent.
To Thee, now high ex - alt - - ed, Our mel - o - dy we raise.
Who in all good de - light - est, Thou good and gra - cious King.

After each verse.

{ All glo - ry, laud, and hon - or To Thee, Re - deem-er, King,
{ To whom the lips of chil - dren Made sweet ho - san - nas ring. } A - men.

Beneath the cross of Jesus.

E. C. CLEPHANE, 1868.   "ST. CHRISTOPHER."   F. C. MAKER, 1881.

1. Be - neath the cross of Je - sus I fain would take my stand, The
2. Up - on the cross of Je - sus, Mine eye at times can see The
3. I take, O Cross, thy shad - ow For my a - bid - ing - place; I

shad - ow of a might - y rock With - in a wea - ry land; A
ver - y dy - ing form of one Who suf - fer'd there for me. And
ask no oth - er sun - shine than The sun - shine of His face; Con -

home with - in the wil - der - ness, A rest up - on the way, From the
from my smit - ten heart with tears, These won - ders I con - fess,—The.......
tent to let the world go by, To know no gain nor loss, My........

burn - ing of the noon-tide heat, And the bur - den of the day. A - men.
won - der of His glo - rious love, And..... my own worth-less-ness.
sin - ful self my on - ly shame, My...... glo - ry all the cross.

114

There is a green hill far away.

C. F. ALEXANDER, 1848.   "ILFRACOMB." (LAMBETH.)   S. WEBBE [?] (1740—1816).

1. There is a green hill far a - way, With-out a cit - y wall,.....
2. He died that we might be for - giv'n, He died to make us good,.....
3. Oh, dear - ly, dear - ly has He lov'd! And we must love Him too,.......

Where the dear Lord was cru - ci - fied, Who died to save us all....... A - men.
That we might go at last to heav'n, Sav'd by His pre - cious blood....
And trust in His re - deem - ing blood, And try His works to do........

SECOND TUNE.

"CAROL."   R. S. WILLIS, 1849.

1. There is a green hill far a - way, With - out a cit - y wall,
2. He died that we might be for - giv'n, He died to make us good,
3. Oh, dear - ly, dear - ly has He lov'd! And we must love Him too,

Where the dear Lord was cru - ci - fied, Who died to save us all.....
That we might go at last to heav'n, Sav'd by His pre - cious blood.
And trust in His re - deem - ing blood. And try His works to do.....

There is a green hill far away.—*Concluded.*

We may not know, we can-not tell, What pains He had to bear,
There was none oth - er good e - nough To pay the price of sin,
For there's a green hill far a - way, With-out a cit - y wall,

But we be - lieve it was for us He hung and suf - fer'd there. *A-men.*
He on - ly could un - lock the gate Of heav'n, and let us in.....
Where the dear Lord was cru - ci - fied, Who died to save us all....

Jesus lives! thy terrors now. 115

C. F. GELLERT, 1757.
Tr. Miss F. E. COX, 1841. Alt. Abr.   "ST. ALBINUS."   H. J. GAUNTLETT (1805—1876).

1. Je - sus lives! thy ter-rors now Can no lon - ger, death, ap - pall us; Je - sus
2. Je - sus lives! for us He died; Then, a - lone to Je - sus liv - ing, Pure in
3. Je - sus lives! our hearts know well Naught from us His love shall sev - er, Life, nor
4. Je - sus lives! to Him the throne O - ver all the world is giv - en; May we

lives! by this we know Thou, O grave, canst not en-thrall us. Al - le - lu - ia! *A-men.*
heart may we a - bide, Glo - ry to ou: Sav-iour giv - ing, Al - le - lu - ia!
death, nor pow'rs of hell Tear us from His keep-ing ev - er. Al - le - lu - ia!
go where He has gone, Rest and reign with Him in heav - en. Al - le - lu - ia!

116

Welcome, happy morning!

V. H. C. FORTUNATUS (6th Cent.).
Tr. J. ELLERTON, 1868.

"WELCOME, HAPPY MORNING."

J. B. CALKIN (1827—).

1. Wel - come, hap-py morn - ing! age to age shall say, Hell to - day is
2. Earth her joy con - fess - es, cloth-ing her for spring, All good gifts re-
3. Months in due suc - ces - sion, days of length'ning light, Hours and pass - ing

van-quish'd, heav'n is won to - day. Lo! the Dead is liv - ing,
turned with her re - turn - ing King; Bloom in ev - er - y mead - ow,
mo - ments praise Thee in their flight; Bright-ness of the morn - ing,

God for ev - er - more; Him, their true Cre - a - tor, all His works a - dore.
leaves on ev-ery bough, Speak His sor - row end - ed, hail His tri - umph now.
sky and fields and sea, Van - quish-er of darkness, bring their praise to Thee.

ff Refrain in unison.

Wel-come, hap - py morn - ing! age to age shall say, Hell to - day is

Welcome, happy morning!—*Concluded.*

van-quish'd, heav'n is won to-day. Lo! the Dead is liv-ing,

God for ev-er-more; Him, their true Cre-a-tor, all His works a-dore. A-men.

4 Maker and Redeemer, life and health of all,
    Thou from heaven beholding human nature's fall,
    Of the Father's Godhead true and only Son,
    Manhood to deliver, manhood didst put on.—*Ref.*

5 Thou, of life the author, death didst undergo,
    Tread the path of darkness, saving strength to show;
    Come then, True and Faithful, now fulfill Thy word;
    'T is Thine own third morning: rise, O buried Lord!—*Ref.*

6 Loose the souls long prisoned, bound with Satan's chain,
    All that now is fallen raise to life again;
    Show Thy face in brightness, bid the nations see,
    Bring again our daylight; day returns with Thee.—*Ref.*

8 E

117

Christ is risen, Christ is risen!

A. T. Gurney, 1862. "RESURREXIT." A. S. Sullivan (1874—).

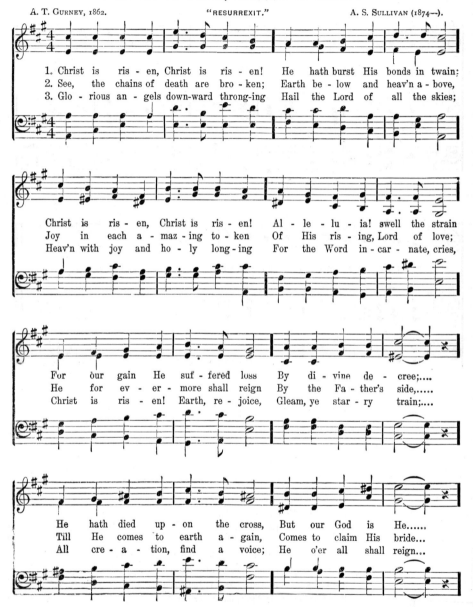

1. Christ is ris - en, Christ is ris - en! He hath burst His bonds in twain;
2. See, the chains of death are bro - ken; Earth be - low and heav'n a - bove,
3. Glo - rious an - gels down-ward throng-ing Hail the Lord of all the skies;

Christ is ris - en, Christ is ris - en! Al - le - lu - ia! swell the strain
Joy in each a - maz - ing to - ken Of His ris - ing, Lord of love;
Heav'n with joy and ho - ly long-ing For the Word in - car - nate, cries,

For our gain He suf - fered loss By di - vine de - cree;....
He for ev - er - more shall reign By the Fa - ther's side,.....
Christ is ris - en! Earth, re - joice, Gleam, ye star - ry train;....

He hath died up - on the cross, But our God is He......
Till He comes to earth a - gain, Comes to claim His bride...
All cre - a - tion, find a voice; He o'er all shall reign...

Christ is risen, Christ is risen!—*Concluded.*

Refrain.

Refrain for last verse.

Christ is ris - en, Christ is ris - en! He hath burst His bonds in twain;
Christ is ris - en, Christ is ris - en! He hath burst His bonds in twain;

Christ is ris - en, Christ is ris - en! Al - le - lu - ia! swell the strain. A - men.
Christ is ris - en, Christ is ris - en! O'er the u - ni - verse to reign.

The golden gates are lifted up. 118

Mrs. C. F. Alexander, 1858. "TREVES." H. Hiles.

1. The gold - en gates are lift - ed up, The doors are o - pen'd wide,
2. Thou art gone up be - fore us, Lord, To make for us a place,
3. Lift up our hearts, lift up our minds, Let Thy dear grace be giv'n,
4. That where Thou art, at God's right hand, Our hope, our love may be;

The King of glo - ry is gone in Un - to His Fa - ther's side. A - men.
That we may be where now Thou art And look up - on God's face.
That while we tar - ry here be - low, Our treas-ure be in heav'n;—
Dwell Thou in us, that we may dwell For ev - er - more in Thee!

119

The fishers sat within their boat.

"DAWNING."

H. ELLIOT BUTTON, 1893.

1. The fish-ers sat with-in their boat, The long and wea-ry night; And
2. A form sub-lime stood on the shore, A-mid the melt-ing gloom; It
3. And O what won-drous ti-dings then! That Je-sus, who was slain, Had

hop'd and toil'd and watch'd their nets, Till morning's dawn-ing light. And then up-on the
was the form of Him they lov'd, All-glo-rious from the tomb. And then up-on the
burst the might-y bars of death, And con-quer'd life a-gain. And still up-on the

si-lent air They heard that voice once more That woke such thrills of bliss and love
si-lent air Rang out those tones once more That woke such thrills of bliss and love
si-lent air We hear that voice once more; It calls us with the same sweet words

Refrain.

In wea-ry hearts be-fore:
In wea-ry hearts be-fore:
It call'd to them be-fore:

"Come, chil-dren, toil no lon-ger, Thro' night's long lin-g'ring

The fishers sat within their boat.—*Concluded.*

gloom; For morn-ing sweet is dawn-ing O-ver the con-quer'd tomb." A-men.

The strife is o'er, the battle done.　120

Anon. (Latin). Tr. F. Pott, 1861.　　　"VICTORY."　　　Arr. fr. Palestrina (1515?—1594).

Al - le - lu - ia! Al - le - lu - ia! Al - le - lu - ia!

Org.

1. The strife is o'er, the bat - tle done,　The vic - to - ry of life is won;
2. The pow'rs of death have done their worst,　But Christ their le - gions hath dis - pers'd;
3. The three sad days are quick - ly sped,　He ris - es glo - rious from the dead;
4. He clos'd the yawn - ing gates of hell,　The bars from heav'n's high por - tals fell;
5. Lord, by the stripes which wound - ed Thee,　From death's dread sting Thy serv - ants free,

The song of tri - umph has be - gun.　Al - le - lu - ia!　A - men.
Let shout of ho - ly joy out - burst,　Al - le - lu - ia!
All glo - ry to our ris - en Head!　Al - le - lu - ia!
Let hymns of praise His tri - umphs tell.　Al - le - lu - ia!
That we may live and sing to Thee,　Al - le - lu - ia!

121

The day of Resurrection.

John of Damascus (8th Cent.).
Tr. J. M. Neale, 1862.   "LANCASHIRE."   H. Smart, 1866.

1. The day of Res - ur - rec - tion, Earth, tell it out a - broad,
2. Our hearts be pure from e - vil That we may see a - right
3. Now let the heav'ns be joy - ful, Let earth her song be - gin,

The Pass - o - ver of glad - ness, The Pass - o - ver of God.
The Lord in rays e - ter - nal Of Res - ur - rec - tion light;
Let the round world keep tri - umph, And all that is there - in;

From death to life e - ter - nal, From this world to the sky,...
And, list - 'ning to His ac - cents, May hear so calm and plain
In - vis - i - ble and vis - i - ble Their notes let all things blend,

Our Christ hath brought us o - ver, With hymns of vic - to - ry. A - men.
His Own "All hail," and hear - ing May raise the vic - tor strain.
For Christ the Lord is ris - en, Our joy that hath no end.

Come, ye faithful, raise the strain.

JOHN OF DAMASCUS (8th Cent.).
Tr. J. M. NEALE, 1850.

"ST. KEVIN."

A. S. SULLIVAN, 1872.

1. Come, ye faith-ful, raise the strain Of tri-umph-ant glad-ness,
2. 'Tis the spring of souls to-day, Christ hath burst His pris-on,
3. Now the queen of sea-sons, bright With the day of splen-dor,
4. Nei-ther might the gates of death, Nor the tomb's dark por-tal,

God hath brought His Is-ra-el In-to joy from sad-ness;
And from three days' sleep in death As a sun hath ris-en;
With the roy-al feast of feasts Comes its joy to ren-der;
Nor the watch-ers, nor the seal, Hold Thee as a mor-tal;

Loos'd from Pha-raoh's bit-ter yoke Ja-cob's sons and daugh-ters,
All the win-ter of our sins, Long and dark, is fly-ing,
Comes to glad Je-ru-sa-lem, Who with true af-fec-tion
But to-day a-midst the twelve Thou didst stand, be-stow-ing

Led them with un-moist-en'd foot Thro' the Red Sea wa-ters. *A-men.*
From His light, to whom we give Laud and praise un-dy-ing.
Wel-comes, in un-wea-ried strains, Je-sus' res-ur-rec-tion.
That Thy peace, which ev-er-more Pass-eth hu-man know-ing.

123 Jesus Christ is risen to-day.

ANON. (Latin, 14th Cent.).
Tr. TATE AND BRADY.

"WORGAN."

LYRA DAVIDICA, 1708.

1. Je - sus Christ is ris'n to - day,... Al - - - le - lu - ia!
2. Hymns of praise then let us sing.. Al - - - le - lu - ia!
3. But the pains which He en - dured, Al - - - le - lu - ia!
4. Now be God the Fa - ther praised, Al - - - le - lu - ia!

Our tri - umph - ant ho - ly day,... Al - - - le - lu - ia!
Un - to Christ, our heav'n - ly King, Al - - - le - lu - ia!
Our sal - va - tion have pro - cured; Al - - - le - lu - ia!
With the Son, from death up - raised, Al - - - le - lu - ia!

Who did once up - on the cross, Al - - - le - lu - ia!
Who en - dured the cross and grave, Al - - - le - lu - ia!
Now a - bove the sky He's King, Al - - - le - lu - ia!
And the Spir - it, ev - er blest, Al - - - le - lu - ia!

Suf - fer to re - deem our loss. Al - - - le - lu - ia! A - men.
Sin - ners to re - deem and save. Al - - - le - lu - ia!
Where the an - gels ev - er sing, Al - - - le - lu - ia!
One true God, by all con - fessed. Al - - - le - lu - ia!

Sweetly the birds are singing.

Miss E. D. CHAPMAN.　　　　　　"EASTER."　　　　　　L. DAMROSCH, 1885.

1. Sweet-ly the birds are.... sing - ing At Eas - ter dawn, Sweet-ly the
2. Birds,... for-get not your sing - ing At Eas - ter dawn; Bells, be ye
3. Buds, ye will soon be..... flow - ers, Cher - ry and white; Snow-storms are
4. Eas - ter...... buds were.. grow - ing A - ges a - go; Eas - ter

bells are..... ring - ing On Eas - ter morn, And the words that they say On
ev - er...... ring - ing On Eas - ter morn. In the spring of the year, When
chang-ing to show - ers, Dark-ness to light. With... wak - 'ning of spring, O
lil - ies were blow - ing By wa - ter's flow. All...... na - ture was glad, No

Eas - ter - Day Are— "Christ the Lord...... is ris - - - - en!" A - men.
Eas - ter is here, Sing— "Christ the Lord...... is ris - - - - en!"
sweet - ly sing—"Lo! Christ the Lord...... is ris - - - - en!"
creature was sad, For Christ the Lord...... was ris - - - - en!

Copyright, 1885, by The Century Co.

125

Christ is risen, Alleluia!

J. S. B. MONSELL, 1863: verse 2, l. 2, alt.   "NOYES."   F. C. MAKER.

1. Christ is ris - en, Al - le - lu - ia! Ris - en our vic - to - rious Head!
2. Christ is ris - en; all the sad - ness Of His earth - ly life is o'er:
3. Christ is ris - en; hence-forth nev - er Death or hell shall us en - thrall;

Sing His prais - es, Al - le - lu - ia! Christ is ris - en from the dead.
Thro' the o - pen gates of glad - ness He re - turns to life once more.
Be we Christ's, in Him for ev - er, We have tri - umphed o - ver all;

Grate - ful - ly our hearts a - dore Him, As His light once more ap - pears,
Death and hell be - fore Him bend - ing, See Him rise, the Vic - tor now;
All the doubt - ing and de - jec - tion Of our trem - bling hearts have ceased:

Bow - ing down in joy be - fore Him, Ris - ing up from grief and tears.
An - gels on His steps at - tend - ing, Glo - ry round His wound - ed brow.
'Tis His day of res - ur - rec - tion; Let us rise and keep the feast.

Christ is risen, Alleluia!—*Concluded.*

Refrain.

Christ is ris - en, Al - le - lu - ia! Ris - en our vic - to - rious Head!

Sing His prais-es, Al - le - lu - ia! Christ is ris - en from the dead. *A - men.*

Christ the Lord is risen to-day. 126

C. WESLEY, 1739 : verse 3, l. 3, alt. "RESURRECTION." H. J. GAUNTLETT, 1848.

1. "Christ the Lord is ris'n to - day, Sons of men and an - gels say:
2. Vain the stone, the watch, the seal! Christ has burst the gates of hell:
3. Lives a - gain our glo - rious King: Where, O death, is now thy sting?
4. Soar we now where Christ has led, Fol - lowing our ex - alt - ed Head:
5. Hail the Lord of earth and heav'n! Praise to Thee by both be giv'n:

Raise your joys and tri-umphs high; Sing ye heav'ns, and earth, re - ply. *A - men.*
Death in vain for - bids His rise; Christ has o - pened Par - a - dise.
Once He died, our souls to save: Where thy vic - to - ry, O grave?
Made like Him, like Him we rise; Ours the cross, the grave, the skies.
Thee we greet tri - umph-ant now: Hail, the Res - ur - rec - tion Thou!

127

Alleluia! Alleluia!

C. WORDSWORTH, 1862. Abr.   "ST. ANDREW."   J. BARNBY, 1870.

1. Al - le - lu - ia! Al - le - lu - ia! Hearts to heav'n and voic - es raise;
2. Now the i - ron bars are bro - ken, Christ from death to life is born,
3. Christ is ris - en, Christ the first-fruits Of the ho - ly har - vest-field,

Sing to God a hymn of glad - ness, Sing to God a hymn of praise;
Glo - rious life, and life im - mor - tal, On this ho - ly Eas - ter morn,
Which will all its full a - bun - dance At His sec - ond com - ing yield:

He who on the cross a vic - tim For the world's sal - va - tion bled,
Christ has tri-umph'd, and we con - quer By His might - y en - ter - prise,
Then the gold - en ears of har - vest Will their heads be - fore Him wave,

Je - sus Christ, the King of glo - ry, Now is ris - en from the dead. A - men.
We with Him to life e - ter - nal By His res - ur - rec - tion rise.
Ri - pen'd by His glo - rious sun-shine From the fur - rows of the grave.

Alleluia! Alleluia!—*Concluded.*

4 Christ is risen, we are risen!
   Shed upon us heavenly grace,
  Rain and dew and gleams of glory
   From the brightness of Thy face;
  That, with hearts in heaven dwelling,
   We on earth may fruitful be,
  And by angel-hands be gathered,
   And be ever, Lord, with Thee.

5 Alleluia! Alleluia!
   Glory be to God on high;
  Alleluia to the Saviour
   Who has won the victory;
  Alleluia to the Spirit,
   Fount of love and sanctity;
  Alleluia! Alleluia!
   To the Triune Majesty.

On wings of living light. 128

W. W. How, 1872.   "MANSFIELD."   J. Barnby, 1893.

Vivace.

1. On wings of liv-ing light, At ear-liest dawn of day,
2. The keep-ers watch-ing near, At that dread sight and sound,
3. Then rose from death's dark gloom, Un-seen by mor-tal eye,
4. Ye chil-dren of the light, A-rise with Him, a-rise:
5. Leave in the grave be-neath The old things pass'd a-way;

Came down the an-gel bright, And roll'd the stone a-way.
Fell down with sud-den fear, Like dead men, to the ground.
Tri-um-phant o'er the tomb, The Lord of earth and sky.
See, how the Day-star bright Is burn-ing in the skies!
Bur-ied with Him in death, O live with Him to-day.

Your voic-es raise with one ac-cord To bless and praise your ris-en Lord. A-men.

129

Golden harps are sounding.

F. R. HAVERGAL, 1872.   "HERMAS."   F. R. HAVERGAL, 1872.

1. Gold - en harps are sound - ing, An - gel-voic - es ring, Pearl - y gates are o - pened,
2. He who came to save us, He who bled and died, Now is crown'd with glo - ry,
3. Plead - ing for His chil - dren In that bless-ed place, Call - ing them to glo - ry,

O - pened for the King. Christ, the King of Glo - ry, Je - sus, King of love,
At His Fa - ther's side. Nev - er more to suf - fer, Nev - er more to die;
Send - ing them His grace, His bright home pre - par - ing, Faith-ful ones, for you,

Refrain.

Is gone up in tri - umph To His throne a - bove.
Je - sus, King of glo - ry, Is gone up on high.   All His work is end - ed;
Je - sus ev - er liv - eth, Ev - er lov - eth too.

Joy - ful - ly we sing, Je - sus hath as - cend - ed, Glo - ry to our King! A - men.

Hail the day that sees Him rise.

C. WESLEY, 1739.   "ASCENSION."   W. H. MONK, 1861.

1. Hail the day that sees Him rise, Al - - le - lu - - ia!
2. Him though high - est heav'n re - ceives, Al - - le - lu - - ia!
3. Still for us His death He pleads; Al - - le - lu - - ia!
4. Lord, though part - ed from our sight Al - - le - lu - - ia!

To His throne a - bove the skies. Al - - le - lu - - ia!
Still He loves the earth He leaves Al - - le - lu - - ia!
Prev - a - lent He in - ter - cedes; Al - - le - lu - - ia!
High a - bove yon a - zure height, Al - - le - lu - - ia!

Christ, a - while to mor - tals given, Al - - le - lu - - ia!
Though re - turn - ing to His throne, Al - - le - lu - - ia!
Near Him - self pre - pares our place, Al - - le - lu - - ia!
Grant our hearts may thith - er rise, Al - - le - lu - - ia!

Re - as - cends His na - tive heav'n. Al - le - lu - ia!   A - men.
Still He calls man - kind His own. Al - le - lu - ia!
Har - bin - ger of hu - man race. Al - le - lu - ia!
Fol - lowing Thee be - yond the skies. Al - le - lu - ia!

131

Lo! He comes, with clouds descending.

Verse 1, 2, 4, C. WESLEY, 1758.
Verse 3, J. CENNICK, 1752.

"HOLLYWOOD."

S. WEBBE (1740—1816).

1. Lo! He comes with clouds de - scend - ing, Once for fa - vored sin - ners slain;
2. Ev - ery eye shall now be - hold Him Robed in dread-ful maj - es - ty;

Thou - sand thou - sand saints at - tend - ing Swell the tri - umph of His train:
Those who set at naught and sold Him, Pierc'd, and nailed Him to the tree,

Al - le - lu - ia! Al - le - lu - ia! God ap - pears on earth to reign. A - men.
Deep-ly wail - ing, Deep-ly wail-ing, Shall the true Mes - si - ah see.

3 Now redemption, long expected
See in solemn pomp appear;
All His saints, by man rejected,
Now shall meet Him in the air
Alleluia!
See the day of God appear.

4 Yea, Amen! let all adore Thee,
High on Thine eternal throne;
Saviour, take the power and glory,
Claim the kingdom for Thine own:
Alleluia!
Thou shalt reign, and Thou alone.

Rejoice, all ye believers.

L. Laurenti, 1700.
Tr. S. B. Findlater, 1853.   "GREENLAND."   Lausanne Psalter.

1. Re - joice, all ye be - liev - ers, And let your lights ap - pear;
2. See that your lamps are burn - ing, Re - plen - ish them with oil;
3. Our hope and ex - pec - ta - tion, O Je - sus, now ap - pear;

The eve - ning is ad - vanc - ing, And dark - er night is near.
Look now for your sal - va - tion, The end of earth - ly toil.
A - rise, Thou Sun so longed for, O'er this be - night - ed sphere.

The Bride-groom is a - ris - ing, And soon He draw - eth nigh;
The watch - ers on the moun - tain Pro - claim the Bride - groom near;
With hearts and hands up - lift - ed, We plead, O Lord, to see

Up, pray, and watch, and wres - tle: At mid - night comes the cry. A - men.
Go meet Him as He com - eth, With al - le - lu - ias clear.
The day of earth's re - demp - tion, That brings us un - to Thee.

9 E

133

Alleluia! sing to Jesus.

W. C. Dix, 1866.   "ALLELUIA."   S. S. Wesley, 1868.

1. Al - le - lu - ia! sing to Je - sus; His the scep - tre, His the throne;
2. Al - le - lu - ia! not as or - phans Are we left in sor - row now;
3. Al - le - lu - ia! Bread of heav - en, Thou on earth our food, our stay!

Al - le - lu - ia! His the tri - umph, His the vic - to - ry a - lone:
Al - le - lu - ia! He is near us, Faith be - lieves, nor ques - tions how.
Al - le - lu - ia! here the sin - ful Flee to Thee from day to day:

Hark! the songs of peace - ful Zi - on Thun - der like a might - y flood;
Tho' the cloud from sight re - ceived Him, When the for - ty days were o'er,
In - ter - ces - sor, friend of sin - ners, Earth's Re - deem - er, plead for me,

Je - sus out of ev - ery na - tion Hath re - deemed us by His blood. A - men.
Shall our hearts for - get His prom - ise, "I am with you ev - er - more"?
Where the songs of all the sin - less Sweep a - cross the crys - tal sea.

Mighty God, while angels bless Thee.

R. ROBINSON (1735—1790).   "KENSINGTON NEW."   J. TILLEARD (1827—1876)
(Or to ALLELUIA, opposite).

1. Might - y God, while an - gels bless Thee, May a mor - tal sing Thy name?
2. Lord of ev - ery land and na - tion, An - cient of e - ter - nal days,
3. For the gran - deur of Thy na - ture—Grand be - yond a ser - aph's thought;
4. For Thy prov - i - dence that gov - erns Thro' Thine em - pire's wide do - main,

Lord of men as well as an - gels, Thou art ev - ery crea - ture's theme;
Sound - ed through the wide cre - a - tion Be Thy just and end - less praise.
For the won - ders of cre - a - tion, Works with skill and kind - ness wrought;
Wings an an - gel, guides a spar - row; Bless - ed be Thy gen - tle reign.

Al - le - lu - ia! Al - le - lu - ia! Al - le - lu - ia, A - men. A - men.

5 But Thy rich, Thy free redemption,
    Bright, though veiled in darkness long,—
Thought is poor, and poor expression,—
    Who can sing that wondrous song?
        Alleluia!
        Alleluia, Amen.

6 Brightness of the Father's glory,
    Shall Thy praise unuttered lie?
Break, my tongue, such guilty silence!
    Sing the Lord who came to die.
        Alleluia!
        Alleluia, Amen.

7 From the highest throne of glory
    To the cross of deepest woe,
Thou didst stoop to ransom captives;
    Flow, my praise, forever flow,
        Alleluia!
        Alleluia, Amen.

8 Re-ascend, Immortal Saviour,
    Leave Thy footstool, take Thy Throne:
Thence return, and reign for ever:
    Be the kingdom all Thine own!
        Alleluia!
        Alleluia, Amen.

135

Rejoice! rejoice! for Jesus reigns.

M. E. Servoss, 1884.　　　　"REJOICE."　　　　Adam Geibel.

1. Re-joice! re-joice! for Je-sus reigns, The Prince of peace and love, To guide the chil-dren
2. Re-joice! re-joice! the Christ has come, The Sav-iour of man-kind, To seek the lost ones

of His grace To heav'n, their home a - bove. And they who seek His lov - ing care Thro'
of His fold, And heal the halt and blind. O err - ing and re - pent - ant soul, Look

dark and sun - ny days, Shall know how safe-ly they may walk When God di-rects their ways.
up, and thou shalt live, The Friend of sin-ners comes to save, To ran - som and for - give.

Chorus.

Re-joice! re-joice for ev-er-more! Em-man-uel's praises sing. They must re-joice who sure-ly

know That Je - sus is their King. A - men.

3 Rejoice! rejoice for evermore,
　　Nor let one soul repine.
Though friends forget, and hearts grow cold,
　　A Father's love is thine.
And if the world seem dark with frowns,
　　Just meet them with a smile;
And, with the hope of future bliss,
　　All present ills beguile.

All hail the power of Jesus' name!

E. PERRONET (1779—80). "MILES LANE." W. SHRUBSOLE, 1785.

1. All hail the pow'r of Je-sus' name! Let an-gels pros-trate fall; Bring forth the roy-al
2. Crown Him, ye mar-tyrs of your God, Who from His al-tar call; Ex-tol the stem of
3. Ye seed of Is-rael's chos-en race, Ye ran-som'd of the fall, Hail Him who saves you
4. Sin-ners, whose love can ne'er for-get The wormwood and the gall, Go spread your trophies

di-a-dem, And crown Him, crown Him, crown Him, crown Him Lord of all! A-men.
Jes-se's rod, And crown Him, crown Him, crown Him, crown Him Lord of all!
by His grace, And crown Him, crown Him, crown Him, crown Him Lord of all!
at His feet, And crown Him, crown Him, crown Him, crown Him Lord of all!

5 Let every kindred, every tribe,
  On this terrestrial ball,
To Him all majesty ascribe,
  And crown Him Lord of all!

6 Oh, that with yonder sacred throng
  We at His feet may fall,
Join in the everlasting song,
  And crown Him Lord of all!

SECOND TUNE.

"CORONATION." O. HOLDEN, 1793.

1. All hail the pow'r of Je-sus' name! Let an-gels prostrate fall; Bring forth the roy-al di-a-dem,

And crown Him Lord of all! Bring forth the royal di-a-dem, And crown Him Lord of all! A-men.

137

Gracious Spirit, Holy Ghost.

C. WORDSWORTH, 1862.　　　　"CHARITY."　　　　J. STAINER, 1868.

1. Gra - cious Spir - it, Ho - ly Ghost, Taught by Thee we cov-et most Of Thy gifts at Pen-te - cost,
2. Love is kind, and suffers long, Love is meek, and thinks no wrong, Love than death itself more strong;
3. Proph-e - cy will fade a-way, Melt-ing in the light of day; Love will ev-er with us stay;

Voices in Unison. rall.

Ho - ly heav'n-ly Love.　A - men.
There-fore, give us Love.
There-fore, give us Love.

4 Faith will vanish into sight;
　Hope be emptied in delight;
　Love in heaven will shine more bright;
　　Therefore, give us Love.

5 Faith and Hope and Love we see,
　Joining hand in hand, agree,
　But the greatest of the three,
　　And the best, is Love.

138

Our blest Redeemer, ere He breathed.

H. AUBER, 1829.　　　　"ST. CUTHBERT."　　　　J. B. DYKES, 1861.

1. Our blest Re-deem-er, ere He breathed His ten-der, last fare - well, A Guide, a Com-fort-
2. He came sweet influence to im-part, A gra-cious, will-ing guest, While He can find one
3. And His that gen - tle voice we hear, Soft as the breath of even, That checks each tho't, that

er, be-queath'd With us to dwell. A - men.
hum - ble heart Where-in to rest.
calms each fear, And speaks of heav'n.

4 And every virtue we possess,
　And every victory won,
　And every thought of holiness
　　Are His alone.

5 Spirit of purity and grace,
　Our weakness, pitying, see:
　O make our hearts Thy dwelling-place,
　And worthier Thee.

Holy Ghost, come down upon Thy children.

F. W. FABER, 1854.   "SENOJWILL."   B. TOURS (1838—1897).

Refrain.

*1. Ho - ly Ghost, come down up - on Thy chil - dren, Give us grace and make us Thine;

Thy ten-der fires with-in us kin - dle, Bless-ed Spir - it, Dove di-vine! A - men. FINE.

* The first verse to be sung as refrain after each succeeding verse.

2. For all with - in us, good and ho - ly, Is from Thee, Thy pre - cious gift;
3. For Thou to us art more than fa - ther, More than sis - ter in Thy love,
4. Oh, we have grieved Thee, gra - cious Spir - it! Way-ward, wan - ton, cold are we;
5. Now, if our hearts do not de - ceive us, We would take Thee for our Lord,

In all our joys, in all our sor-rows, Wist - ful hearts to Thee we lift. D. C.
So gen - tle, pa - tient, and for - bear - ing, Ho - ly Spir - it, Heav'n - ly Dove!
And still our sins, new ev - ery morn-ing, Nev - er yet have wea - ried Thee.
O dear - est Spir - it, make us faith - ful To Thy least and light - est word.

140

O Word of God incarnate.

W. W. How, 1867.   "MUNICH."   J. G. C. Störl's Choralbuch, 1710.

1. O Word of God in-car-nate, O Wis-dom from on high,
2. The Church from her dear Mas-ter Re-ceived the gift di-vine,
3. It float-eth like a ban-ner Be-fore God's host un-furled;
4. Oh, make Thy Church, dear Sav-iour, A lamp of pur-est gold,

O Truth un-changed, un-chang-ing, O Light of our dark sky;
And still that light she lift-eth O'er all the earth to shine.
It shin-eth like a bea-con A-bove the dark-ling world;
To bear be-fore the na-tions Thy true light as of old;

We praise Thee for the ra-diance That from the hal-low'd page,
It is the gold-en cas-ket Where gems of truth are stored,
It is the chart and com-pass That o'er life's surg-ing sea,
O teach Thy wan-d'ring pil-grims By this their path to trace,

A lan-tern to our foot-steps, Shines on from age to age. A-men.
It is the heav'n-drawn pic-ture Of Christ, the liv-ing Word.
Mid mists and rocks and quick-sands, Still guides, O Christ, to Thee.
Till, clouds and dark-ness end-ed, They see Thee face to face.

Lord, Thy Word abideth.

H. W. BAKER, 1861   "ST. CYPRIAN."   H. R. CHOPE, 1862.

1. Lord, Thy Word a - bid - eth, And our foot-steps guid - eth; Who its truth be -
2. When our foes are near us, Then Thy Word doth cheer us, Word of con - so -
3. When the storms are o'er us, And dark clouds be - fore us, Then its light di -

liev - eth, Light and joy re - ceiv - eth. A - men.
la - tion, Mes - sage of sal - va - tion.
rect - eth, And our way pro - tect - eth.

4 Word of mercy, giving
Succor to the living;
Word of life, supplying
Comfort to the dying!—

5 O that we, discerning
Its most holy learning
Lord, may love and fear Thee,
Evermore be near Thee!

Thy Word is like a garden, Lord.

141. 142

E. HODDER 1868.   "TIVERTON."   "GRIGG," IN RIPPON'S COLL., 1806.

1. Thy Word is like a gar - den, Lord, With flow - ers bright and fair;
2. Thy Word is like a deep, deep mine; And jew - els rich and rare;
3. O may I love Thy pre - cious Word, May I ex - plore the mine,
4. O may I find my ar - mor there, Thy Word my trust - y sword;

And ev - ery one who seeks may pluck A love - ly nose - gay there. A - men.
Are hid - den in its might - y depths For ev - ery search - er there.
May I its fra - grant flow - ers glean, May light up - on me shine;
I'll learn to fight with ev - ery foe The bat - tle of the Lord.

143

Come unto Me, ye weary.

W. C. Dix, 1867.   "COME UNTO ME."   J. B. Dykes, 1875.

Org.

1. "Come un-to Me, ye wea-ry, And I will give you rest."
2. "Come un-to Me, dear chil-dren, And I will give you light."
3. "Come un-to Me, ye wea-ry, And I will give you life."
4. "And who-so-ev-er com-eth I will not cast him out."

cres.

O bless-ed voice of Je-sus, Which comes to hearts op-prest!
O lov-ing voice of Je-sus, Which comes to cheer the night.
O cheer-ing voice of Je-sus, Which comes to aid our strife,
O wel-come voice of Je-sus, Which drives a-way our doubt,

mf

It tells of ben-e-dic-tion, Of par-don, grace, and peace,
Our hearts were filled with sad-ness And we had lost our way;
The foe is stern and ea-ger, The fight is fierce and long;
Which calls us, ver-y sin-ners, Un-wor-thy though we be

f   rall.

Of joy that hath no end-ing, Of love which can-not cease. A-men.
But He has brought us glad-ness And songs at break of day.
But Thou hast made us might-y And stron-ger than the strong.
Of love so free and bound-less, To come, dear Lord, to Thee.

Art thou weary, art thou languid.

J. M. NEALE, 1862. Abr.   "STEPHANOS."   H. W. BAKER, 1861.

1. Art thou wea - ry, art thou lan - guid, Art thou sore dis - trest? "Come to Me," saith
2. Hath He marks to lead me to Him, If He be my guide? "In His feet and
3. Is there di - a - dem, as mon - arch, That His brow a - dorns? "Yea, a crown, in
4. If I find Him, if I fol - low, What His guer - don here? "Many a sor - row,

One, "and, com - ing, Be at rest." A - men.
hands are wound-prints, And His side."
ver - y sure - ty, But of thorns."
many a la - bor, Many a tear."

5 If I ask Him to receive me,
　　Will He say me nay?
"Not till earth and not till heaven
　　Pass away."

6 Finding, following, keeping, struggling,
　　Is He sure to bless?
"Saints, apostles, prophets, martyrs,
　　Answer, Yes"

I am trusting Thee, Lord Jesus. **145**

F. R. HAVERGAL, 1874. Abr.   "BULLINGER."   E. W. BULLINGER, 1877.

1. I am trust-ing Thee, Lord Je-sus, Trust-ing on - ly Thee; Trust-ing Thee for full sal-
2. I am trust-ing Thee for par-don; At Thy feet I bow; For Thy grace and ten - der

va - tion, Great........ and free. A - men.
mer - cy, Trust - - ing now.

3 I am trusting Thee to guide me;
　　Thou alone shalt lead,
Every day and hour supplying
　　All my need.

4 I am trusting Thee, Lord Jesus;
　　Never let me fall;
I am trusting Thee for ever,
　　And for all.

146

Tell me the old, old story.

K. HANKEY, 1866.   "ANGEL'S STORY."   A. H. MANN.

1. Tell me the old, old sto - ry Of un - seen things a - bove,
2. Tell me the sto - ry slow - ly, That I may take it in—
3. Tell me the sto - ry soft - ly, With ear - nest tones and grave;
4. Tell me the same old sto - ry, When you have cause to fear

Of Je - sus and His glo - ry, Of Je - sus and His love.
That won - der - ful Re - demp - tion, God's rem - e - dy for sin!
Re - mem - ber! I'm the sin - ner Whom Je - sus came to save.
That this world's emp - ty glo - ry Is cost - ing me too dear.

Tell me the sto - ry sim - ply, As to a lit - tle child,
Tell me the sto - ry oft - en, For I for - get so soon!
Tell me that sto - ry al - ways, If you would real - ly be,
Yes, and when that world's glo - ry Is draw - ing on my soul,

For I am weak and wea - ry, And help - less and de - filed.   A - men.
The "ear - ly dew" of morn - ing Has passed a - way at noon.
In a - ny time of trou - ble, A com - fort - er to me.
Tell me the old, old sto - ry: "Christ Je - sus makes thee whole."

REF.—Tell me the old, old sto - ry, Of Je - sus and His love.

There were ninety and nine.

E. C. CLEPHANE, 1874.   "NINETY AND NINE."   A. H. MANN, 1895.

1. There were nine-ty and nine that safe-ly lay In the shel-ter of the
2. "Lord, Thou hast here Thy nine-ty and nine: Are they not e-nough for
3. But none of the ran-som'd ev-er knew How deep were the wa-ters
4. "Lord, whence are those blood-drops all the way That mark out the moun-tain's
5. And all through the moun-tains, thun-der-riv'n, And up from the rock-y

fold; But one was out on the hills a-way, Far
Thee?" But the Shep-herd made an-swer: "This of Mine Has
cross'd, Nor how dark was the night that the Lord pass'd through Ere He
track?" "They were shed for one who had gone a-stray Ere the
steep, There rose a cry to the gate of heav'n, "Re-

off from the gates of gold, A-way on the moun-tains
wan-der'd a-way from Me; And al-though the road be
found His sheep that was lost. Out in the des-ert He
Shep-herd could bring Him back" "Lord, whence are Thy hands so
joice, I have found My sheep." And the an-gels ech-oed a

wild and bare, A-way from the ten-der Shep-herd's care. A-men.
rough and steep, I go to the des-ert to find My sheep."
heard its cry,......... Sick, and help-less, and read-y to die.
rent and torn?" "They are pierc'd to-night by ma-ny a thorn."
round the throne, "Re-joice, for the Lord brings back His own."

148

Just as I am, without one plea.

C. ELLIOTT, 1836.　　　　"ST. CRISPIN."　　　　G. J. ELVEY (1816—1893).

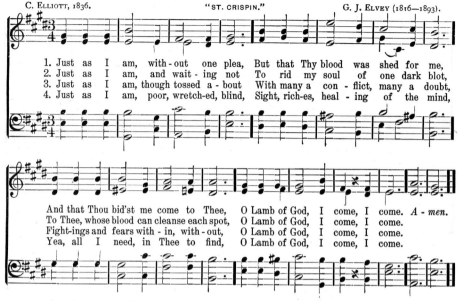

1. Just as I am, with-out one plea, But that Thy blood was shed for me,
2. Just as I am, and wait-ing not To rid my soul of one dark blot,
3. Just as I am, though tossed a-bout With many a con-flict, many a doubt,
4. Just as I am, poor, wretch-ed, blind, Sight, rich-es, heal-ing of the mind,

And that Thou bid'st me come to Thee, O Lamb of God, I come, I come. A-men.
To Thee, whose blood can cleanse each spot, O Lamb of God, I come, I come.
Fight-ings and fears with-in, with-out, O Lamb of God, I come, I come.
Yea, all I need, in Thee to find, O Lamb of God, I come, I come.

5 Just as I am, Thou wilt receive,
　Wilt welcome, pardon, cleanse, relieve;
　Because Thy promise I believe,
　　O Lamb of God, I come.

6 Just as I am, Thy love unknown
　Has broken every barrier down,
　Now to be Thine, yea, Thine alone,
　　O Lamb of God, I come.

SECOND TUNE.

C. ELLIOTT, 1836.　　　　"WOODWORTH."　　　　W. B. BRADBURY, 1849.

1. Just as I am, with-out one plea, But that Thy blood was shed for me,

And that Thou bid'st me come to Thee, O Lamb of God, I come, I come. A-men.

O Jesus, Thou art standing.

W. W. How, 1867.   "ST. HILDA."   J. H. KNECHT, 1799, and E. HUSBAND, 1871.

1. O Je - sus, Thou art stand - ing Out - side the fast - closed door,
2. O Je - sus, Thou art knock - ing, And lo! that hand is scarred,
3. O Je - sus, Thou art plead - ing In ac - cents meek and low,

In low - ly pa - tience wait - ing To pass the thresh - old o'er:
And thorns Thy brow en - cir - cle, And tears Thy face have marred:
"I died for you, My chil - dren, And will ye treat Me so?"

Shame on us, Chris - tian broth - ers, His Name and sign who bear:
O love that pass - eth knowl - edge, So pa - tient - ly to wait!
O Lord, with shame and sor - row We o - pen now the door:

Oh, shame, thrice shame up - on us, To keep Him stand - ing there! A - men.
O sin that hath no e - qual, So fast to bar the gate!
Dear Sav - iour, en - ter, en - ter, And leave us nev - er more.

150

Father, I know that all my life.

A. L. WARING, 1580. Alt.   "ST. BEDE."   J. B. DYKES (1823—1876).

1. Fa - ther, I know that all my life Is por - tioned out for me;
2. I ask Thee for a thought-ful love, Thro' con - stant watch - ing wise,
3. I would not have the rest - less will That hur - ries to and fro,
4. Wher - ev - er in the world I am, In what - so - e'er es - tate,

The chang - es that are sure to come, I do not fear to see:
To meet the glad with joy - ful smiles, To wipe the weep - ing eyes;
Seek - ing for some great thing to do, Or se - cret thing to know;
I have a fel - low - ship with hearts To keep and cul - ti - vate;

I ask Thee for a pres - ent mind, In - tent on pleas - ing Thee. A - men.
A heart at lei - sure from it - self To soothe and sym - pa - thize.
I would be treat - ed as a child, And guid - ed where I go.
A work of low - ly love to do For Him on whom I wait.

5 I ask Thee for the daily strength,
   To none that ask denied,
A mind to blend with outward life,
   While keeping at Thy side,
Content to fill a little space,
   If Thou be glorified.

6 In service which Thy will appoints
   There are no bonds for me;
My secret heart is taught the truth
   That makes Thy children free;
A life of self-renouncing love
   Is one of liberty.

O Lamb of God, still keep me.

151

J. G. DECK, 1842.   "DAVENPORT."   M. D. BABCOCK, 1896.

1. O Lamb of God, still keep me Near to Thy wound-ed side;
2. 'Tis on-ly in Thee hid-ing I feel my life se-cure;
3. Soon shall mine eyes be-hold Thee, With rap-ture face to face;

'Tis on-ly there in safe-ty And peace I can a-bide.
On-ly in Thee a-bid-ing The con-flict can en-dure.
One half hath not been told me Of all Thy pow'r and grace:

What foes and snares sur-round me! What doubts and fears with-in!
Thine arm the vic-t'ry gain-eth O'er ev-ery hurt-ful foe;
Thy beau-ty, Lord, and glo-ry, The won-ders of Thy love,

The grace that sought and found me A-lone can keep me clean. A - men.
Thy love my heart sus-tain-eth In all its care and woe.
Shall be the end-less sto-ry Of all Thy saints a-bove.

152 Nearer, my God, to Thee.

S. F. ADAMS, 1841. "HORBURY." J. B. DYKES, 1861.

1. Near - er, my God, to Thee, Near - er to Thee! E'en tho' it be a cross That rais-eth
2. Though like the wan-der-er, The sun gone down, Dark-ness be o - ver me, My rest a
3. There let the way ap - pear Steps un - to heav'n; All that Thou send'st to me In mer-cy

me; Still all my song shall be, Near - er, my God, to Thee, Near - er to Thee! A - men.
stone; Yet in my dreams I'd be Near - er, my God, to Thee, Near - er to Thee!
giv'n; An - gels to beck - on me Near - er, my God, to Thee, Near - er to Thee!

4 Then, with my waking thoughts
 Bright with Thy praise,
Out of my stony griefs,
 Bethel I'll raise;
So by my woes to be
 Nearer, my God, to Thee,
  Nearer to Thee!

5 Or if on joyful wing,
 Cleaving the sky,
Sun, moon, and stars forgot,
 Upward I fly,
Still all my song shall be,
 Nearer, my God, to Thee,
  Nearer to Thee!

(SECOND TUNE).

"BETHANY." L. MASON, 1856.

1. Near - er, my God, to Thee, Near-er to Thee! E'en tho' it be a cross
D.S.—Near - er, my God, to Thee,

Nearer, my God, to Thee.—*Concluded.*

That rais - eth me;... Still all my song shall be, Near - er, my God, to Thee, A - men.
Near - er to Thee!..

Nearer, O God, to Thee! 153

W. W. How, 1864.   "PROPIOR DEO."   A. S. SULLIVAN, 1872.

1. Near - er, O God, to Thee! Hear Thou my prayer; E'en though a heav - y cross
2. If where they led my Lord, I too am borne, Plant - ing my steps in His,
3. If Thou the cup of pain Giv - est to drink, Let not my trem-bling lip
4. And when Thou, Lord, once more Glo - rious shalt come, Oh, for a dwell-ing-place,

Faint - ing I bear; Still all my pray'r shall be, Near - er, O
Wea - ry and worn; There e - ven let me be Near - er, O
From the draught shrink; So by my woes to be Near - er, O
In Thy bright home! Through all e - ter - ni - ty Near - er, O

God, to Thee, Near - er to Thee!... Near - er to Thee! A - men.
God, to Thee, Near - er to Thee!... Near - er to Thee!
God, to Thee, Near - er to Thee!... Near - er to Thee!
God, to Thee, Near - er to Thee!... Near - er to Thee!

154

My faith looks up to Thee.

R. PALMER, 1830.   "ST. AMBROSE."   W. H. MONK (1823—1889).

1. My faith looks up to Thee, Thou Lamb of Cal - va - ry,
2. May Thy rich grace im - part Strength to my faint - ing heart,
3. While life's dark maze I tread, And griefs a - round me spread,
4. When ends life's tran - sient dream, When death's cold sul - len stream

Sav - iour di - vine! Now hear me while I pray, Take all my
My zeal in - spire, As Thou hast died for me, Oh, may my
Be Thou my guide; Bid dark - ness turn to day, Wipe sor - row's
Shall o'er me roll; Blest Sav - iour, then, in love, Fear and dis -

guilt a - way, Oh, let me from this day Be whol - ly Thine. A - men.
love to Thee Pure, warm, and changeless be, A liv - ing fire.
tears a - way, Nor let me ev - er stray From Thee a - side.
trust re - move; Oh, bear me safe a - bove, A ran - somed soul!

SECOND TUNE.

"OLIVET."   L. MASON, 1832.

1. My faith looks up to Thee, Thou Lamb of Cal-va-ry, Saviour divine! Now hear me while I pray,

My faith looks up to Thee.—*Concluded.*

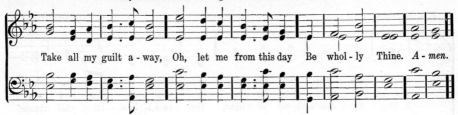

Take all my guilt a - way, Oh, let me from this day Be whol - ly Thine. *A - men.*

I lift my heart to Thee.

155

C. E. MUDIE, 1873.   "BUDLEIGH."   T. M. MUDIE (1809—1876).

1. I lift my heart to Thee, Sav - iour di - vine, For Thou art all to
2. To Thee, Thou bleed - ing Lamb, I all things owe All that I have and
3. How can I, Lord, with - hold life's bright - est hou; From Thee; or gath - ered
4. I pray Thee, Sav - iour, keep me in Thy love, Un - til death's ho - ly

me, and I am Thine. Is there on earth a clos - er bond than
am, and all I know. All that I have is now no lon - ger
gold, or a - ny pow'r? Why should I keep one pre - cious thing from
sleep shall me re - move To that fair realm, where sin and sor - row

this, That "my Be - lov - ed's mine and I am His"? *A - men.*
mine, And I am not mine own; Lord, I am Thine.
Thee, When Thou hast giv'n Thine own dear self for me?
o'er, Thou and Thine own are one for ev - er - more.

156

Thy life was given for me.

F. R. HAVERGAL, 1858.　　　　　"FALCONER."　　　　　A. C. FALCONER (1850—)

1. Thy life was giv'n for me, Thy blood, O Lord, was shed,
2. Long years were spent for me In wea - ri - ness and woe,
3. Thy Fa - ther's home of light, Thy rain - bow - cir - cled throne

That I might ran - somed be, And quick - ened from the dead.
That through e - ter - ni - ty Thy glo - ry I might know.
Were left for earth - ly night, For wan - d'rings sad and lone.

Thy life was giv'n for me: What have I giv'n for Thee? A - men.
Long years were spent for me: Have I spent one for Thee?
Yea, all was left for me: Have I left aught for Thee?

4 And Thou hast brought to me,
　Down from Thy home above,
Salvation full and free,
　Thy pardon and Thy love.
Great gifts Thou broughtest me:
What have I brought to Thee?

5 Oh, let my life be given,
　My years for Thee be spent,
World-fetters all be riven,
　And joy with suffering blent!
Thou gavest Thyself for me;
I give myself to Thee.

Saviour, Thy dying love.

S. D. Phelps, 1867.　　　　　　　"EDEN."　　　　　　　S. S. Wesley (1810—1876).

1. Sav - iour, Thy dy - ing love Thou gav - est me,
2. O'er the blest mer - cy - seat Plead - ing for me,
3. Give me a faith - ful heart, Like - ness to Thee,
4. All that I am and have, Thy gifts so free,

Nor should I aught with - hold, My Lord, from Thee;
My fee - ble faith looks up, Je - sus, to Thee.
That each de - part - ing day Hence - forth may see
In joy, in grief, through life, O Lord, for Thee!

In love my soul would bow, My heart ful - fil its vow,
Help me the cross to bear, Thy won - drous love de - clare,
Some work of love be - gun, Some deed of kind - ness done,
And when Thy face I see, My ran - somed soul shall be,

Some of - f'ring bring Thee now, Some - thing for Thee. A - men.
Some song to raise, or prayer, Some - thing for Thee.
Some wan - d'rer sought and won, Some - thing for Thee.
Through all e - ter - ni - ty, Some - thing for Thee.

158

Father, lead me day by day.

J. P. HOPPS, 1877. "TICHFIELD." J. RICHARDSON, 1853.
From "CROWN OF JESUS."

1. Fa - ther, lead me day by day, Ev - er in Thine own sweet way;
2. When I'm tempt-ed to do wrong, Make me stead-fast, wise, and strong;
3. May I see the good and bright, When they pass be - fore my sight;

Teach me to be pure and true, Show me what I ought to do.
And when all a - lone I stand, Shield me with Thy might - y hand.
May I hear the heav'n - ly voice When the pure and wise re - joice.

When in dan - ger, make me brave; Make me know that Thou canst save:
When my heart is full of glee, Help me to re - mem - ber Thee,—
May I do the good I know, Be Thy lov - ing child be - low,

Keep me safe by Thy dear side; Let me in Thy love a - bide. A - men.
Hap - py most of all to know That my Fa - ther loves me so.
Then at last go home to Thee, Ev - er-more Thy child to be.

Saviour! teach me, day by day.

J. E. Leeson, 1842.   "EMMELAR."   Arr. from A. S. Sullivan.

1. Sav - iour! teach me, day by day, Love's sweet les - son to o - bey;
2. Teach me all Thy steps to trace, Strong to fol - low in Thy grace;

Sweet - er les - son can - not be, Lov - ing Him who first loved me.
Learn - ing how to love from Thee; Lov - ing Him who first loved me.

With a child - like heart of love, At Thy bid - ding may I move;
Thus may I re - joice to show That I feel the love I owe;

Prompt to serve and fol - low Thee, Lov - ing Him who first loved me. A - men
Sing - ing, till Thy face I see, Of His love who first loved me.

160

Jesus, Shepherd of the sheep.

H. COOKE, 1881.   "SHEPHERD."   S. P. WARREN, 1887.

The melody is the same for all the verses.

1. Je - sus, Shep-herd of the sheep, Who Thy Fa - ther's flock dost keep, Safe we wake and safe we sleep, Guard-ed still by Thee.

2. In Thy prom-ise firm we stand, None can pluck us from Thy hand, Speak,—we hear; at Thy com - mand We will fol - low Thee.

3. By Thy blood our souls were bought, By Thy life sal - va-tion wrought, By Thy Word our

Jesus, Shepherd of the sheep.—*Concluded.*

feet are taught, Lord, to fol-low Thee. 4. Fa-ther, draw us to Thy Son,

We with joy will fol-low on, Till the work of grace is done, And, from sin set

free— 5. We in robes of glo-ry dress'd Join th' as-sem-bly of the blest,

Gath-er'd to e-ter-nal rest,..... In the fold with Thee..................

161

Take my life, and let it be.

F. R. HAVERGAL, 1874. "CEASELESS PRAISE." ANON.

1. Take my life, and let it be Con - se - crat - ed, Lord, to Thee;
2. Take my voice, and let me sing Al - ways, on - ly, for my King;
3. Take my will, and make it Thine, It shall be no lon - ger mine;

Take my mo - ments and my days, Let them flow in cease - less praise;
Take my lips, and let them be Fill'd with mes - sag - es from Thee;
Take my heart, it is Thine own, It shall be Thy roy - al throne;

Take my hands, and let them move At the im - pulse of Thy love;
Take my sil - ver and my gold, Not a mite would I with - hold;
Take my love, my Lord, I pour At Thy feet its treas - ure - store;

Take my feet, and let them be Swift and beau - ti - ful for Thee. A - men.
Take my in - tel - lect, and use Ev - ery pow'r as Thou shalt choose.
Take my - self, and I will be Ev - er, on - ly, all for Thee.

Shepherd of tender youth.

"KIRBY BEDON."   E. BUNNETT, 1887.

1. Shep - herd of ten - der youth, Guid - ing in love and truth,
2. Thou art our ho - ly Lord, The all - sub - du - ing Word,
3. Thou art the great High Priest; Thou hast pre - pared the feast

Through de - vious ways; Christ our tri - umph - ant King, We come Thy
Heal - er of strife; Thou didst Thy - self a - base, That from sin's
Of heav'n - ly love: In all our mor - tal pain None call on

name to sing, And here our chil - dren bring To shout Thy praise. A - men.
deep dis - grace Thou might - est save our race, And give us life.
Thee in vain; Help Thou didst not dis - dain, Help from a - bove.

4 Ever be Thou our guide,
  Our shepherd and our pride,
    Our staff and song;
Jesus, Thou Christ of God,
By Thy perennial word,
Lead us where Thou hast trod,
    Make our faith strong.

5 So now, and till we die,
  Sound we Thy praises high,
    And joyful sing;
Let all the holy throng
Who to Thy church belong,
Unite and swell the song
    To Christ our King!

This beautiful hymn from the third book of Clement of Alexandria, is said to be the earliest known hymn of the Primitive Christian Church. About 200. Tr. H. M. Dexter, 1846.

163

To Thee, O dear, dear Saviour!

J. S. B. MONSELL, 1863.   "SAVOY CHAPEL."   J. B. CALKIN (1827—).

1. To Thee, O dear, dear Sav - iour! My spir - it turns for rest,
2. In Thee my trust a - bid - eth, On Thee my hope re - lies,
3. A - las, that I should ev - er Have failed in love to Thee,
4. Oh, for that choic - est bless - ing Of liv - ing in Thy love,

My peace is in Thy fa - vor, My pil - low on Thy breast;
O Thou whose love pro - vid - eth For all be - neath the skies;
The on - ly One who nev - er For - got or slight - ed me!
And thus on earth pos - sess - ing The peace of heav'n a - bove;

Though all the world de - ceive me, I know that I am Thine,
O Thou whose mer - cy found me, From bond - age set me free,
Oh, for a heart to love Thee More tru - ly as I ought,
Oh, for the bliss that by it The soul se - cure - ly knows

And Thou wilt nev - er leave me, O bless - ed Sav - iour mine. A - men.
And then for ev - er bound me, With three-fold cords to Thee.
And noth - ing place a - bove Thee In deed, or word, or thought.
The ho - ly calm and qui - et Of faith's se - rene re - pose!

Saviour! while my heart is tender.

164

J. Burton, 1850.   "BEECROFT."   R. DeWitt Mallary, 1890.

1. Sav - iour! while my heart is ten - der, I would yield that heart to Thee;
2. Send me, Lord, where Thou wilt send me, On - ly do Thou guide my way:
3. May this sol - emn con - se - cra - tion Nev - er once for - got - ten be;

All my powers to Thee sur - rend - er, Thine and on - ly Thine to be.
May Thy grace through life at - tend me, Glad - ly then shall I o - bey.
Let it know no rev - o - ca - tion, Reg - is - tered, con - firmed by Thee.

Take me now, Lord Je - sus! take me, Let my youth - ful heart be Thine:
Let me do Thy will, or bear it, I would know no will but Thine;
Thine I am, O Lord, for ev - er To Thy serv - ice set a - part;

Thy de - vot - ed serv - ant make me: Fill my soul with love di - vine. A - men.
Shouldst Thou take my life, or spare it, I that life to Thee re - sign.
Suf - fer me to leave Thee nev - er: Seal Thine im - age on my heart.

165

Rock of ages, cleft for me.

A. M. TOPLADY, 1776.   "GETHSEMANE."   R. REDHEAD, 1853.

1. Rock of a-ges, cleft for me, Let me hide my-self in Thee;
2. Not the la-bors of my hands Can ful-fill Thy law's de-mands;
3. Noth-ing in my hand I bring; Sim-ply to Thy cross I cling;
4. While I draw this fleet-ing breath, When mine eye-lids close in death,

Let the wa-ter and the blood, From Thy riv-en side which flowed,
Could my zeal no res-pite know, Could my tears for-ev-er flow,
Nak-ed, come to Thee for dress; Help-less, look to Thee for grace;
When I soar to worlds un-known, See Thee on Thy judg-ment throne;

Be of sin the dou-ble cure, Cleanse me from its guilt and power. A-men.
All for sin could not a-tone; Thou must save, and Thou a-lone.
Foul, I to the foun-tain fly: Wash me, Sav-iour, or I die?
Rock of a-ges, cleft for me, Let me hide my-self in Thee!

SECOND TUNE.

"TOPLADY."   T. HASTINGS, 1830.

FINE.   D. C.

Jesus, the very thought of Thee.

Tr E. CASWALL, 1848. "ST. AGNES." J. B. DYKES, 1866.

1. Je - sus, the ver - y thought of Thee With sweetness fills my breast; But sweeter far Thy face to
2. Nor voice can sing, nor heart can frame Nor can the memory find, A sweeter sound than Thy blest
3. O hope of ev - ery con-trite heart, O joy of all the meek, To those who fall, how kind Thou

see, And in Thy pres-ence rest. A - men.
name, O Sav - iour of man - kind.
art, How good to those who seek.

4 But what to those who find? Ah, this
  Nor tongue nor pen can show;
The love of Jesus, what it is
  None but His loved ones know

5 Jesus, our only joy be Thou,
  As Thou our prize shalt be;
Jesus, be Thou our glory now,
  And through eternity.

Children of the heavenly King.

J. CENNICK, 1742. Abr. "PLEYEL'S HYMN." I. J. PLEYEL, 1790.

1. Chil-dren of the heav'nly King, As ye jour-ney, sweetly sing; Sing our Saviour's worthy praise,
2. We are trav'ling home to God, In the way the fathers trod: They are hap-py now, and we
3. Lift your eyes, ye sons of light, Zi - on's cit - y is in sight: There our endless home shall be,

Glo - rious in His works and ways. A - men.
Soon their hap - pi - ness shall see.
There our Lord we soon shall see.

4 Fear not, brethren; joyful stand
  On the borders of your land;
Jesus Christ, your Father's Son,
  Bids you undismayed go on.

5 Lord, obediently we go,
  Gladly leaving all below;
Only Thou our Leader be,
  And we still will follow Thee.

11E

168

When, His salvation bringing.

J. King.   "HOMELAND."   A. S. Sullivan, 1867.

1. When, His sal - va - tion bring - ing, To Zi - on Je - sus came,
2. And since the Lord re - tain - eth His love for chil - dren still,
3. For should we fail pro - claim - ing Our great Re - deem - er's praise,

The chil - dren all stood sing - ing Ho - san - na to His name.
Though now as King He reign - eth On Zi - on's heav'n - ly hill,
The stones, our si - lence sham - ing, Would their ho - san - nas raise.

Nor did their zeal of - fend Him; But, as He rode a - long,
We'll flock a - round His ban - ner, Who sits up - on the throne,
But should we on - ly ren - der The trib - ute of our words?

He let them still at - tend Him, And smil'd to hear their song.   A - men.
And raise a loud ho - san - na To Da - vid's roy - al Son.
No, while our hearts are ten - der, They, too, should be the Lord's.

(Or to Berthold, No. 207.)

Jesus, name of wondrous love.

W. W. How, 1854.   "REDHEAD 45"   R. Redhead, 1853.

1. Je - sus, name of wondrous love, Name all oth-er names a-bove! Unto which must ev - ery knee
2. Je - sus, name decreed of old, To the maid-en moth-er told, Kneeling in her low-ly cell,
3. Je - sus, name of priceless worth To the fall-en sons of earth, For the promise that it gave,
4. Je - sus, name of mer-cy mild, Giv-en to the ho-ly Child, When the cup of hu-man woe

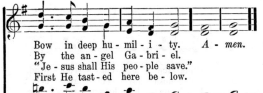

Bow in deep hu - mil - i - ty.   A - men.
By the an - gel Ga - bri - el.
"Je - sus shall His peo - ple save."
First He tast - ed here be - low.

5 Jesus, only name that's given
Under all the mighty heaven,
Whereby man, to sin enslaved,
Bursts his fetters, and is saved.

6 Jesus, name of wondrous love,
Human name of God above:
Pleading only this we flee,
Helpless, O our God, to Thee.

There is an eye that never sleeps.   170

J. C. Wallace.   "NORTHREPPS."   J. Booth, 1887.

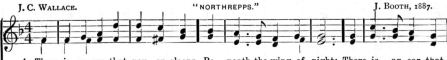

1. There is an eye that nev - er sleeps, Be - neath the wing of night; There is an ear that
2. There is an arm that nev - er tires, When human strength giv's way; There is a love that
3. That eye is fixed on ser-aph throngs; That arm up-holds the sky; That ear is fill'd with

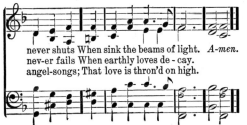

never shuts When sink the beams of light.   A-men.
nev-er fails When earthly loves de - cay.
angel-songs; That love is thron'd on high.

4 But there's a power which man can wield
When mortal aid is vain,
That eye, that arm, that love to reach,
That listening ear to gain.

5 That power is prayer, which soars on high
Through Jesus to the throne,
And moves the hand which moves the world,
To bring salvation down.

171

I lay my sins on Jesus.

H. Bonar, 1843. "ELIM." (MOSCOW). J. B. Calkin, 1867.

1. I lay my sins on Je - sus, The spot - less Lamb of God;
2. I lay my wants on Je - sus; All full - ness dwells in Him;
3. I rest my soul on Je - sus, This wea - ry soul of mine;
4. I long to be like Je - sus, Meek, lov - ing, low - ly, mild;

He bears them all, and frees us From the ac - curs - ed load.
He heals all my dis - eas - es He doth my soul re - deem:
His right hand me em - brac - es, I on His breast re - cline:
I long to be like Je - sus, The Fa - ther's ho - ly child.

I bring my guilt to Je - sus, To wash my crim - son stains
I lay my griefs on Je - sus, My bur - dens and my cares;
I love the name of Je - sus, Im - man - uel, Christ, the Lord;
I long to be with Je - sus A - mid the heav'n - ly throng,

White in His blood most pre - cious, Till not a stain re - mains. A - men
He from them all re - leas - es, He all my sor - rows shares.
Like fra-grance on the breez - es, His name a - broad is poured.
To sing with saints His prais - es, To learn the an - gels' song.

I need Thee, precious Jesus.

F. WHITFIELD, 1855.   "FRANKSCOT."   J. BARNBY, 1883.

1. I need Thee, pre-cious Je-sus, For I am full of sin;
2. I need Thee, bless-ed Je-sus, For I am ver-y poor;
3. I need Thee, bless-ed Je-sus, I need a friend like Thee,
4. I need Thee, bless-ed Je-sus, And hope to see Thee soon,

My soul is dark and guilt-y, My heart is dead with-in;
A stran-ger and a pil-grim, I have no earth-ly store.
A friend to soothe and pit-y, A friend to care for me.
En-cir-cled with the rain-bow And seat-ed on Thy throne:

I need the cleans-ing foun-tain Where I can al-ways flee,
I need the love of Je-sus To cheer me on my way,
I need the heart of Je-sus To feel each anx-ious care,
There, with Thy blood-bought chil-dren, My joy shall ev-er be

The blood of Christ most pre-cious, The sin-ner's per-fect plea. *A-men.*
To guide my doubt-ing foot-steps, To be my strength and stay.
To tell my ev-ery tri-al, And all my sor-rows share.
To sing Thy praise, Lord Je-sus, To gaze, my Lord, on Thee.

173

Hushed was the evening hymn.

J. D. BURNS, 1856.   "SAMUEL."   A. S. SULLIVAN, 1874.

1. Hushed was the eve-ning hymn, The tem-ple courts were dark;.... The
2. The old man, meek and mild, The priest of Is-rael, slept;... His
3. Oh! give me Sam-uel's ear, The o-pen ear, O Lord, ... A-
4. Oh! give me Sam-uel's heart, A low-ly heart that waits,... Where
5. Oh! give me Sam-uel's mind, A sweet un-murmuring faith,... O-

lamp was burn-ing dim Be-fore the sa-cred ark; When sud-den-
watch the tem-ple-child, The lit-tle Le-vite, kept; And what from
live and quick to hear Each whis-per of Thy word, Like him to
in Thy house Thou art, Or watch-es at Thy gates By day and
be-dient and re-signed To Thee in life and death, That I may

ly a voice di-vine Rang thro' the si-lence of the shrine. A-men.
E-li's sense was sealed, The Lord to Han-nah's son re-vealed.
an-swer at Thy call, And to o-bey Thee first of all.
night, a heart that still Moves at the breath-ing of Thy will.
read with child-like eyes Truths that are hid-den from the wise.

Lead, kindly Light, amid the encircling gloom.

J. H. NEWMAN, 1833.   "LUX BENIGNA."   J. B. DYKES (1823—1876).

1. Lead, kind-ly Light, a-mid th' en-cir-cling gloom,... Lead Thou me on;
2. I was not ev-er thus, nor pray'd that Thou..... Shouldst lead me on;
3. So long Thy pow'r has blest me, sure it still..... Will lead me on;

The night is dark, and I am far from home; Lead Thou me on:
I loved to choose and see my path; but now.. Lead Thou me on.
O'er moor and fen, o'er crag and tor-rent, till.. The night is gone;

Keep Thou my feet; I do not ask to see.........
I loved the gar--ish day, and, spite of fears,......
And with the morn those an-gel fa-ces smile,.....

The dis-tant scene,—one step e-nough for me...... A-men.
Pride ruled my will: re-mem-ber not.... past years...
Which I have loved long since, and lost... a-while...

175

When the weary, seeking rest.

H. BONAR, 1866. Abr. "INTERCESSION, NEW." W. W. CALCOTT, 1867.
Last 2 l. fr. MENDELSSOHN, 1846.

1. When the wea-ry, seeking rest, To Thy goodness flee; When the heavy - la - den cast
2. When the worldling, sick at heart, Lifts his soul a - bove; When the prod-i - gal looks back
3. When the stranger asks a home, All his toils to   end; When the hungry crav-eth food,
4. When the child,with loving heart, Youth, or maiden fair; When the a - ged, trusting still,

All their load on Thee; When the trou-bled, seek-ing peace, On Thy name shall call;
To   his Fa-ther's love; When the proud man,from his pride, Stoops to seek Thy face;
And the poor a friend; When the sail - or   on the wave Bows the fer - vent knee;
Seek Thy face in pray'r; When the wid - ow weeps to Thee, Sad and lone and low;

When the sin - ner, seek - ing life, At Thy feet shall fall:........ Hear then in
When the burdened brings his guilt To Thy throne of grace:...... Hear then in
When the sol - dier on the field Lifts his heart to Thee:....... Hear then in
When the or - phan brings to Thee All his or - phan woe:........ Hear then in

love, O Lord, the cry In heav'n, Thy dwell - ing - place on high. A - men.

Go when the morning shineth.

J. C. SIMPSON, 1831.   "CRATHIE."   J. F. BRIDGE, 1895.

1. Go when the morn-ing shin-eth, Go when the moon is bright,
2. Re-mem-ber all who love thee, All who are loved by thee;
3. But if 'tis e'er de-nied thee In sol-i-tude to pray;
4. O, not a joy or bless-ing With this can we com-pare,

Go when the eve de-clin-eth, Go in the hush of night:
Pray too for those that hate thee, If a-ny such there be;
Should ho-ly thoughts come o'er thee When friends are round thy way;
The pow'r that He hath giv'n us To pour our souls in pray'r.

Go with pure mind and feel-ing, Fling earth-ly thoughts a-way,
Then for thy-self in meek-ness A bless-ing hum-bly claim,
E'en then the si-lent breath-ing Of thy spir-it raised a-bove
When-e'er thou pin'st in sad-ness, Be-fore His foot-stool fall;

And in thy cham-ber, kneel-ing, Do thou in se-cret pray. A-men.
And link with each pe-ti-tion Thy great Re-deem-er's Name.
Shall reach His throne of glo-ry, Of mer-cy, truth, and love.
Re-mem-ber in thy glad-ness His love Who gave thee all.

177

Jesus, my Lord, my God, my all.

H. COLLINS, 1854.   "ADORO."   J. BARNBY, 1872.

1. Je - sus, my Lord, my God, my all, Hear me, blest Sav - iour,
2. Je - sus, too late I Thee have sought: How can I love Thee
3. Je - sus, what didst Thou find in me, That Thou hast dealt so
4. Je - sus, of Thee shall be my song, To Thee my heart and

when I call; Hear me, and from Thy dwell - ing - place
as I ought? And how ex - tol Thy match - less fame,
lov - ing - ly? How great the joy that Thou hast brought,
soul be - long: All that I have or am is Thine,

Pour down the rich - es of Thy grace. Je - sus, my Lord, I
The glo - rious beau - ty of Thy name? Je - sus, my Lord, I
So far ex - ceed - ing hope or thought. Je - sus, my Lord, I
And Thou, blest Sav - iour, Thou art mine. Je - sus, my Lord, I

Thee a - dore: Oh, make me love Thee more and more. A - men.

Sweet is Thy mercy, Lord! 178

J. S. B. MONSELL, 1862.　　　"MONSELL."　　　J. BARNBY, 1866.

1. Sweet is Thy mer-cy, Lord! Be - fore Thy mer-cy-seat My soul, a-dor-ing, pleads Thy word,
2. My need, and Thy de-sires, Are all in Christ complete; Thou hast the jus-tice truth requires
3. Where'er Thy name is blest, Where'er Thy peo-ple meet, There I de-light in Thee to rest,

And owns Thy mer - cy sweet. A - men.
And I Thy mer - cy sweet.
And find Thy mer - cy sweet.

4 Light Thou my weary way,
   Lead Thou my weary feet,
   That while I stay on earth I may
   Still find Thy mercy sweet.

5 Thus shall the heavenly host
   Hear all my songs repeat,
   To Father, Son, and Holy Ghost,
   My joy, Thy mercy sweet.

Searcher of hearts, from mine erase. 179

G. P. MORRIS, 1838.　　　"GRATITUDE."　　　J. B. DYKES, 1875.

1. Searcher of hearts, from mine e - rase All thoughts that should not be,
2. Hear-er of pray'r, O guide a - right Each word and deed of mine;
3. Giv - er of all— for ev - ery good In the Re - deem - er came—
4. Fa - ther, and Son, and Ho - ly Ghost, Thou glo-rious Three in One,

And in its deep re - cess - es trace My grat - i - tude to Thee. A - men.
Life's bat-tle teach me how to fight, And be the vic - t'ry Thine.
For rai-ment, shel - ter, and for food, I thank Thee in His Name.
Thou knowest best what I need most, And let Thy will be done.

180

Love divine, all loves excelling.

C. WESLEY, 1746.　　　　　　"LOVE DIVINE."　　　　　　G. F. LE JEUNE, 1872.

1. Love di - vine, all loves ex - cel - ling, Joy of heav'n, to earth come down,
2. Breathe, oh breathe Thy lov - ing Spir - it In - to ev - ery trou - bled breast;
3. Come, Al - might - y to de - liv - er! Let us all Thy life re - ceive;
4. Fin - ish, then, Thy new cre - a - tion, Pure and spot - less let us be;

Fix in us Thy hum - ble dwell - ing, All Thy faith - ful mer - cies crown.
Let us all in Thee in - her - it, Let us find Thy prom - ised rest;
Sud - den - ly re - turn, and nev - er, Nev - er - more Thy tem - ples leave.
Let us see Thy great sal - va - tion, Per - fect - ly se - cured by Thee,

Je - sus, Thou art all com - pas - sion, Pure, un - bound - ed love Thou art;
Take a - way the love of sin - ning, Al - pha and O - me - ga be;
Thee we would be al - ways bless - ing; Serve Thee as Thy hosts a - bove;
Chang'd from glo - ry in - to glo - ry, Till in heav'n we take our place;

Vis - it us with Thy sal - va - tion, En - ter ev - ery trembling heart. A - men.
End of faith, as its be - gin - ning, Set our hearts at lib - er - ty.
Pray, and praise Thee with-out ceas - ing, Glo - ry in Thy per - fect love.
Till we cast our crowns be - fore Thee, Lost in won - der, love, and praise.

The King of love my Shepherd is.

H. W. Baker, 1868. Abr.   "DOMINUS REGIT ME."   J. B. Dykes, 1868.

1. The King of love my Shep-herd is, Whose good-ness fail-eth nev - er;
2. Where streams of liv - ing wa - ter flow My ran - som'd soul He lead - eth,
3. Per - verse and fool - ish oft I stray'd, But yet in love He sought me,
4. In death's dark vale I fear no ill With Thee, dear Lord, be - side me;
5. And so through all the length of days, Thy good-ness fail-eth nev - er;

I noth-ing lack if I am His And He is mine for - ev - er.   A - men.
And, where the ver - dant pas - tures grow, With food ce - les - tial feed - eth.
And on His shoul-der gen - tly laid, And home, re - joic-ing, brought me.
Thy rod and staff my com - fort still, Thy cross be - fore to guide me.
Good Shep-herd, may I sing Thy praise With - in Thy house for ev - er.

SECOND TUNE.

C. Wesley, 1746.   "BEECHER."   J. Zundel, 1870.

1. Love di-vine, all loves excelling, Joy of heav'n, to earth come down, Fix in us Thy humble dwelling,

D. S.—Vis-it us with Thy sal-va-tion,

FINE.   D. S.

All Thy faithful mercies crown. Jesus, Thou art all compassion, Pure, unbounded love Thou art; A - men.
Enter every trembling heart.

182

Sometimes a light surprises.

W. COWPER, 1779.   "BENTLEY."   J. HULLAH, 1867.

1. Some - times a light sur - pris - es The Chris - tian while he sings;
2. In ho - ly con - tem - pla - tion, We sweet - ly then pur - sue
3. It can bring with it noth - ing, But He will bear us through;
4. Though vine, nor fig - tree nei - ther, Their wont - ed fruit shall bear,

It is the Lord, who ris - es With heal - ing in His wings,
The theme of God's sal - va - tion, And find it ev - er new;
Who gives the lil - ies cloth - ing, Will clothe His peo - ple too;
Though all the field should with - er, Nor flocks nor herds be there;

When com - forts are de - clin - ing, He grants the soul a - gain
Set free from pres - ent sor - row, We cheer - ful - ly can say,
Be - neath the spread - ing heav - ens, No crea - ture but is fed;
Yet God the same a - bid - ing, His praise shall tune my voice,

A sea - son of clear shin - ing, To cheer it aft - er rain. A - men.
E'en let th' un-known to - mor - row Bring with it what it may.
And He who feeds the ra - vens, Will give His chil - dren bread.
For, while in Him con - fid - ing, I can - not but re - joice.

Dear Jesus, ever at my side.

F. W. FABER, 1849. "AUDIENTES." A. S. SULLIVAN, 1875.

Voices in unison.

Organ.

1. Dear Je - sus, ev - er at my side, How lov - ing must Thou be
2. I can - not feel Thee touch my hand With press - ure light and mild,
3. And when, dear Sav - iour, I kneel down, Morn - ing and night, to pray'r,

To leave Thy home in heav'n to guard A lit - tle child like me!
To check me, as my moth - er did When I was but a child.
Some-thing there is with - in my heart Which tells me Thou art there.

Voices in harmony.

Thy beau - ti - ful and shin - ing face I see not, though so near;
But I have felt Thee in my thoughts Fight-ing with sin for me;
Yes, when I pray, Thou pray - est too; Thy prayer is all for me'

The sweet - ness of Thy soft, low voice I am too deaf to hear. A - men.
And when my heart loves God, I know The sweet-ness is from Thee.
But when I sleep, Thou sleep - est not, But watch-est pa - tient - ly.

184

As helpless as a child who clings.

J. D. BURNS, 1856. "FATHERHOOD." J. B. CALKIN (1827—).

1. As help-less as a child who clings Fast to his fa-ther's arm,
2. As trust-ful as a child who looks Up in his moth-er's face,
3. As lov-ing as a child who sits Close by his par-ent's knee,

And casts his weak-ness on the strength That keeps him safe from harm,
And all his lit-tle griefs and fears For-gets in her em-brace,—
And knows no want while he can have That sweet so-ci-e-ty,

So I, my Fa-ther, cling to Thee, And thus I ev-ery hour
So I to Thee, my Sav-iour, look, And in Thy face di-vine,
So, sit-ting at Thy feet, my heart Would all its love out-pour,

Would link my earth-ly fee-ble-ness To Thine Al-might-y pow'r. A-men.
Can read the love that will sus-tain As weak a faith as mine.
And pray that Thou wouldst teach me, Lord, To love Thee more and more.

I've found a Friend.

J. G. SMALL, 1886. "CONSTANCE." A. S. SULLIVAN (1842—).

1. I've found a Friend; O! such a Friend! He loved me ere I knew Him!
2. I've found a Friend; O! such a Friend! He bled, He died to save me;
3. I've found a Friend; O! such a Friend! So kind, and true, and ten - der,

He drew me with the cords of love, And thus He bound me to Him:
And not a - lone the gift of life, But His own self He gave me.
So wise a Coun - sel - lor and Guide, So might - y a De - fend - er.

And round my heart still close - ly twine Those ties which nought can sev - er,
Nought that I have my own I call, I hold it for the Giv - er:
From Him, Who loves me now so well, What pow'r my soul can sev - er?

For I am His, and He is mine, For - ev - er and for - ev - er. A - men.
My heart, my strength, my life, my all, Are His, and His for - ev - er.
Shall life?—or death?—or earth?—or hell? No! I am His for - ev - er.

186
Dear Lord and Father of mankind.

J. G. WHITTIER, 1872.   "ELTON."   F. C. MAKER (1844—).

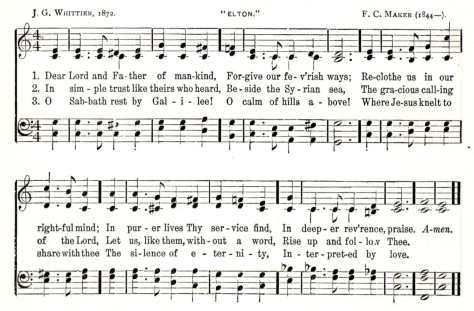

1. Dear Lord and Fa-ther of man-kind, For-give our fe-v'rish ways; Re-clothe us in our
2. In sim - ple trust like theirs who heard, Be-side the Sy - rian sea, The gra-cious call-ing
3. O Sab-bath rest by Gal - i - lee! O calm of hills a - bove! Where Je-sus knelt to

right-ful mind; In pur - er lives Thy ser - vice find, In deep - er rev'rence, praise. A-men.
of the Lord, Let us, like them, with - out a word, Rise up and fol - low Thee.
share with thee The si - lence of e - ter - ni - ty, In - ter - pret-ed by love.

4 Drop thy still dews of quietness
  Till all our strivings cease;
  Take from our souls the strain and stress,
  And let our ordered lives confess
  The beauty of thy peace.

5 Breathe through the heats of our desire
  Thy coolness and thy balm;
  Let sense be dumb, let flesh retire:
  Speak thro' the earthquake, wind, and fire,
  O still small voice of calm!

187
Awake, my soul, stretch every nerve.

P. DODDRIDGE, 1755.   "CHRISTMAS."   Arr. fr. G. F. HÄNDEL, 1728.

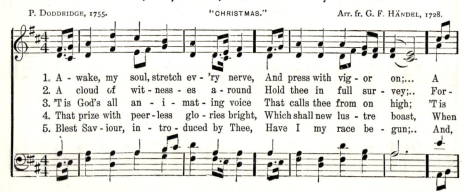

1. A - wake, my soul, stretch ev - 'ry nerve, And press with vig - or on;... A
2. A cloud of wit - ness - es a - round Hold thee in full sur - vey;.. For-
3. 'T is God's all an - i - mat - ing voice That calls thee from on high; 'T is
4. That prize with peer-less glo - ries bright, Which shall new lus - tre boast, When
5. Blest Sav - iour, in - tro - duced by Thee, Have I my race be - gun;.. And,

Awake, my soul, stretch every nerve.—*Concluded.*

heav'nly race demands thy zeal, And an im-mor-tal crown, And an im-mor-tal crown. *A-men.*
get the steps al-read-y trod, And onward urge thy way, And on-ward urge thy way.
His own hand presents the prize To thine up-lift-ed eye, To thine up-lift-ed eye:
victors' wreaths and monarchs' gems Shall blend in common dust, Shall blend in com-mon dust.
crown'd with vict'ry, at Thy feet I'll lay my hon-ors down, I'll lay my hon-ors down.

Rejoice, ye pure in heart.

188

E. H. PLUMPTRE, 1865. Abr. "MARION." A. H. MESSITER, 1883.

1. Re - joice, ye pure in heart, Rejoice, give thanks and sing; Your fes-tal ban-ner wave on high,
2. Bright youth and snow-crown'd age, Strong men and maidens meek, Raise high your free, exulting song,
3. With voice as full and strong As o-cean's surging praise, Send forth the hymns our fathers lov'd,
4. Yes on, thro' life's long path, Still chanting as ye go; From youth to age, by night and day,

Refrain.

The cross of Christ your King.)
God's wondrous praises speak. } Re-joice, re-joice, Rejoice, give thanks and sing. *A - men.*
The psalms of an-cient days. }
In glad-ness and in woe.)

Re-joice, re-joice,

5 Still lift your standard high,
   Still march in firm array,
As warriors through the darkness toil
   Till dawns the golden day.

6 At last the march shall end,
   The wearied ones shall rest,
The pilgrims find their Father's house,
   Jerusalem the blest.

189

Oh, happy band of pilgrims.

Tr. J. M. NEALE, 1862. "GLADNESS, NO. 1." (ST. ANSELM.) J. BARNBY, 1869.

1. Oh, hap - py band of pil - grims, If on - ward ye will tread
2. The cross that Je - sus car - ried, He car - ried as your due:
3. The tri - als that be - set you, The sor - rows ye en - dure,
4. O hap - py band of pil - grims, Look up - ward to the skies,

With Je - sus as your fel - low, To Je - sus as your head!
The crown that Je - sus wear - eth, He wear - eth it for you.
The man - i - fold tempt - a - tions That death a - lone can cure
Where such a light af - flic - tion Shall win so great a prize!

Oh, hap - py if ye la - bor As Je - sus did for men!
The faith by which ye see Him, The hope in which ye yearn,
What are they but His jew - els, Of right ce - les - tial worth?
To Fa - ther, Son, and Spir - it, The God whom we a - dore,

Oh, hap - py if ye hun - ger As Je - sus hun - ger'd then! A - men.
The love that thro' all trou - bles To Him a - lone will turn;
What are they but the lad - der Set up to heav'n on earth?
Be loft - i - est prais - es giv'n, Now and for ev - er - more.

Saviour, blessed Saviour.

G. Thring, 1862. Abr.   "BACON."   L. C. Jacoby, 1895.

1. Sav - iour, bless-ed Sav - iour, List - en while we sing;... Hearts and voic - es rais - ing
2. Near - er, ev - er near - er, Christ, we draw to Thee,.. Deep in ad - o - ra - tion
3. Bright-er still and bright-er Glows the west-ern sun, ... Shed - ding all its glad-ness
4. On - ward, ev - er on - ward, Journeying o'er the road... Worn by saints be - fore us,

Prais - es to our King. All we have we of - fer, All we hope to be,......
Bend - ing low the knee: Thou for our re - demp-tion Cam'st on earth to die;....
O'er our work that's done: Time will soon be o - ver, Toil and sor - row past, ...
Journeying on to God; Leav - ing all be - hind us, May we hast - en on, ...

All........ we yield to Thee. **Refrain.**

Bod - y, soul, and spir - it, All we yield to Thee.
Thou, that we might fol - low, Hast gone up on high.
May we, bless-ed Sav - iour, Find a rest at last.
Back-ward nev - er look - ing Till the prize is won.

Sav - iour, bless - ed Sav - iour.

List - en while we sing; Hearts and voic - es rais - ing Prais-es to our King. *A-men.*

191

Forward! be our watchword.

H. ALFORD, 1871. Abr.   "WATCHWORD."   H. SMART, 1872.

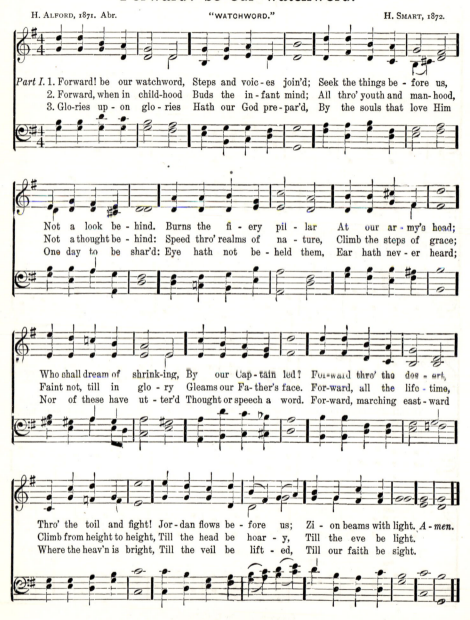

Part I. 1. Forward! be our watchword, Steps and voic-es join'd; Seek the things be-fore us,
2. Forward, when in child-hood Buds the in-fant mind; All thro' youth and man-hood,
3. Glo-ries up-on glo-ries Hath our God pre-par'd, By the souls that love Him

Not a look be-hind. Burns the fi-ery pil-lar At our ar-my's head;
Not a thought be-hind: Speed thro' realms of na-ture, Climb the steps of grace;
One day to be shar'd: Eye hath not be-held them, Ear hath nev-er heard;

Who shall dream of shrink-ing, By our Cap-tain led? Forward thro' the des-ert,
Faint not, till in glo-ry Gleams our Fa-ther's face. For-ward, all the life-time,
Nor of these have ut-ter'd Thought or speech a word. For-ward, marching east-ward

Thro' the toil and fight! Jor-dan flows be-fore us; Zi-on beams with light. *A-men.*
Climb from height to height, Till the head be hoar-y, Till the eve be light.
Where the heav'n is bright, Till the veil be lift-ed, Till our faith be sight.

Far o'er yon horizon.

H. ALFORD, 1871. Abr. "BONIFACE." H. R. GADSBY (1842—).

Part II.
1. Far o'er yon ho - ri - zon Rise the cit - y tow'rs, Where our God a - bid - eth;
2. In - to God's high tem - ple On - ward as we press, Beau - ty spreads a - round us,
3. Naught that cit-y need - eth Of these aisles of stone; Where the God-head dwell - eth,

That fair home is ours. Flash the streets with jas - per, Shine the gates with gold,
Born of ho - li - ness; Arch, and vault, and carv - ing, Lights of va - ried tone,
Tem - ple there is none; All the saints, that ev - er In these courts have stood,

Flows the gladd'ning riv - er, Shed-ding joys un - told. Thith - er, on - ward thith - er,
Soft - ened words and ho - ly, Pray'r and praise a - lone: Ev - ery thought up-rais - ing
Are but babes, and feed - ing On the chil-dren's food. On thro' sign and to - ken,

In the Spir - it's might, Pil-grims to your coun - try, For - ward in - to light. A- men.
To our cit - y bright, Where the tribes as-sem - ble Round the throne of light.
Stars a - mid the night, For-ward thro' the dark - ness, For - ward in - to light.

193

I love to tell the story.

K. Hankey, 1870.   "HANKEY."   W. G. Fischer, 1869.

1. I love to tell the sto - ry Of un - seen things a-bove, Of Je - sus and His glo-ry,
2. I love to tell the sto - ry; More won - der - ful it seems Than all the gold-en fan-cies
3. I love to tell the sto - ry; 'Tis pleas-ant to re - peat What seems, each time I tell it,
4. I love to tell the sto - ry; For those who know it best Seem hun-ger-ing and thirsting

Of Je - sus and His love. I love to tell the sto - ry, Be - cause I know it's true;
Of all our gold-en dreams. I love to tell the sto - ry, It did so much for me;
More won - der-ful-ly sweet. I love to tell the sto - ry, For some have never heard
To hear it, like the rest. And when, in scenes of glo - ry, I sing the new, new song.

Refrain.

It sat - is - fies my long-ings As noth - ing else would do.
And that is just the rea - son I tell it now to thee.
The mes-sage of sal - va - tion From God's own ho-ly word.
'T will be the old, old sto - ry That I have loved so long.

I love to tell the sto - ry,

'T will be my theme in glo - ry, To tell the old, old sto - ry Of Je-sus and His love. A - men.

Who is on the Lord's side?

F. R. HAVERGAL, 1877.　　　　"ARMAGEDDON."　　　　ARR. by J. GOSS, 1871.

1. Who is on the Lord's side? Who will serve the King? Who will be His help-ers
2. Not for weight of glo - ry, Not for crown and palms, En - ter we the ar - my,
3. Je - sus, Thou hast bought us, Not with gold or gem, But with Thine own life - blood,
4. Fierce may be the con - flict, Strong may be the foe, But the King's own ar - my

Oth - er lives to bring? Who will leave the world's side? Who will face the foe?
Raise the war - rior psalm; But for Love that claim - eth Lives for whom He died:
For Thy di - a - dem: With Thy bless-ing fill - ing Each who comes to Thee,
None can o - ver-throw: Round His standard rang - ing, Vic - t'ry is se - cure;

Refrain.

Who is on the Lord's side? Who for Him will go? By Thy call of mer - cy,
He whom Je - sus nam - eth Must be on His side. By Thy love con - strain-ing,
Thou hast made us will - ing, Thou hast made us free. By Thy grand re - demp - tion,
For His truth un-chang-ing Makes the tri - umph sure. Joy - ful - ly en - list - ing

By Thy grace Di - vine, We are on the Lord's side, Sav - iour, we are Thine. A-*men*.

Courage, brother! do not stumble.

195

NORMAN MACLEOD, 1857. "TRUSTING." A. S. SULLIVAN.

1. Cour - age, broth - er! do not stum - ble, Though thy path be
2. Per - ish pol - i - cy and cun - ning, Per - ish all that

dark as night; There's a star to guide the hum - ble:
fears the light! Wheth - er los - ing, wheth - er win - ning,

'Trust in God, and do the right.' Let the road be rough and drear - y,
Trust in God, and do the right. Trust no par - ty, sect, or fac - tion;

And its end far out of sight, Foot it brave - ly; strong or wea - ry,
Trust no lead - ers in the fight; But in ev - ery word or ac - tion

Courage, brother! do not stumble.—*Concluded.*

Trust in God, trust in God, trust in God, and do the right. A - men.

3 Trust no lovely forms of passion,—
   Friends may look like angels bright;
Trust no custom, school, or fashion:
   Trust in God, and do the right.
Some will hate thee, some will love thee,
   Some will flatter, some will slight;
Cease from man, and look above thee:
   Trust in God, and do the right.

4 Simple rule, and safest guiding,
   Inward peace, and inward might,
Star upon our path abiding,—
   Trust in God, and do the right.
Courage, brother! do not stumble,
   Though thy path be dark as night;
There's a star to guide the humble:
   'Trust in God, and do the right.'

Oft in danger, oft in woe. 196

H. K. WHITE, 1806.   "UNIVERSITY COLLEGE."   H. J. GAUNTLETT, 1848.

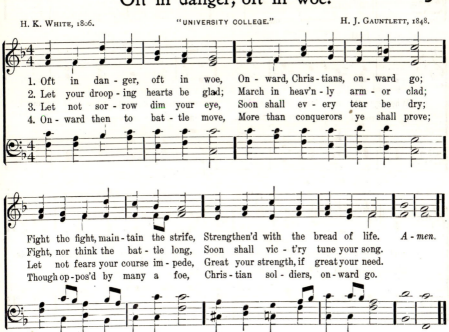

1. Oft in dan - ger, oft in woe, On - ward, Chris - tians, on - ward go;
2. Let your droop - ing hearts be glad; March in heav'n - ly arm - or clad;
3. Let not sor - row dim your eye, Soon shall ev - ery tear be dry;
4. On - ward then to bat - tle move, More than conquerors ye shall prove;

Fight tho fight, main - tain the strife, Strengthen'd with the bread of life. A - men.
Fight, nor think the bat - tle long, Soon shall vic - t'ry tune your song.
Let not fears your course im - pede, Great your strength, if great your need.
Though op - pos'd by many a foe, Chris - tian sol - diers, on - ward go.

197

There is a blessed home.

H. W. BAKER, 1861.   "BLESSED HOME."   J. STAINER, 1875.

1. There is a bless - ed home...... Be - yond this land of woe,
2. There is a land of peace,...... Good an - gels know it well;

Where tri - als nev - er come, Nor tears of sor - row flow;
Glad songs that nev - er cease With - in its por - tals swell;

Where faith is lost in sight, And pa - tient hope is crown'd,
A round its glo - rious throne Ten thou - sand saints a - dore

And ev - er - last - ing light Its glo - ry throws a - round. *A - men.*
Christ, with the Fa - ther One, And Spir - it, ev - er - more.

There is a blessed home.—*Concluded.*

3 O joy all joys beyond,
  To see the Lamb who died,
  And count each sacred wound
  In hands, and feet, and side;
  To give to Him the praise
  Of every triumph won,
  And sing through endless days
  The great things He hath done!

4 Look up, ye saints of God,
  Nor fear to tread below
  The path your Saviour trod
  Of daily toil and woe:
  Wait but a little while
  In uncomplaining love,
  His own most gracious smile
  Shall welcome you above.

I do not ask, O Lord, that life may be. 198

A. A. PROCTER, 1862.   "SUBMISSION, No. 2."   A. L. PEACE, 1889.

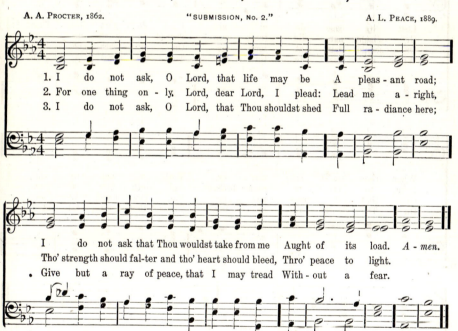

1. I do not ask, O Lord, that life may be A pleas-ant road;
2. For one thing on-ly, Lord, dear Lord, I plead: Lead me a-right,
3. I do not ask, O Lord, that Thou shouldst shed Full ra-diance here;

I do not ask that Thou wouldst take from me Aught of its load. A-men.
Tho' strength should fal-ter and tho' heart should bleed, Thro' peace to light.
Give but a ray of peace, that I may tread With-out a fear.

4 I do not ask my cross to understand,
  My way to see;
  Better in darkness just to feel Thy hand,
  And follow Thee.

5 Joy is like restless day; but peace divine
  Like quiet right.
  Lead me, O Lord, till perfect day shall shine,
  Through peace to light.

199

In the hour of trial.

J. Montgomery, 1834.   "MARY MAGDALENE."   J. B. Dykes, 1862.

1. In the hour of tri - al, Je - sus, plead for me,
2. With for - bid - den pleas - ures Would this vain world charm;
3. Should Thy mer - cy send me Sor - row, toil, and woe;
4. When my last hour com - eth, Fraught with strife and pain,

Lest by base de - ni - al I de - part from Thee;
Or its sor - did treas - ures Spread to work me harm;
Or should pain at - tend me On my path be - low;
When my dust re - turn - eth To the dust a - gain;

When Thou see'st me wav - er, With a look re - call.
Bring to my re - mem - brance Sad Geth - sem - a - ne,
Grant that I may nev - er Fail Thy hand to see;
On Thy truth re - ly - ing, Through that mor - tal strife,

Nor for fear or fa - vor Suf - fer me to fall. A - men.
Or, in dark - er sem - blance, Cross-crown'd Cal - va - ry.
Grant that I may ev - er Cast my care on Thee.
Je - sus, take me, dy - ing, To e - ter - nal life.

(Or to PENITENCE, opposite.)

Purer yet and purer.

J. W. Von Goethe, 1858.　　　　　　"PENITENCE."　　　　　　S. Lane, 1878.

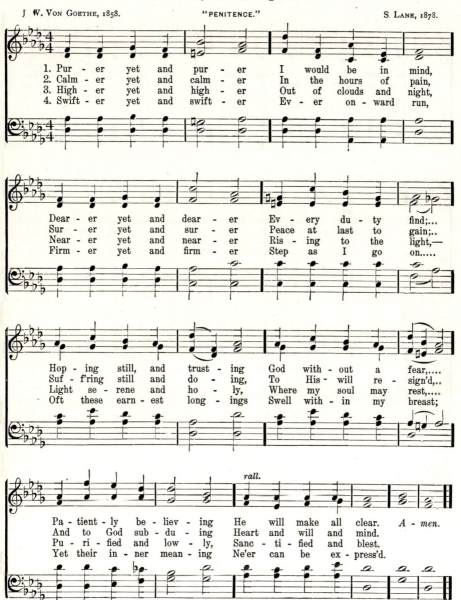

1. Pur - er yet and pur - er I would be in mind,
2. Calm - er yet and calm - er In the hours of pain,
3. High - er yet and high - er Out of clouds and night,
4. Swift - er yet and swift - er Ev - er on - ward run,

Dear - er yet and dear - er Ev - ery du - ty find;...
Sur - er yet and sur - er Peace at last to gain;..
Near - er yet and near - er Ris - ing to the light,—
Firm - er yet and firm - er Step as I go on.....

Hop - ing still, and trust - ing God with - out a fear,....
Suf - f'ring still and do - ing, To His - will re - sign'd,..
Light se - rene and ho - ly, Where my soul may rest,....
Oft these earn - est long - ings Swell with - in my breast;

Pa - tient - ly be - liev - ing He will make all clear. A - men.
And to God sub - du - ing Heart and will and mind.
Pu - ri - fied and low - ly, Sanc - ti - fied and blest.
Yet their in - ner mean - ing Ne'er can be ex - press'd.

201

Jesus, lover of my soul.

C. WESLEY, 1740. "HOLLINGSIDE." J. B. DYKES, 1861.

1. Je - sus, lov - er of my soul, Let me to Thy bo - som fly,
2. Oth - er ref - uge have I none; Hangs my help - less soul on Thee;
3. Thou, O Christ, art all I want, More than all in Thee I find:
4. Plen - teous grace with Thee is found, Grace to cov - er all my sin;

While the near - er wa - ters roll, While the tem - pest still is high!
Leave, ah! leave me not a - lone, Still sup - port and com - fort me.
Raise the fall - en, cheer the faint, Heal the sick, and lead the blind.
Let the heal - ing streams a - bound; Make and keep me pure with - in.

Hide me, O my Sav - iour, hide, Till the storm of life be past;
All my trust on Thee is stay'd, All my help from Thee I bring;
Just and ho - ly is Thy name; I am all un - right - eous - ness;
Thou of life the foun - tain art, Free - ly let me take of Thee;

Safe in - to the ha - ven guide; Oh, re - ceive my soul at last! A - men.
Cov - er my de - fence - less head With the shad - ow of Thy wing!
False and full of sin I am, Thou art full of truth and grace.
Spring Thou up with - in my heart; Rise to all e - ter - ni - ty!

(Or to ST. FABIAN, opposite.)

God of mercy, throned on high.

HENRY NEALE, Pub. 1829. "ST. FABIAN." J. BARNBY, 1866.

1. God of mer - cy, thron'd on high, List - en from Thy loft - y seat;
2. Je - su, Lov - er of the young, Cleanse us with Thy blood di - vine;
3. Let us ev - er hear Thy voice, Ask Thy coun - sel ev - ery day;

Hear, O hear our fee - ble cry; Guide, O guide our wan - d'ring feet.
Ere the tide of sin grow strong, Save us, Lord, and keep us Thine.
Saints and an - gels will re - joice, If we walk in wis - dom's way.

Young and err - ing trav - 'lers, we All our dan - gers do not know;
When per - plex'd in dan - ger's snare, Thou a - lone our Guide canst be;
Sav - iour, give us faith, and pour Hope and love on ev - ery soul!

Scarce - ly fear the storm - y sea, Hard - ly feel the temp - est blow. A - men.
When op-press'd with woe and care, Whom have we to trust but Thee?
Hope, till time shall be no more! Love, while end - less a - ges roll!

203

My God, I thank Thee.

A. A. PROCTER, 1858. Abr. "WENTWORTH." F. C. MAKER, 1876.

1. My God, I thank Thee, Who hast made The earth so bright; So full of splen-dor and of joy,
2. I thank Thee too that Thou hast made Joy to a - bound; So ma - ny gen-tle thoughts and deeds
3. I thank Thee, Lord, that Thou hast kept The best in store; We have e-nough, yet not too much
4. I thank Thee, Lord, that here our souls, Though amply blest, Can nev - er find, al-though they seek,

Beau - ty and light; So ma - ny glo-rious things are here, No - ble and right. A-men.
Cir - cling us round, That in the dark-est spot of earth Some love is found.
To long for more: A yearn-ing for a deep-er peace, Not known be - fore.
A per - fect rest; Nor ev - er shall, un - til they lean On Je - sus' breast.

204

Lead us, heavenly Father.

J. EDMESTON, 1821. "FARMER." H. FARMER, 1893.

1. Lead us, heav'n-ly Fa - ther, lead us O'er the world's tem - pes-tuous sea;
2. Sav - iour, breathe for - give - ness o'er us; All our weak - ness Thou dost know;
3. Spir - it of our God, de - scend - ing, Fill our hearts with heav'n-ly joy;

Guard us, guide us, keep us, feed us, For we have no help but Thee:
Thou didst tread this earth be - fore us; Thou didst feel its keen - est woe;
Love with ev - ery pas - sion blend - ing, Pleas - ure that can nev - er cloy

Lead us, heavenly Father.--*Concluded.*

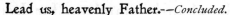

rall.

Yet pos-sess-ing Ev-ery bless-ing, If our God our Fa-ther be. A-men.
Lone and drear-y, Faint and wea-ry, Thro' the des-ert Thou didst go.
Thus pro-vid-ed, Par-doned, guid-ed, Noth-ing can our peace de-stroy.

Jesus, Saviour, pilot me. 205

E. HOPPER, 1871.   "PILOT."   J. E. GOULD, 1871.

1. Je - sus, Sav - iour, pi - lot me O - ver life's tem - pest - uous sea;
2. As a moth - er stills her child, Thou canst hush the o - cean wild;
3. When at last I near the shore, And the fear - ful break - ers roar

Un - known waves be - fore me roll,... Hid - ing rock and treach'rous shoal;
Bois-t'rous waves o - bey Thy will When Thou say'st to them, "Be still."
'Twixt me and the peace-ful rest, Then, while lean - ing on Thy breast,

Chart and com - pass came from Thee: Je - sus, Sav - iour, pi - lot me. A - men.
Won - drous Sov - 'reign of the sea, Je - sus, Sav - iour, pi - lot me.
May I hear Thee say to me, "Fear not, I will pi - lot thee."

206

Stand up!—stand up for Jesus!

G. DUFFIELD, 1858.　　　　　　　"WEBB."　　　　　　　G. J. WEBB, 1830.

1. Stand up!— stand up for Je - sus! Ye sol - diers of the cross;
2. Stand up!— stand up for Je - sus! The trum - pet call o - bey;
3. Stand up!— stand up for Je - sus! Stand in His strength a - lone;
4. Stand up!— stand up for Je - sus! The strife will not be long;

Lift high His roy - al ban - ner, It must not suf - fer loss;
Forth to the might - y con - flict, In this His glo - rious day.
The arm of flesh will fail you, Ye dare not trust your own:
This day the noise of bat - tle, The next, the vic - tor's song.

From vic - t'ry un - to vic - t'ry His ar - my shall He lead,
Ye that are men, now serve Him A - gainst un - num - bered foes;
Put on the gos - pel ar - mor, Each piece put on with pray'r,
To him that o - ver - com - eth, A crown of life shall be;

Till ev - 'ry foe is van - quish'd, And Christ is Lord in - deed. A - men.
Let cour - age rise with dan - ger, And strength to strength op - pose.
Where du - ty calls, or dan - ger, Be nev - er want - ing there.
He with the King of Glo - ry Shall reign e - ter - nal - ly!

Go forward, Christian soldier.

L. TUTTIETT, 1861.   "BERTHOLD."   B. TOURS, 1872.

1. Go for-ward, Chris-tian sol-dier, Be-neath His ban-ner true;
2. Go for-ward, Chris-tian sol-dier, Fear not the se-cret foe;
3. Go for-ward, Chris-tian sol-dier, Nor dream of peace-ful rest,
4. Go for-ward, Chris-tian sol-dier, Fear not the gath-'ring night;

The Lord Him-self, thy lead-er, Shall all thy foes sub-due.
Far more o'er thee are watch-ing Than hu-man eyes can know.
Till Sa-tan's host is van-quished And heav'n is all pos-sessed;
The Lord has been thy shel-ter; The Lord will be thy light.

His love fore-tells thy tri-als; He knows thine hour-ly need;
Trust on-ly Christ, thy Cap-tain; Cease not to watch and pray;
Till Christ him-self shall call thee To lay thine ar-mor by,
When morn His face re-veal-eth, Thy dan-gers all are past:

He can with bread of heav-en Thy faint-ing spir-it feed. A-men.
Heed not the treach'rous voic-es That lure thy soul a-stray.
And wear in end-less glo-ry The crown of vic-to-ry.
Oh, pray that faith and vir-tue May keep thee to the last!

208

The Son of God goes forth to war.

R. HEBER, 1827. "ALL SAINTS." H. S. CUTLER, 1872.

1. The son of God goes forth to war, A king-ly crown to gain;....
2. That mar-tyr first, whose ea-gle eye Could pierce be-yond the grave;....
3. A no-ble band, the chos-en few, On whom the Spir-it came,.....
4. A no-ble ar-my, men and boys, The ma-tron and the maid,.....

His blood-red ban-ner streams a-far: Who fol-lows in His train?
Who saw His Mas-ter in the sky, And called on Him to save;
Twelve val-iant saints, their hope they knew And mocked the torch of flame;
A-round the throne of God re-joice, In robes of light ar-rayed.

Who best can drink his cup of woe, Tri-umph-ant o-ver pain,.....
Like Him, with par-don on His tongue, In midst of mor-tal pain,.....
They met the ty-rant's brandish'd steel, The li-on's go-ry mane,....
They climb'd the steep as-cent of heav'n Thro' per-il, toil, and pain;.....

Who pa-tient bears his cross be-low, He fol-lows in His train. A-men.
He pray'd for them that did the wrong: Who fol-lows in His train?
They bow'd their necks the stroke to feel: Who fol-lows in their train?
O God, to us may grace be giv'n To fol-low in their train.

Onward, Christian soldiers.

S. Baring-Gould, 1865. "ST. GERTRUDE." A. S. Sullivan, 1871.

1. On - ward, Christian sol - diers, March-ing as to war, With the cross of Je - sus
2. Like a might - y ar - my Moves the Church of God; Broth-ers, we are tread - ing
3. Crowns and thrones may per - ish, King-doms rise and wane, But the Church of Je - sus
4. On - ward, then, ye peo - ple! Join our hap - py throng! Blend with ours your voic - es

Go - ing on be - fore! Christ the roy - al Mas - ter Leads a - gainst the foe;
Where the saints have trod; We are not di - vid - ed, All one bod - y we,
Con - stant will re - main; Gates of hell can nev - er 'Gainst that Church pre-vail;
In the tri - umph song! Glo - ry, laud, and hon - or, Un - to Christ the King;

Refrain.

For-ward in - to bat - tle, See, His ban-ners go.
One in hope and doc - trine, One in char - i - ty.
We have Christ's own prom-ise, And that can - not fail.
This thro' countless a - ges Men and an - gels sing.

On-ward, Christian sol - diers,

Marching as to war, With the cross of Je - sus Go - ing on be - fore! A - men.

war, With the cross of

With the cross of

210

Christian, dost thou see them.

Tr. J. M. NEALE, 1862. "ST. ANDREW OF CRETE." J. B. DYKES (1823—1876).

1. Chris - tian, dost thou see them On the ho - ly ground,
2. Chris - tian, dost thou hear them, How they speak thee fair?...
3. "Well I know thy trou - ble, O my serv - ant true;...

How the hosts of dark - ness Com - pass thee a - round?
"Al - ways fast and vig - il? Al - ways watch and pray'r?"
Thou art ver - y wea - ry, I was wea - ry too;

Chris - tian, up and smite them, Count - ing gain but loss;
Chris - tian, an - swer bold - ly: "While I breathe I pray:"
But that toil shall make thee Some day all Mine own,

Smite them, Christ is with thee, Sol - dier of the cross. A - men.
Peace shall fol - low bat - tle, Night shall end in day.
And the end of sor - row Shall be near My throne."

SECOND TUNE.

St. Andrew of Crete, 700.
Tr. J. M. Neale, 1862.

"HOLY WAR."

J. Booth (1852—).

Voices in Unison.

1. Chris - tian, dost thou see them On the ho - ly ground,
2. Chris - tian, dost thou hear them, How they speak thee fair?
3. "Well I know thy trou - ble, O my serv - ant true;

How the hosts of dark - ness Com - pass thee a - round?
"Al - ways fast and vig - il? Al - ways watch and pray'r?"
Thou art ver - y wea - ry, I was wea - ry too;

Harmony.

f

Chris - tian, up and smite them, Count - ing gain but loss;
Chris - tian, an - swer bold - ly: "While I breath and pray:"
But that toil shall make thee Some day all Mine own,

Organ Ped.

Smite them, Christ is with thee, Sol - dier of........ the cross. *A - men.*
Peace shall fol - low bat - tle, Night shall end....... in day.
And the end of sor - row Shall be near...... My throne."

2II

There's a fight to be fought.

SARAH G. STOCK, 1888.   "WATCHWORD."   A. L. PEACE, 1890.

1. There's a fight to be fought, there's a work to be done, And a foe to be met ere the
2. O'er the wa - ters it sound-eth, from lands far a - way, Where the reb - el u - surp - er holds
3. O, true hearts have gone forth, glad and strong, to the war, And the fame of their ex-ploits has

set of the sun. And the call is gone out o'er the land far and wide;
fair realms in sway: There are chains to be sev - er'd, and souls to be freed;
ech - oed a - far; And though brave ones have fall - en, yet rich their re - ward,

Verses 1, 4 & 5.   *Verses 2 & 3.*

Who'll fol - low the ban - ner, who's on the Lord's side?
Our Cap tain is call - ing, Him - - - - self takes the lead.
Who dies is crown'd vic - tor by (*Omit.....................*) Je - sus our Lord.

Refrain.

ff

O hark! the call of bat - tle re-sounds far and wide: Who'll fol - low the
Refrain after 5th verse.
O hark! the shout of tri-umph re-sounds far and wide; O, joy to the

There's a fight to be fought.—*Concluded.*

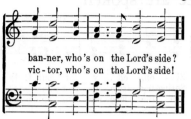

ban-ner, who's on the Lord's side?
vic-tor, who's on the Lord's side!

4 'T is not each one is called in the front rank to fight,
And there's room for us all though our strength may be
    slight,
And the weakest and poorest some succor may bring,
If only he follows the flag of his King.—Ref.

5 When the warfare is finished, the long struggle o'er,
And the name of our Master all nations adore,
Then the glad shout of triumph shall ring far and wide;
O, joy to the victor who's on the Lord's side!—Ref.

Breast the wave, Christian.   212

J. Stammers, 1830.   "ONWARD."   W. C. Filby (1836–).

1. Breast the wave, Chris-tian, When it is stron-gest; Watch for day, Chris-tian,
2. Fight the fight, Chris-tian, Je-sus is o'er thee; Run the race, Chris-tian,
3. Lift thine eye, Chris-tian, Just as it clos-eth; Raise thy heart, Chris-tian,

When the night's lon-gest; On-ward and on-ward still, Be thine en-deav-or;
Heav'n is be-fore thee; He who hath prom-is-ed Fal-ter-eth nev-er;
Ere it re-pos-eth; Thee from the love of Christ Noth-ing shall sev-er;

The rest that re-main-eth, Will be for-ev-er.   A-men.
He who hath lov'd so well, Lov-eth for-ev-er.
And, when thy work is done, Praise Him for-ev-er.

213

Glorious things of thee are spoken.

J. NEWTON, 1779. "AUSTRIA." F. J. HAYDN, 1797.

1. Glo - rious things of thee are spo - ken, Zi - on, cit - y of our God;
2. See, the streams of liv - ing wa - ters Spring-ing from e - ter - nal love,
3. Round each hab - it - a - tion hov - 'ring, See the cloud and fire ap - pear
4. Blest in - hab - it - ants of Zi - on, Wash'd in the Re - deem-er's blood!

He whose word can - not be bro - ken, Form'd thee for His own a - bode;
Well sup - ply thy sons and daugh-ters, And all fear of want re - move.
For a glo - ry and a cov - 'ring, Show - ing that the Lord is near;
Je - sus, whom their souls re - ly on, Makes them kings and priests to God.

On the Rock of A - ges found - ed, What can shake thy sure re - pose?
Who can faint, while such a riv - er Ev - er flows their thirst t' as-suage
Thus de - riv - ing from their ban - ner, Light by night, and shade by day,
'Tis His love His peo - ple rais - es O - ver self to reign as kings:

With sal - va - tion's walls sur - round - ed, Thou may'st smile at all thy foes. A-men.
Grace which, like the Lord, the giv - er, Nev - er fails from age to age.
Safe they feed up - on the man - na Which He gives them when they pray.
And as priests, His sol - emn prais - es Each for a thank - of - f'ring brings.

The Church's one foundation.

S. J. STONE, 1866.   "AURELIA."   S. S. WESLEY, 1864.

1. The Church's one foun - da - tion Is Je - sus Christ our Lord;
2. E - lect from ev - ery na - tion, Yet one o'er all the earth,
3. 'Mid toil and trib - u - la - tion, And tu - mult of her war,
4. Yet she on earth hath un - ion With God the Three in One,

She is His new cre - a - tion By wa - ter and the word;
Her char - ter of sal - va - tion One Lord, one faith, one birth;
She waits the con - sum - ma - tion Of peace for ev - er - more;
And mys - tic sweet com - mun - ion With those whose rest is won;

From heav'n He came and sought her To be His ho - ly bride;
One ho - ly name she bless - es, Par - takes one ho - ly food,
Till with the vi - sion glo - rious Her long - ing eyes are blest,
O hap - py ones and ho - ly! Lord, give us grace, that we,

With His own blood He bought her, And for her life He died. A - men.
And to one hope she press - es, With ev - ery grace en - dued.
And the great church vic - to - rious Shall be the church at rest.
Like them, the meek and low - ly, On high may dwell with Thee.

215 For all the saints who from their labors rest.

W. W. How, 1864.   "SARUM."   J. Barnby, 1869.

1. For all the saints who from their la - bors rest, Who Thee by
2. Thou wast their rock, their fort - ress and their might: Thou, Lord, their
3. Oh, may Thy sol - diers, faith - ful, true, and bold, Fight as the
4. Oh, blest com - mun - ion, fel - low - ship di - vine! We fee - bly

faith be - fore the world con - fessed, Thy name, O Je - sus
cap - tain in the well - fought fight; Thou, in the dark - ness
saints who no - bly fought of old, And win, with them, the
strug - gle, they in glo - ry shine; Yet all are one in

be for - ev - er blest. Al - le - lu - ia! Al - le - lu - ia! A - men.
drear, their light of light. Al - le - lu - ia! Al - le - lu - ia!
vic - tors' crown of gold. Al - le - lu - ia! Al - le - lu - ia!
Thee, for all are Thine. Al - le - lu - ia! Al - le - lu - ia!

5 And when the strife is fierce, the warfare long,
Steals on the ear the distant triumph-song,
And hearts are brave again, and arms are strong. Alleluia!

6 The golden evening brightens in the west;
Soon, soon to faithful warriors cometh rest;
Sweet is the calm of Paradise the blest. Alleluia!

7 But lo! there breaks a yet more glorious day;
The saints triumphant rise in bright array;
The King of glory passes on His way. Alleluia!

8 From earth's wide bounds, from ocean's farthest coast,
Through gates of pearl streams in the countless host,
Singing to Father, Son, and Holy Ghost. Alleluia!

Through the night of doubt and sorrow.

B. S. Ingeman, 1825.
Tr. S. Baring-Gould, 1867, 1875.   "ST. ASAPH."   W. S. Bambridge, 1872.

1. Thro' the night of doubt and sor - row On - ward goes the pil - grim band,
2. One, the light of God's own pres - ence, O'er His ran - som'd peo - ple shed,
3. One, the strain which lips of thou - sands Lift as from the hearts of one,
4. On - ward there - fore, pil - grim broth - ers, On - ward, with the cross our aid;

Sing - ing songs of ex - pec - ta - tion, March - ing to the prom - ised land.
Chas - ing far the gloom and ter - ror, Bright-'ning all the path we tread:
One the con - flict, one the per - il, One, the march in God be - gun:
Bear its shame, and fight its bat - tle, Till we rest be - neath its shade.

Clear be - fore us through the dark-ness Gleams and burns the guid - ing light;
One, the ob - ject of our jour-ney, One, the faith which nev - er tires,
One, the glad - ness of re - joic - ing On the far e - ter - nal shore,
Soon shall come the great a - wak - ing; Soon the rend - ing of the tomb;

Broth - er clasps the hand of broth-er, Step - ping fear - less thro' the night. A - men.
One, the ear - nest look - ing for - ward, One, the hope our God in - spires,
Where the One Al - might - y Fa - ther Reigns in love for ev - er - more.
Then, the scat - t'ring of all shad-ows, And the end of toil and gloom.

217

Hark the bugle-call of God.

A. T. Pierson, 1894.   "BUGLE-CALL."   A. T. Pierson, 1894.

1. Hark the bu-gle-call of God Down the a-ges sound-ing,
2. Let the sa-cred her-alds go Thro' the vales and moun-tains;
3. Go to wom-an now en-slaved In her house-hold pris-on.
4. Hosts of God, march round the wall, While the trum-pet's peal-ing;

"Go ye, and pro-claim a-broad News of grace a-bound-ing!"
Stead-y streams of treas-ure flow From the gold-en foun-tains.
Tell her, you whom Je-sus saved, He was dead— is ris-en.
Sa-tan's might-y tow'rs will fall, God's own pow'r re-veal-ing.

Refrain.

Tell the news! Tell the news! Let the far-thest na-tion

Hear the sound, the world a-round, Ti-dings of sal-va-tion. A-men.

O Zion, haste, thy mission high.

MARY A. THOMSON, 1870. "PROCLAMATION." J. WALCH, 1876.

1. O Zi - on, haste, thy mis - sion high ful - fill - ing, To tell to all the
2. Be - hold how ma - ny thou-sands still are ly - ing Bound in the dark - some
3. Pro - claim to ev - ery peo-ple, tongue, and na - tion That God, in whom they
4. Give of thy sons to bear the mes-sage glo - rious; Give of thy wealth to
5. He comes a - gain: O Zi - on, ere thou meet Him, Make known to ev - ery

world that God is Light; That He who made all na - tions is not will - ing
pris - on - house of sin, With none to tell them of the Sav-iour's dy - ing,
live and move, is Love: Tell how He stooped to save His lost cre - a - tion,
speed them on their way; Pour out thy soul for them in pray'r vic - to - rious;
heart His sav - ing grace; Let none whom He hath ran-somed fail to greet Him,

Refrain.

One soul should per - ish, lost in shades of night.
Or of the life He died for them to win.
And died on earth that man might live a - bove. } Pub - lish glad ti - dings.
And all thou spend-est Je - sus will re - pay.
Thro' thy neg - lect, un - fit to see His face.

ti - dings of peace, Ti - dings of Je - sus, re - demp-tion and re - lease. A - *men.*

14 E

219

From Greenland's icy mountains.

R. HEBER, 1819.   "MISSIONARY HYMN."   L. MASON, 1823.

1. From Green-land's i - cy moun - tains, From In - dia's cor - al strand,
2. What though the spi - cy breez - es Blow soft o'er Cey - lon's isle;
3. Shall we whose souls are light - ed With wis - dom from on high,
4. Waft, waft, ye winds, His sto - ry, And you, ye wa - ters, roll,

Where Af - ric's sun - ny foun - tains Roll down their gold - en sand;
Though ev - ery pros - pect pleas - es, And on - ly man is vile;
Shall we to men be - night - ed The lamp of life de - ny?
Till, like a sea of glo - ry, It spreads from pole to pole;

From many an an - cient riv - er, From many a palm - y plain,
In vain with lav - ish kind - ness The gifts of God are strown;
Sal - va - tion! oh, sal - va - tion! The joy - ful sound pro - claim,
Till o'er our ran - somed na - ture The Lamb for sin - ners slain,

They call us to de - liv - er Their land from er - ror's chain.   A - men.
The hea - then in his blind - ness Bows down to wood and stone.
Till earth's re - mot - est na - tion Has learn'd Mes - si - ah's name.
Re - deem - er, King, Cre - a - tor, In bliss re - turns to reign.

Rise, crowned with light.

A. POPE, 1720.   "MOSCOW."   A. F. LWOFF, 1833.

1. Rise, crown'd with light,.... im - pe - rial Sa - lem, rise; Ex - alt thy
2. See a long race..... thy spa - cious courts a - dorn: See fu - ture

tow - 'ring head and lift thine eyes; See heav'n its spark - ling por - tals wide dis-
sons, and daugh-ters yet un - born, In crowd-ing ranks on ev - ery side a -

play, And break up - on thee in a flood of day. A - men.
rise, De - mand - ing life, im - pa - tient for the skies.

3 See barbarous nations at thy gates attend,
   Walk in thy light, and in thy temple bend;
   See thy bright altars thronged with prostrate kings,
   While every land its joyous tribute brings.

4 The seas shall waste, the skies to smoke decay,
   Rocks fall to dust, and mountains melt away;
   But fixed His word, His saving power remains,
   Thy realms shall last, thy own Messiah reigns.

221

Fling out the banner!

G. W. DOANE, 1848.   "WALTHAM."   J. B. CALKIN, 1872.

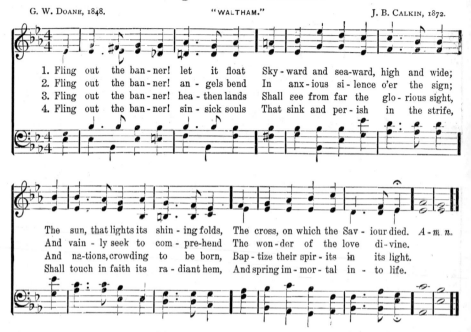

1. Fling out the ban-ner! let it float Sky-ward and sea-ward, high and wide,
2. Fling out the ban-ner! an - gels bend In anx-ious si - lence o'er the sign;
3. Fling out the ban-ner! hea-then lands Shall see from far the glo - rious sight,
4. Fling out the ban-ner! sin - sick souls That sink and per - ish in the strife,

The sun, that lights its shin - ing folds, The cross, on which the Sav - iour died. A - men.
And vain - ly seek to com - pre-hend The won-der of the love di - vine.
And na-tions, crowding to be born, Bap - tize their spir - its in its light.
Shall touch in faith its ra - diant hem, And spring im - mor - tal in - to life.

5 Fling out the banner! let it float
  Skyward and seaward, high and wide,
Our glory, only in the cross;
  Our only hope, the Crucified!

6 Fling out the banner! wide and high,
  Seaward and skyward, let it shine:
Nor skill, nor might, nor merit ours;
  We conquer only in that sign.

222   Lord, lead the way the Saviour went.

W. CROSSWELL, 1831.   "HOLY TRINITY."   J. BARNBY, 1861.

1. Lord, lead the way the Sav - iour went, By lane and cell ob - scure,
2. Like Him thro' scenes of deep dis - tress, Who bore the world's sad weight,
3. For Thou hast placed us side by side, In this wide world of ill,
4. Mean are the of - f'rings we can make, But Thou hast taught us, Lord,

Lord, lead the way the Saviour went.—*Concluded.*

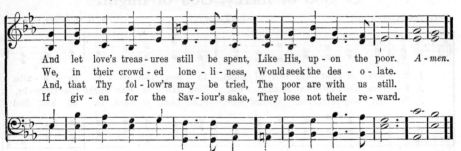

And let love's treas-ures still be spent, Like His, up-on the poor. *A-men.*
We, in their crowd-ed lone-li-ness, Would seek the des-o-late.
And, that Thy fol-low'rs may be tried, The poor are with us still.
If giv-en for the Sav-iour's sake, They lose not their re-ward.

O Lord of heaven and earth and sea. 223

C. WORDSWORTH, 1872.   "BELAUGH."   A. H. MANN.

1. O Lord of heav'n and earth and sea, To Thee all praise and glo-ry be; How shall we show our
2. The gold-en sun-shine, ver-nal air, Sweet flow'rs and fruit Thy love declare; When harvests ripen,
3. For peaceful homes, and healthful days, For all the blessings earth displays, We owe Thee thankful-

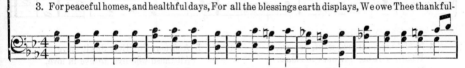

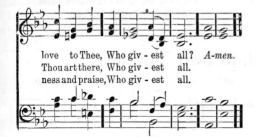

love to Thee, Who giv-est all? *A-men.*
Thou art there, Who giv-est all.
ness and praise, Who giv-est all.

6 For souls redeemed, for sins forgiven,
  For means of grace and hopes of heaven,
  What can to Thee, O Lord, be given,
    Who givest all?

7 We lose what on ourselves we spend,
  We have, as treasure without end,
  Whatever, Lord, to Thee we lend,
    Who givest all.

4 Thou didst not spare Thine only Son,
  But gav'st Him for a world undone,
  And freely with that blessèd one
    Thou givest all.

5 Thou giv'st the Spirit's holy dower,
  Spirit of life, and love, and power,
  And dost His sevenfold graces shower
    Upon us all.

8 Whatever, Lord, we lend to Thee,
  Repaid a thousand-fold will be;
  Then gladly will we give to Thee
    Who givest all.

9 To Thee, from whom we all derive
  Our life, our gifts, our power to give;
  Oh, may we ever with Thee live,
    Who givest all!

224

O God of mercy, God of might.

G. THRING, 1879. Abr. "ELMHURST." E. D. DREWETT, 1887.

1. O God of mer - cy, God of might, In love and pit - y in - fi - nite,
2. And Thou who cam'st on earth to die, That fall - en man might live there - by,
3. For all are breth-ren, far and wide Since Thou, O Lord, for all hast died:

Teach us, as ev - er in Thy sight, To live our life to Thee. A - men.
O hear us, for to Thee we cry, In hope, O Lord, to Thee.
Then teach us, what - so - e'er be - tide, To love them all in Thee.

4 In sickness, sorrow, want, or care,
　Whate'er it be, 't is ours to share;
　May we, where help is needed, there
　Give help as unto Thee.

5 And may Thy Holy Spirit move
　All those who live, to live in love,
　Till Thou shalt greet in heaven above
　All those who give to Thee.

225 # Fountain of good, to own Thy love.

P. DODDRIDGE, 1755. E. OSLER, 1836. "ARMAGH." J. TURLE (1802—1882).

1. Foun-tain of good, to own Thy love Our thank - ful hearts in - cline;
2. But Thou hast need - y breth - ren here, Par - tak - ers of Thy grace,
3. In each sad ac - cent of dis - tress Thy plead - ing voice is heard;
4. Help us then, Lord, Thy yoke to wear, And joy to do Thy will;
5. Thy face with rev - 'rence and with love We in Thy poor would see:

Fountain of good, to own Thy love.—*Concluded.*

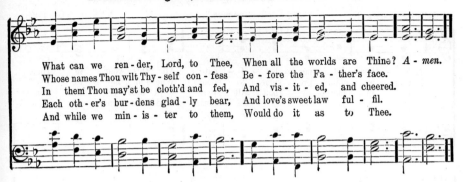

What can we ren - der, Lord, to Thee, When all the worlds are Thine? A - *men.*
Whose names Thou wilt Thy - self con - fess Be - fore the Fa - ther's face.
In them Thou may'st be cloth'd and fed, And vis - it - ed, and cheered.
Each oth - er's bur - dens glad - ly bear, And love's sweet law ful - fil.
And while we min - is - ter to them, Would do it as to Thee.

My blessed Saviour, is Thy love. 226

J. STENNETT, 1697.   "NORTH ADAMS."   W. S. PRATT, 1887.

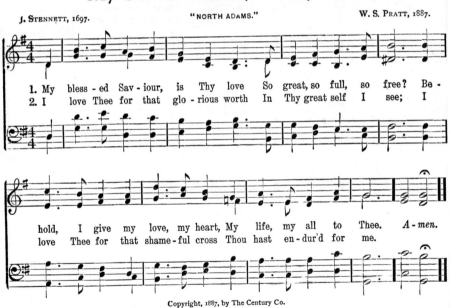

1. My bless - ed Sav - iour, is Thy love So great, so full, so free? Be -
2. I love Thee for that glo - rious worth In Thy great self I see; I

hold, I give my love, my heart, My life, my all to Thee. A - *men.*
love Thee for that shame - ful cross Thou hast en - dur'd for me.

3 No man of greater love can boast
   Than for his friend to die;
But for Thy foes, Lord, Thou wast slain:
   What love with Thine can vie?

4 Make us like Thee in meekness, love,
   In every beauteous grace,
From glory thus to glory changed
   As we behold Thy face.

227

Father, let me dedicate.

L. Tuttiett (1825—).   "GORDON."   J. Barnby (1838—1896).

1. Fa - ther, let me ded - i - cate All this year to Thee,
In what - ev - er world - ly state Thou wilt have me be.
Not from sor - row, pain, or care, Free - dom dare I claim;
This a - lone shall be my pray'r: Glo - ri - fy Thy name. A - men.

2. Can a child pre - sume to choose Where or how to live?
Can a Fa - ther's love re - fuse All the best to give?
More Thou giv - est ev - ery day Than the best can claim,
Nor with - hold - est aught that may Glo - ri - fy Thy name.

3. If in mer - cy Thou wilt spare Joys that yet are mine;
If on life, se - rene and fair, Bright - er rays may shine,—
Let my glad heart, while it sings, Thee in all pro - claim,
And, what - e'er the fu - ture brings, Glo - ri - fy Thy name.

4. If Thou call - est to the cross, And its shad - ow come,
Turn - ing all my gain to loss, Shroud - ing heart and home,—
Let me think how Thy dear Son To His glo - ry came,
And in deep - est woe pray on; "Glo - ri - fy Thy name."

Standing at the portal.

F. R. Havergal, 1873. "NEW YEAR." F. A. Mann.

1. Stand-ing at the por - tal of the o-p'ning year, Words of com-fort meet us,
2. I, the Lord, am with thee, be not thou a - fraid, I will help and strengthen,
3. For the year be - fore us, oh, what rich sup - plies! For the poor and need - y
4. He will nev - er fail us, He will not for - sake; His e - ter - nal cov-e-nant

hush - ing ev - ery fear; Spo - ken thro' the si - lence by our Fa - ther's voice,
be thou not dis - mayed! Yea, I will up - hold thee with my own right hand,
liv - ing streams shall rise; For the sad and sin - ful shall his grace a - bound;
He will nev - er break. Rest-ing on His prom - ise, what have we to fear?

Ten - der, strong and faith - ful, Mak - ing us re - joice.
Thou art called and chos - en in my sight to stand.
For the faint and fee - ble per - fect strength be found.
God is all - suf - fi - cient for the com - ing year.

Refrain.

On-ward, then, and fear not,

chil - dren of the day! For His word shall nev - er, nev - er pass a - way! *A-men.*

229

We plough the fields, and scatter.

M. CLAUDIUS, 1782.
Tr. JANE M. CAMPBELL, 1861.　　　"GIVE THANKS."　　　CALEB SIMPER.

Andante.

1. We plough the fields, and scat - ter　The good seed on the land,　But it is fed and
2. He on - ly is the Mak - er　Of all things near and far;　He paints the way - side
3. We thank Thee, then, O Fa - ther,　For all things bright and good,　The seed-time and the

wa - ter'd　By God's al - might-y hand;　He sends the snow in win - ter, The warmth to
flow - er,　He lights the eve - ning star;　The winds and waves o - bey Him, By Him the
har - vest,　Our life, our health, our food;　Ac - cept the gifts we of - fer, For all Thy

swell the grain,　The breez - es and the sun - shine, And soft re - fresh-ing rain.
birds are fed;　Much more to us, His chil - dren, He gives our dai - ly bread.
love im - parts,　And, what Thou most de - sir - est, Our hum - ble, thank-ful hearts.

Refrain.

All Thy works shall praise Thee, Thy saints give thanks and sing;...... Thy

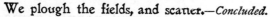

We plough the fields, and scatter.—*Concluded.*

Glo - rious Name shall men pro-claim Je - ho - vah, Lord, and King! A - men.

Summer suns are glowing.　230

W. W. How, 1871.　　　"RUTH."　　　Samuel Smith (1804—1873).

1. Sum - mer suns are glow - ing　O - ver land and sea;　Hap - py light is
2. God's free mer - cy stream-eth　O - ver all the world,　And His ban - ner
3. Lord, up - on our blind - ness,　Thy pure ra-diance pour,　For Thy lov - ing
4. We will nev - er doubt Thee,　Tho' Thou vail Thy light;　Life is dark with -

flow - ing, Boun - ti - ful and free;　Ev - 'ry-thing re - joic - es
gleam - eth, Ev - ery-where un - furl'd;　Broad and deep and glo - rious,
kind - ness Makes us love Thee more;　And when clouds are drift - ing
out Thee, Death with Thee is bright;　Light of light, shine o'er us

In the mel - low rays;　All earth's thousand voic - es　Swell the psalm of praise.
As the heav'n a - bove,　Shines in might vic - to - rious　His e - ter - nal love.
Dark a - cross the sky,　Then, the vail up - lift - ing,　Fa - ther, be Thou nigh.
On our pil - grim way,　Go Thou still be - fore us　To the end - less day.

231

Come, ye thankful people, come.

H. ALFORD, 1845. "ST. GEORGE'S, WINDSOR." G. J. ELVEY, 1858.

1. Come, ye thank-ful peo-ple, come, Raise the song of Har-vest-Home:
2. All the world is God's own field, Fruit un-to His praise to yield;
3. For the Lord our God shall come, And shall take His har-vest home;
4. E-ven so, Lord, quick-ly come, To Thy fi-nal Har-vest-Home!

All is safe-ly gath-ered in, Ere the win-ter storms be-gin;
Wheat and tares to-geth-er sown, Un-to joy or sor-row grown:
From His field shall in that day All of-fenc-es purge a-way;
Gath-er Thou Thy peo-ple in, Free from sor-row free from sin;

God, our Mak-er, doth pro-vide For our wants to be sup-plied;
First the blade, and then the ear, Then the full corn shall ap-pear:
Give His an-gels charge at last In the fire the tares to cast,
There for ev-er pu-ri-fied, In Thy Pres-ence to a-bide:

Come to God's own tem-ple, come, Raise the song of Har-vest-Home. A-men.
Lord of har-vest, grant that we Wholesome grain and pure may be.
But the fruit-ful ears to store In His Gar-ner ev-er-more.
Come, with all Thine an-gels, come, Raise the glo-rious Har-vest-Home.

Now let us raise our Harvest song.

AMY S. WOODS.   "ELMCOURT."   CALEB SIMPER.

1. Now let us raise our Har - vest song, And wake ex - ult - ant sing - ing;
2. The gold - en grain now gath - er'd in, His boun-teous Hand be - stow - eth;
3. The sea - sons all God's love pro-claim, Each month His good - ness shew - eth,
4. Then raise, O raise your Har - vest song! For heav'n and earth are sing - ing;

Hark! how the house of God to - day With joy - ful praise is ring - ing!
He sends the sun - shine and the rain To bless it as it grow - eth.
Who day by day with gra - cious Hand Our dai - ly bread be - stow - eth.
The an - them of our Fa - ther's Love Round all the world is ring - ing.

Refrain.

Then prais - es bring our Lord and King, Whose prom - ise fail - eth nev - er:

Who will His chil - dren's needs supply For ev - er and for ev - er. A - men.

233

The sower went forth sowing.

W. St. Hill Bourne. "ST. BEATRICE." J. F. Bridge, 1896.

1 The sow - er went forth sow - ing, The seed in
se - cret slept Through weeks of faith and pa - tience,
Till out the green blade crept; And warmed by gold - en sun - shine,
And fed by sil - ver rain, At last the fields were whit - ened

2. Be - hold! the heav'n - ly Sow - er, Goes forth with
bet - ter seed, The word of sure sal - va - tion,
With Feet and Hands that bleed; Here in His Church 'tis scat - tered,
Our spir - its are the soil; Then let an am - ple fruit - age

The sower went forth sowing.—*Concluded.*

To har - vest once a - gain. O praise the heav'n - ly
Re - pay His pain and toil. Oh, beau - teous is the

Sow - er, Who gave the fruit - ful seed, And watched and
har - vest Where - in all good - ness thrives, And this the

wa - tered du - ly, And rip - ened for our need. A - men.
true thanks - giv - ing, The first - fruits of our lives.

3 Within a hallowed acre
   He sows yet other grain,
When peaceful earth receiveth
   The dead He died to gain;
For though the growth be hidden,
   We know that they shall rise;
Yea, even now they ripen
   In sunny Paradise.
O summer land of harvest,
   O fields for ever white
With souls that wear Christ's raiment,
   With crowns of golden light!

4 One day the heavenly Sower
   Shall reap where He hath sown,
And come again rejoicing,
   And with Him bring His own;
And then the fan of judgment
   Shall winnow from His floor
The chaff into the furnace
   That flameth evermore.
O holy, awful Reaper,
   Have mercy in the day
Thou puttest in Thy sickle,
   And cast us not away.

234 My country 't is of thee.

S. F. SMITH, 1832.   "AMERICA."   H. CAREY, 1743.

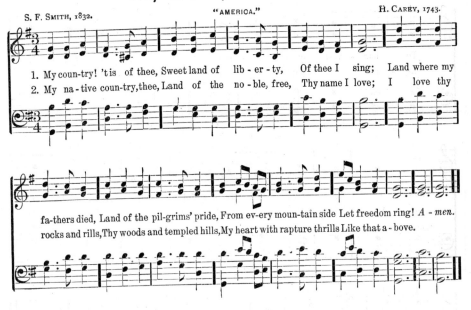

1. My coun-try! 't is of thee, Sweet land of lib-er-ty, Of thee I sing; Land where my
2. My na-tive coun-try,thee, Land of the no-ble, free, Thy name I love; I love thy

fa-thers died, Land of the pil-grims' pride, From ev-ery moun-tain side Let freedom ring! *A - men.*
rocks and rills,Thy woods and templed hills,My heart with rapture thrills Like that a-bove.

3 Let music swell the breeze,
And ring from all the trees
  Sweet freedom's song:
Let mortal tongues awake,
Let all that breathe partake,
Let rocks their silence break,
  The sound prolong.

4 Our fathers' God, to Thee,
Author of liberty,
  To Thee we sing:
Long may our land be bright
With freedom's holy light;
Protect us by Thy might,
  Great God, our King.

235 God bless our native land!

C. T. BROOKS, 1834.   "UNION."   S. P. WARREN, 1896.

(Or to AMERICA, above.)

1. God bless our na-tive land! Firm may she ev-er stand, Thro' storm and night! When the wild
2. For her our pray'r shall rise To God, a-bove the skies; On Him we wait; Thou who art

God bless our native land!—*Concluded.*

tem-pests rave, Rul - er of wind and wave, Do Thou our coun-try save By Thy great might. *A-men.*
ev - er nigh, Guarding with watchful eye, To Thee a - loud we cry, God save the State!

God the all-merciful! 236

H. F. CHORLEY, 1842.
J. ELLERTON, 1870.

"ULTOR."

A. S. SULLIVAN, 1874.

1. God the all - mer - ci - ful! earth hath for - sak - en Thy ways of
2. God the all - right - eous One! man hath de - fied Thee; Yet to e-
3. God the all - wise! by the fire of Thy chast - 'ning, Earth shall to
4. So will Thy peo - ple, with thank - ful de - vo - tion, Praise Him Who

bless - ed - ness, slight - ed Thy word; Bid not Thy wrath in its
ter - ni - ty stand - eth Thy word, False-hood and wrong shall not
free - dom and truth be re - stored; Thro' the thick dark - ness Thy
saved them from per - il and sword, Shout - ing in cho - rus from

p

ter - rors a - wak - en; Give to us peace in our time, O Lord. *A-men.*
tar - ry be - side Thee; Give to us peace in our time, O Lord.
king - dom is hast - 'ning; Thou wilt give peace in Thy time, O Lord.
o - cean to o - cean, Peace to the nations, and praise to the Lord.

15 E

237

O Lord of Hosts! Almighty King!

O. W. HOLMES.　　　　　　　　"DUKE STREET."　　　　　　J. HATTON (—1793), c. 1790.

1. O Lord of Hosts! Al - might - y...... King! Be - hold the
2. Wake in our breast the... liv - ing.... fires, The ho - ly
3. Be Thou a pil - lared flame to..... show The mid - night

sac - ri - fice we bring: To ev - ery arm Thy
faith that warmed our sires; Thy hand hath made our
snare, the si - lent foe; And when the bat - tle

strength im - part, Thy Spir - it shed.... thro' ev - ery heart. A - men
na - tion free; To die for her..... is serv - ing Thee.
thun - ders loud, Still guide us in...... its mov - ing cloud.

4 God of all nations! Sovereign Lord!
　In Thy dread name we draw the sword,
　We lift the starry flag on high,
　That fills with light our stormy sky.

5 From treason's rent, from murder's stain,
　Guard Thou its folds till peace shall reign,
　Till fort and field, till shore and sea,
　Join our loud anthem, Praise to Thee!

God of our fathers.

D. C. ROBERTS, 1876.   "NATIONAL HYMN."   G. W. WARREN, 1892.

Trumpets, before each verse.

1. God of our fa-thers, Whose al-might-y hand
2. Thy love di-vine hath led us in the past,

Leads forth in beau-ty all the star-ry band   Of shin-ing worlds in
In this free land by Thee our lot is cast;   Be Thou our rul-er,

splendor thro' the skies,   Our grate-ful songs be-fore Thy throne a-rise. A-men.
guardian, guide and stay,   Thy word our law, Thy paths our chos-en way.

From the Tucker (Episcopal) Hymnal.

3 From war's alarms, from deadly pestilence,
Be Thy strong arm our ever sure defence;
Thy true religion in our hearts increase,
Thy bounteous goodness nourish us in peace.

4 Refresh Thy people on their toilsome way,
Lead us from night to never-ending day;
Fill all our lives with love and grace divine,
And glory, laud and praise be ever Thine.

239 Mine eyes have seen the glory.

JULIA WARD HOWE.   "BATTLE HYMN OF THE REPUBLIC."   ANON.

1. Mine.... eyes have seen the glo - ry of the com - ing of the
2. I have seen Him in the watch - fires of a hun - dred cir - cling
3. I have read a fi - ery gos - pel, writ in bur - nish'd rows of

Lord; He is tramp - ling out the vint - age where the
camps; They have build - ed Him an al - tar in the
steel; "As ye deal with my con - tem - ners, so with

grapes of wrath are stor'd, He hath loosed the fate - ful
eve - ning dews and damps, I have read His right - eous
you my grace shall deal: Let the he - ro born of

light - ning of His ter - ri - ble swift sword,
sen - tence by the dim and flar - ing lamps;
wom - an crush the ser - pent with his heel,

Mine eyes have seen the glory.—*Concluded.*

His truth is march - ing on.
His day is march - ing on.
Since God is march - ing on.

Glo - ry! glo - ry! Hal - le - lu - jah! Glo - ry! glo - ry! Hal - le - lu - jah! Glo - ry! glo - ry! Hal - le - lu - jah! His truth is march - ing on.

4 He has sounded forth the trumpet that shall never call retreat;
He is sifting out the hearts of men before His judgment-seat;
Oh be swift, my soul, to answer him,—be jubilant, my feet!
Our God is marching on.—Cho.

5 In the beauty of the lilies Christ was born across the sea,
With a glory in His bosom that transfigures you and me:
As He died to make men holy, let us die to make men free,
While God is marching on.—Cho.

240

Land where the banners wave.

O. W. HOLMES.   "FREEDOM."   S. P. WARREN, 1899.

1. Land where the banners wave last in the sun, Bla - zon'd with
   star - clus - ters, ma - ny in one; Float - ing o'er prai - rie, and
   moun - tain, and sea, Hark! 'tis the voice of thy chil - dren to thee!

2. Here at thine al - tar our vows we re - new, Still to thy
   cause to be loy - al and true, True to thy flag on the
   field and the wave, Liv - ing to hon - or it, dy - ing to save.

3. Moth - er of he - roes! if per - fi - dy's blight Fall on a
   star in thy gar - land of light; Sound but one bu - gle blast!
   Lo! at the sign, Ar - mies all pan - o - plied wheel in - to line.

4. Hope of the world! thou hast bro - ken its chains; Wear thy bright
   arms while a ty - rant re - mains; Stand for the right till the
   na - tion's shall own Free - dom their sov - 'reign with Law for her throne.

5 Freedom! sweet Freedom! our voices resound,
Queen by God's blessing, unsceptred, uncrowned!
Freedom! sweet Freedom, our pulses repeat,
Warm with her life-blood, as long as they beat!

6 Fold the broad barrier-stripes over her breast,
Crown her with star-jewels, Queen of the West!
Earth for her heritage, God for her friend,
She shall reign over us, world without end.

Lord, while for all mankind we pray.

J. R. WREFORD, 1837.   "CONGLETON."   A. H. BROWN.

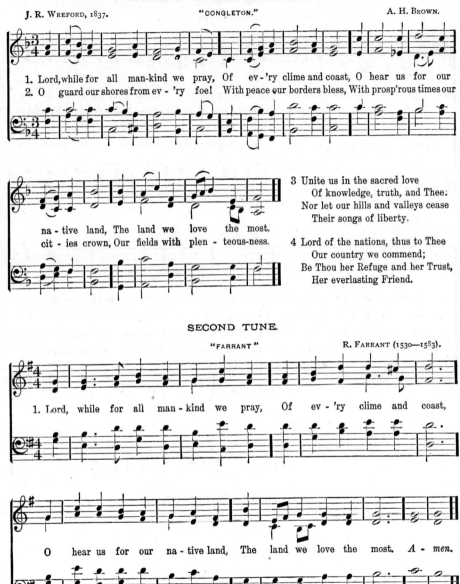

1. Lord, while for all man-kind we pray, Of ev-'ry clime and coast, O hear us for our
2. O guard our shores from ev-'ry foe! With peace our borders bless, With prosp'rous times our

na - tive land, The land we love the most.
cit - ies crown, Our fields with plen - teous-ness.

3 Unite us in the sacred love
　Of knowledge, truth, and Thee:
Nor let our hills and valleys cease
　Their songs of liberty.

4 Lord of the nations, thus to Thee
　Our country we commend;
Be Thou her Refuge and her Trust,
　Her everlasting Friend.

SECOND TUNE.

"FARRANT"   R. FARRANT (1530—1583).

1. Lord, while for all man - kind we pray, Of ev - 'ry clime and coast,

O hear us for our na - tive land, The land we love the most. A - men.

242

The Star-spangled Banner.

F. S. Key.   NATIONAL HYMN.   J. S. Smith, c. 1775.

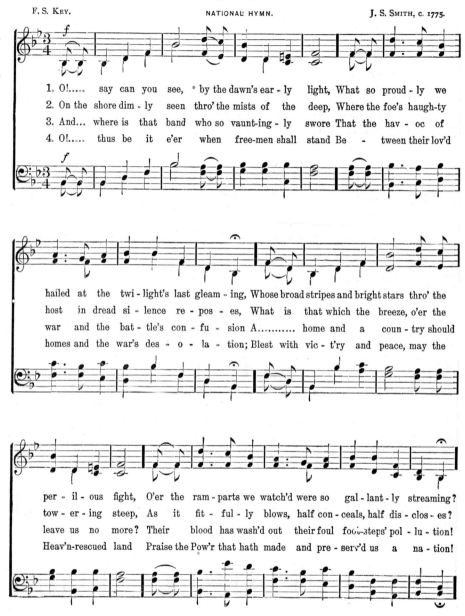

1. O!..... say can you see, by the dawn's ear - ly light, What so proud - ly we
2. On the shore dim - ly seen thro' the mists of the deep, Where the foe's haugh-ty
3. And... where is that band who so vaunt-ing - ly swore That the hav - oc of
4. O!..... thus be it e'er when free-men shall stand Be - tween their lov'd

hailed at the twi - light's last gleam - ing, Whose broad stripes and bright stars thro' the
host in dread si - lence re - pos - es, What is that which the breeze, o'er the
war and the bat - tle's con - fu - sion A.......... home and a coun - try should
homes and the war's des - o - la - tion; Blest with vic - t'ry and peace, may the

per - il - ous fight, O'er the ram - parts we watch'd were so gal - lant - ly streaming?
tow - er - ing steep, As it fit - ful - ly blows, half con - ceals, half dis - clos - es?
leave us no more? Their blood has wash'd out their foul foot-steps' pol - lu - tion!
Heav'n-rescued land Praise the Pow'r that hath made and pre - serv'd us a na - tion!

The Star-spangled Banner.—*Concluded.*

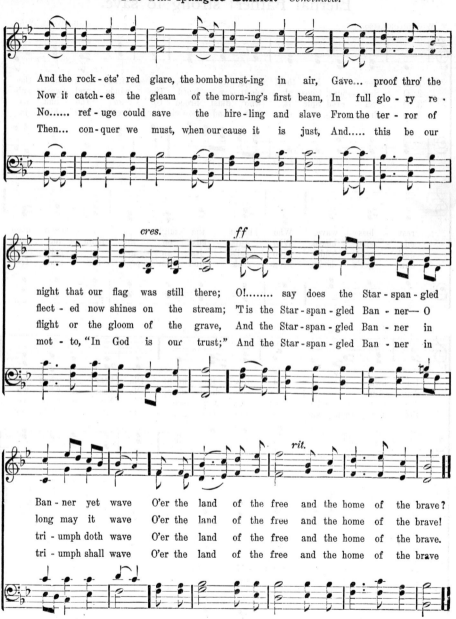

And the rock - ets' red glare, the bombs burst-ing in air, Gave... proof thro' the
Now it catch-es the gleam of the morn-ing's first beam, In full glo - ry re -
No...... ref - uge could save the hire - ling and slave From the ter - ror of
Then... con - quer we must, when our cause it is just, And..... this be our

night that our flag was still there; O!........ say does the Star - span - gled
flect - ed now shines on the stream; 'Tis the Star - span - gled Ban - ner— O
flight or the gloom of the grave, And the Star - span - gled Ban - ner in
mot - to, "In God is our trust;" And the Star - span - gled Ban - ner in

Ban - ner yet wave O'er the land of the free and the home of the brave?
long may it wave O'er the land of the free and the home of the brave!
tri - umph doth wave O'er the land of the free and the home of the brave.
tri - umph shall wave O'er the land of the free and the home of the brave

243

Eternal Father! strong to save.

W. WHITING, 1860. "MELITA." J. B. DYKES, 1861.

1. E - ter - nal Fa - ther! strong to save, Whose arm doth bind the
2. O Sav - iour, whose al - might - y word The winds and waves sub -
3. O Sa - cred Spir - it, who didst brood Up - on the cha - os
4. O Trin - i - ty of love and pow'r! Our breth - ren shield in

rest - less wave, Who bid'st the might - y o - cean deep
mis - sive heard, Who walk - edst on the foam - ing deep,
dark and rude, Who bad'st its an - gry tu - mult cease,
dan - ger's hour; From rock and tem - pest, fire and foe,

Its own ap - point - ed lim - its keep; Oh, hear us when we
And calm a - mid its rage didst sleep; Oh, hear us when we
And gav - est light, and life, and peace; Oh, hear us when we
Pro - tect them where - so - e'er they go, Thus ev - er let there

cry to Thee For those in per - il on the sea! A - men.
cry to Thee For those in per - il on the sea!
cry to Thee For those in per - il on the sea!
rise to Thee Glad hymns of praise from land and sea.

Safe home, safe home in port!

St. Joseph of the Studium, circ. 830.
Tr. J. M. NEALE, 1863.

"SAFE HOME."

A. S. SULLIVAN, 1872.

1. Safe home, safe home in port! Rent cord - age, shat - tered deck,
Torn sails, pro - vi - sions short, And on - ly not a wreck: But oh! the joy up - on the shore To tell our voy - age - per - ils o'er! A - men.

2. The prize, the prize se - cure! The ath - lete near - ly fell,
Bare all he could en - dure, And bare not al - ways well. But he may smile at trou - bles gone, Who sets the vic - tor - gar - land on!

3. No more the foe can harm; No more the leag - uered camp,
And cry of night - a - larm, And need of read - y lamp. And yet how near - ly he had failed,— How near - ly had that foe pre - vailed!

4. The lamb is in the fold, In per - fect safe - ty penn'd;
The li - on once had hold, And thought to make an end; But One came by with Wound - ed Side, And for the sheep the Shep - herd died.

5 The exile is at Home!
 O nights and days of tears,
 O longings not to roam,
 O sins, and doubts and fears.—
What matter now (when so men say)
The King has wiped those tears away?

6 O happy, happy Bride!
 Thy widowed hours are past,
 The Bridegroom at thy side,
 Thou all His Own at last!
The sorrows of thy former cup
In full fruition swallowed up.

245 All is bright and cheerful round us.

J. M. Neale (1818—1866).   "SPRING."   W. H. Walter (1825—1893).

1. All is bright and cheer-ful round us, All a-bove is soft and blue;
2. If the flow'rs that fade so quick-ly, If a day that ends in night,
3. There are leaves that nev-er with-er; There are flow'rs that ne'er de-cay:

Spring at last hath come and found us; Spring and all its pleas-ures too:
If the skies that clouds so thick-ly Oft-en cov-er from our sight,—
Noth-ing e-vil go-eth thith-er; Noth-ing good is kept a-way.

Ev-'ry flow'r is full of glad-ness, Dew is bright and buds are gay;
If they all have so much beau-ty, What must be God's land of rest,
They that came from trib-u-la-tion, Wash'd their robes and made them white,

Earth, with all its sin and sad-ness, Seems a hap-py place to-day.   A - men.
Where His sons that do their du-ty, Af-ter ma-ny toils are blest?
Out of ev-'ry tongue and na-tion, Now have rest, and peace, and light.

From The Tucker Hymnal, by per. of the Editor.

Those eternal bowers.

JOHN OF DAMASCUS.
Tr. J. M. NEALE, 1862.

"WILLIAMS."

T. MORLEY, 1865.

1. Those e - ter - nal bow - ers Man hath nev - er trod, Those un - fad - ing
   flow - ers Round the throne of God: Who may hope to gain them Af - ter
   wea - ry fight? Who at length at - tain them, Clad in robes of white? A - men.

2. He who wakes from slum - ber At the Spir - it's voice, Dar - ing here to
   num - ber Things un - seen his choice. He who casts his bur - den Down at
   Je - sus' cross; Christ's re-proach his guer - don, All be - side but loss.

3. He who glad - ly bar - ters All on earth - ly ground; He who, like the
   mar - tyrs, Says, "I will be crown'd." He whose one ob - la - tion Is a
   life of love, Knit in God's sal - va - tion To the blest a - bove.

4 Shame upon you, legions
    Of the heavenly King,
  Citizens of regions
    Past imagining!
  What, with pipe and tabor
    Dream away the light !
  When He bids you labor,
    When He tells you, "Fight"?

5 Jesus, Lord of glory;
    As we breast the tide,
  Whisper Thou the story
    Of the other side;
  Where the saints are casting
    Crowns before Thy feet,
  Safe for everlasting,
    In Thyself complete.

247
O Paradise, O Paradise.

F. W. FABER, 1862.
H. A. & M., 1868.

"PARADISE."

J. BARNBY, 1866.

1. O Par - a - dise, O Par - a - dise, Who doth not crave for rest?
2. O Par - a - dise, O Par - a - dise, I want to sin no more,
3. O Par - a - dise, O Par - a - dise, I great - ly long to see
4. Lord Je - sus, King of Par - a - dise, Oh, keep me in Thy love,

Who would not seek the hap - py land Where they that loved are blest;
I want to be as pure on earth As on Thy spot - less shore;
The spe - cial place my dear - est Lord Is des - tin - ing for me;
And guide me to that hap - py land Of per - fect rest a - bove.

Refrain.
Where loy - al hearts and true

Where loy - - - al hearts and true Stand ev - er in the light,

All rap - ture, thro' and thro', In God's most ho - ly sight? A - men.

Hark! the sound of holy voices.

C. WORDSWORTH, 1862.   "SANCTUARY."   J. B. DYKES, 1871.

1. Hark! the sound of ho-ly voic-es, Chant-ing at the crys-tal sea,
2. Pa-tri-arch and ho-ly proph-et, Who pre-par'd the way for Christ,
3. March-ing with Thy cross, their ban-ner, They have tri-umph'd, fol-low-ing
4. Now they reign in heav'n-ly glo-ry, Now they walk in gold-en light,

Al-le-lu-ia, Al-le-lu-ia, Al-le-lu-ia, Lord, to Thee;
King, a-pos-tle, saint, con-fes-sor, Mar-tyr and e-van-gel-ist;
Thee, the Cap-tain of sal-va-tion, Thee, their Sav-iour and their King.
Now they drink, as from a riv-er, Ho-ly bliss and in-fi-nite:

Mul-ti-tudes which none can num-ber, Like the stars in glo-ry stand,
Saint-ly maid-en, god-ly ma-tron, Wid-ows who have watch'd to pray'r,
Glad-ly, Lord, with Thee they suf-fer'd; Glad-ly, Lord, with Thee they died;
Love and peace they taste for ev-er, And all truth and knowl-edge see

rall.

Cloth'd in white ap-par-el, hold-ing Palms of vic-t'ry in their hands. *A-men.*
Join'd in ho-ly con-cert, sing-ing To the Lord of all, are there.
And by death to life im-mor-tal They were born and glo-ri-fied.
In the be-a-tif-ic vi-sion Of that bless-ed Trin-i-ty.

249 Around the throne of God in heaven.

A. H. Shepherd, 1835.   "CHILDREN'S PRAISES."   H. E. Matthews, 1854.

1. A - round the throne of God in heav'n Thou - sands of chil - dren stand,
2. In flow - ing robes of spot - less white See ev - ery one ar - rayed;
3. What brought them to that world a - bove, That heav'n so bright and fair,

Chil - dren whose sins are all for - giv'n, A ho - ly hap - py band,
Dwell - ing in ev - er - last - ing light And joys that nev - er fade,
Where all is peace, and joy, and love; How came those chil - dren there,

Refrain.

Sing - ing, "Glo - ry, glo - ry, Glo - ry be to God on high." A - men.

4 Because the Saviour shed His blood
   To wash away their sin;
Bathed in that pure and precious flood,
   Behold them white and clean,
Ref.—Singing, "Glory be to God on high."

5 On earth they sought the Saviour's grace,
   On earth they loved His name;
So now they see His blessed face,
   And stand before the Lamb,
Ref.—Singing, "Glory be to God on high."

Alleluia, song of sweetness.

Tr. J. M. NEALE, 1851.   "ALLELUIA, DULCE CARMEN."   E. J. HOPKINS, 1872.

1. Al - le - lu - ia, song of sweet-ness, Voice of joy that can-not die;
2. Al - le - lu - ia thou re - sound-est, True Je - ru - sa - lem and free;

Al - le - lu - ia is the an - them Ev - er dear to choirs on high;
Al - le - lu - ia, joy - ful moth - er, All thy chil - dren sing with thee;

In the house of God a - bid - ing Thus they sing e - ter - nal - ly. A - men.
But by Bab - y - lon's sad wa - ters Mourning ex - iles now are we.

3 Alleluia cannot always
   Be our song while here below;
Alleluia our transgressions
   Make us for a while forego;
For the solemn time is coming
   When our tears for sin must flow.

4 Therefore in our hymns we pray Thee,
   Grant us, blessèd Trinity,
At the last to see Thy glory
   In our home beyond the sky;
There to Thee forever singing
   Alleulia joyfully.

251

Every morning the red sun.

C. F. Alexander, 1848.　　　"HEAVENLY REST."　　　J. B. Dykes (1823—1876).

1. Ev - ery morn - ing the red sun Ris - es warm and bright;.....
2. Ev - ery spring the sweet young flow'rs O - pen bright and gay,........
3. Lit - tle birds sing songs of praise All the sum - mer long;.......

But the eve - ning com - eth on, And the dark, cold night;
Till the chil - ly au - tumn hours With - er them a - way;
But in cold - er, short - er days They for - get their song:

There's a bright land far a - way, Where is nev - er - end - ing day. A - men.
There's a land we have not seen, Where the trees are al - ways green.
There's a place where an - gels sing Cease - less prais - es to their King.

4 Christ our Lord is ever near
　Those who follow Him!
But we cannot see Him here,
　For our eyes are dim;
There is a most happy place,
Where men always see His face.

5 Who shall go to that bright land,
　All who do the right;
Holy children there shall stand
　In their robes of white;
For that heaven so bright and blest
Is our everlasting rest.

Ten thousand times ten thousand.

H. ALFORD, 1867.　　　　　　　　"ALFORD."　　　　　　　　J. B. DYKES, 1875.

1. Ten thou - sand times ten thou - sand　In spark - ling rai - ment bright,
2. What rush of al - le - lu - ias　Fills all the earth and sky!
3. Oh, then what rap - tur'd greet - ings　On Ca - naan's hap - py shore;
4. Bring near Thy great sal - va - tion,　Thou Lamb for sin - ners slain;

The ar - mies of the ran - som'd saints Throng up the steeps of light:
What ring - ing of a thou - sand harps Be - speaks the tri - umphs nigh!
What knit - ting sev - er'd friend - ships up, Where part - ings are no more!
Fill up the roll of Thine e - lect, Then take Thy pow'r, and reign:

'T is fin - ished! all is fin - ished,　Their fight with death and sin:....
Oh, day for which cre - a - tion　And all its tribes were made;..
Then eyes with joy shall spar - kle　That brimm'd with tears of late;....
Ap - pear, De - sire of na - tions,　Thine ex - iles long for home:..

Fling o - pen wide the gold - en gates, And let the vic - tors in.　A - men.
Oh, joy, for all its for - mer woes, A thou - sand-fold re - paid!
Or - phans no lon - ger fa - ther - less, Nor wi - dows des - o - late.
Show in the heav'ns Thy prom - ised sign: Thou Prince and Sav - iour, come!

253
Upward where the stars are burning.

H. Bonar, 1866. "BONAR." Arr. fr. J. B. Calkin, 1867.
By S. P. Warren, 1896.

1. Up - ward where the stars are burn-ing, Si - lent, si - lent in their turn - ing
2. Far a - bove that arch of glad - ness Far be - yond these clouds of sad - ness,
3. Where the glo - ry bright-ly dwell-eth, Where the new song sweet-ly swell-eth,

Round the nev - er - chang - ing pole; Up - ward where the sky is bright-est,
Are the ma - ny man - sions fair. Far from pain and sin and fol - ly,
And the dis - cord nev - er comes; Where life's stream is ev - er lav - ing,

Up - ward where the blue is light - est, Lift I now my long - ing soul. A-men.
In that pal - ace of the ho - ly, I would find my man - sion there.
And the palm is ev - er wav - ing, That must be the home of homes.

4 Where the Lamb on high is seated,
   By ten thousand voices greeted,
      Lord of lords, and King of kings.
   Son of Man, they crown, they crown Him,
   Son of God, they own, they own Him;
      With His name the palace rings.

5 Blessing, honor, without measure,
   Heavenly riches, earthly treasure,
      Lay we at His blessèd feet:
   Poor the praise that now we render,
   Loud shall be our voices yonder,
      When before His throne we meet.

Jerusalem the golden.

Bernard of Cluny, 12th Cent.
Tr. J. M. Neale, 1851.

"EWING."

A. Ewing, 1853.

1. Je - ru - sa - lem the gold - en, With milk and hon - ey blest,
2. They stand, those halls of Zi - on, All - ju - bi - lant with song,
3. There is the throne of Da - vid,— And there, from care re - leased,
4. O sweet and bless - ed coun - try, The home of God's e - lect!

Be - neath thy con - tem - pla - tion Sink heart and voice op - prest;
And bright with many an an - gel, And all the mar - tyr throng:
The song of them that tri - umph, The shout of them that feast;
O sweet and bless - ed coun - try, That ea - ger hearts ex - pect!

I know not, oh, I know not, What joys a - wait us there;
The Prince is ev - er in them; The day - light is se - rene;
And they, who with their Lead - er, Have con - quered in the fight,
Je - sus, in mer - cy bring us To that dear land of rest;

What ra - dian - cy of glo - ry! What bliss be - yond com - pare! A - men.
The pas - tures of the bless - ed Are decked in glo - rious sheen.
For ev - er and for ev - er Are clad in robes of white.
Who art, with God the Fa - ther, And Spir - it, ev - er blest.

255

Hark! hark, my soul!

F. W. Faber, 1854.　　　　　　"PILGRIMS."　　　　　　　H. Smart, 1868.

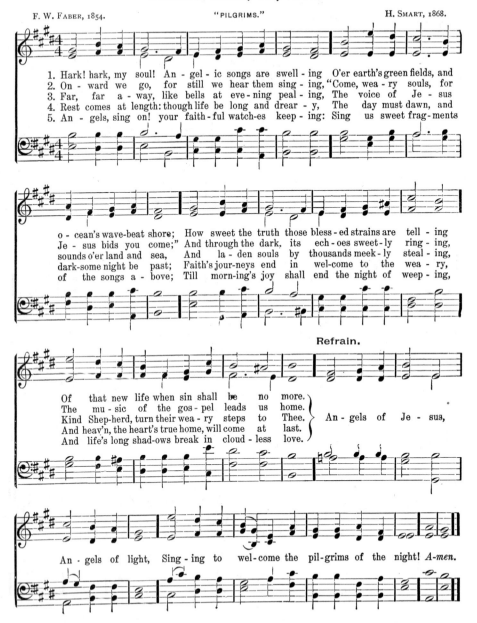

1. Hark! hark, my soul! An - gel - ic songs are swell - ing O'er earth's green fields, and
2. On - ward we go, for still we hear them sing - ing, "Come, wea - ry souls, for
3. Far, far a - way, like bells at eve - ning peal - ing, The voice of Je - sus
4. Rest comes at length: though life be long and drear - y, The day must dawn, and
5. An - gels, sing on! your faith - ful watch - es keep - ing: Sing us sweet frag - ments

o - cean's wave-beat shore; How sweet the truth those bless - ed strains are tell - ing
Je - sus bids you come;" And through the dark, its ech - oes sweet - ly ring - ing,
sounds o'er land and sea, And la - den souls by thousands meek - ly steal - ing,
dark-some night be past; Faith's jour - neys end in wel - come to the wea - ry,
of the songs a - bove; Till morn - ing's joy shall end the night of weep - ing,

Refrain.

Of that new life when sin shall be no more.
The mu - sic of the gos - pel leads us home.
Kind Shep - herd, turn their wea - ry steps to Thee.
And heav'n, the heart's true home, will come at last.
And life's long shad - ows break in cloud - less love.

An - gels of Je - sus,

An - gels of light, Sing - ing to wel - come the pil - grims of the night! A-men.

SECOND TUNE.

"VOX ANGELICA."

J. B. DYKES, 1868.

1. Hark! hark, my soul! An-gel-ic songs are swell-ing O'er earth's green fields, and o-cean's wave-beat shore; How sweet the truth those bless-ed strains are tell-ing Of that new life when sin shall be no more. An-gels of Je-sus, An-gels of light, Sing-ing to wel-come the pil-grims of the night! Sing-ing to wel-come the pil-grims, the pil-grims of the night! A-men.

250

The sands of time are sinking.

A. R. Cousin, 1857.   "RUTHERFORD."   Chrétien D'Urhan, 1834.
Har. E. F. Rimbault, 1867.

1. The sands of time are sink - ing, The dawn of Heav - en breaks,
2. Oh, Christ, He is the foun - tain, The deep, sweet well of love!
3. With mer - cy and with judg - ment My web of time He wove,
4. The bride eyes not her gar - ment, But her dear bride-groom's face;

The sum - mer morn I've sighed for, The fair, sweet morn a - wakes.
The streams of earth I've tast - ed, More deep I'll drink a - bove.
And aye the dews of sor - row Were lus - tred with His love:
I will not gaze at glo - ry, But on my King of grace;

Oh! dark hath been the mid - night, But day - spring is at hand,
There to an o - cean full - ness His mer - cy doth ex - pand,
I'll bless the hand that guid - ed, I'll bless the heart that planned
Not at the crown He giv - eth, But on His pierc - ed hand:

And glo - ry, glo - ry dwell - eth In Em - man - uel's land.   A - men.
And glo - ry, glo - ry dwell - eth In Em - man - uel's land.
When thron'd where glo - ry dwell - eth In Em - man - uel's land.
The Lamb is all the glo - ry Of Em - man - uel's land.

Jerusalem, my happy home.

ANON.   "MATERNA."   S. A. WARD, 1882.

1. Je - ru - sa - lem, my hap - py home, Name ev - er dear to me,......
2. O when, thou Cit - y of my God, Shall I thy courts as - cend,....
3. A - pos - tles, mar - tyrs, proph-ets, there A - round my Sav - iour stand;...

When shall my la - bors have an end In joy, and peace, and thee?.....
Where con - gre - ga - tions ne'er break up, And Sab - baths have no end?......
And soon my friends in Christ be - low Will join the glo - rious band......

When shall these eyes thy heav'n-built walls And pearl - y gates be - hold;....
There hap - pier bow'rs than E - den's bloom, Nor sin nor sor - row know;...
Je - ru - sa - lem, my hap - py home, My soul still pants for thee; ...

Thy bul-warks with sal - va - tion strong, And streets of shin - ing gold? *A - men.*
Blest scats, thro' rude and storm - y scenes I on - ward press to you.
Then shall my la - bors have an end When I thy joys shall see.

Copyright, 1888, by S. A. Ward.

258

Safely, safely gathered in.

H. O. de L. Dobree. "MONICA." M. B. Foster.

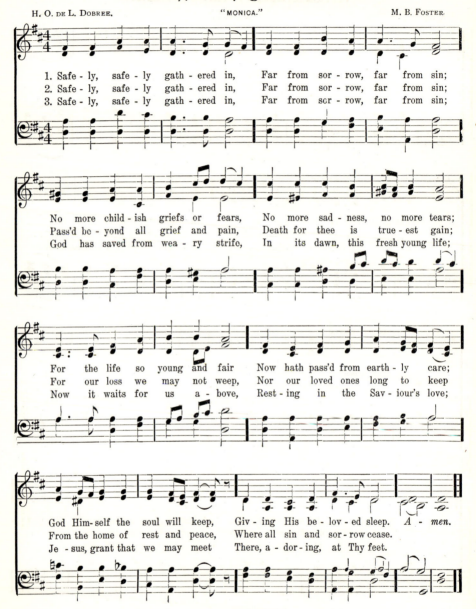

1. Safe - ly, safe - ly gath - ered in, Far from sor - row, far from sin;
2. Safe - ly, safe - ly gath - ered in, Far from sor - row, far from sin;
3. Safe - ly, safe - ly gath - ered in, Far from sor - row, far from sin;

No more child - ish griefs or fears, No more sad - ness, no more tears;
Pass'd be - yond all grief and pain, Death for thee is true - est gain;
God has saved from wea - ry strife, In its dawn, this fresh young life;

For the life so young and fair Now hath pass'd from earth - ly care;
For our loss we may not weep, Nor our loved ones long to keep
Now it waits for us a - bove, Rest - ing in the Sav - iour's love;

God Him - self the soul will keep, Giv - ing His be - lov - ed sleep. A - men.
From the home of rest and peace, Where all sin and sor - row cease.
Je - sus, grant that we may meet There, a - dor - ing, at Thy feet.

Asleep in Jesus!

Mrs. M. Mackay, 1832.   "REPOSE."   F. R. Statham (1844—).

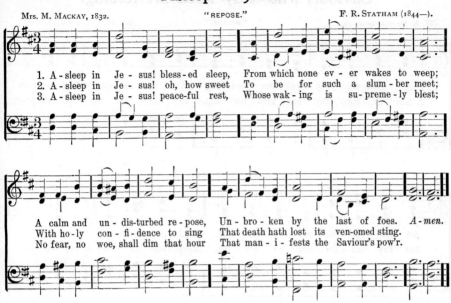

1. A - sleep in   Je - sus! bless-ed   sleep,   From which none ev - er wakes to weep;
2. A - sleep in   Je - sus! oh, how sweet   To   be   for   such   a   slum - ber meet;
3. A - sleep in   Je - sus! peace-ful   rest,   Whose wak - ing   is   su - preme - ly blest;

A calm and   un - dis-turbed re - pose,   Un - bro - ken by   the   last of foes.   A - men.
With ho - ly   con - fi - dence to sing   That death hath lost   its   ven-omed sting.
No fear, no   woe, shall dim that hour   That man - i - fests the   Saviour's pow'r.

4 Asleep in Jesus! oh, for me
  May such a blissful refuge be;
  Securely shall my ashes lie,
  Waiting the summons from on high.

5 Asleep in Jesus! far from thee
  Thy kindred and their graves may be;
  But thine is still a blessèd sleep,
  From which none ever wakes to weep.

SECOND TUNE.

"REST."   W. B. Bradbury, 1843. Arr.

1. A - sleep in   Je - sus! bless-ed   sleep,   From which none ev - er wakes to   weep,

A calm and un - dis-turb'd re - pose,   Un - bro-ken by   the   last of foes.   A - men.

260

Saviour, who Thy flock art feeding.

W. A. MUHLENBERG, 1826.   "HILARY."   KOCHER'S ZIONSHARFE, 1855.

1. Sav - iour, who Thy flock art feed - ing With the Shep-herd's kind - est care,
2. Nev - er, from Thy pas - ture rov - ing, Let them be the li - on's prey;

All the fee - ble gen - tly lead - ing, While the lambs Thy bo - som share,
Let Thy ten - der - ness, so lov - ing, Keep them all life's dan - g'rous way;

Now, these lit - tle ones re - ceiv - ing, Fold them in Thy gra - cious arm;
Then, with - in Thy fold e - ter - nal Let them find a rest - ing - place,

There, we know, Thy word be - liev - ing, On - ly there, se - cure from harm. A - men.
Feed in pas - tures ev - er ver - nal, Drink the riv - ers of Thy grace.

Saviour, like a shepherd lead us.

ANON, c. 1836.   "JESU, BONE PASTOR."   J. H. WILCOX (1827—1875).

1. Sav-iour, like a shep-herd lead us, Much we need Thy ten-der care;
2. We are Thine; do Thou be-friend us, Be the guard-ian of our way;

In Thy pleas-ant pas-tures feed us; For our use Thy folds pre-pare;
Keep Thy flock, from sin de-fend us, Seek us when we go a-stray:

Bless-ed Je-sus! Bless-ed Je-sus! Thou hast bought us, Thine we are. A-men.
Bless-ed Je-sus! Bless-ed Je-sus! Hear the chil-dren when they pray.

From The Tucker Hymnal, by per. of the Editor.

3 Thou hast promised to receive us,
   Poor and sinful though we be;
Thou hast mercy to relieve us,
   Grace to cleanse, and power to free·
     Blessèd Jesus!
   Early let us turn to Thee.

4 Early let us seek Thy favor;
   Early let us do Thy will;
Blessèd Lord and only Saviour,
   With Thy love our bosoms fill:
     Blessèd Jesus!
   Thou hast loved us, love us still.

262

Sing Alleluia forth in duteous praise.

ANON. (Latin, 5th Cent.).
Tr. J. ELLERTON, 1865.

"ALLELUIA PERENNE."

W. H. MONK, 1868.

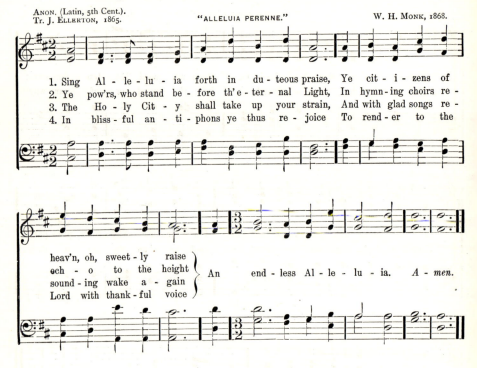

1. Sing Al - le - lu - ia forth in du - teous praise, Ye cit - i - zens of
2. Ye pow'rs, who stand be - fore th' e - ter - nal Light, In hymn - ing choirs re -
3. The Ho - ly Cit - y shall take up your strain, And with glad songs re -
4. In bliss - ful an - ti - phons ye thus re - joice To rend - er to the

heav'n, oh, sweet - ly raise
ech - o to the height
sound - ing wake a - gain
Lord with thank - ful voice

An end - less Al - le - lu - ia. A - men.

5 Ye who have gained at length your palms in bliss,
  Victorious ones, your chant shall still be this,
      An endless Alleluia.

6 There, in one glad acclaim, for ever ring
  The strains which tell the honor of your King,
      An endless Alleluia.

7 This is sweet rest for weary ones brought back,
  This is glad food and drink which ne'er shall lack
      An endless Alleluia.

8 While Thee, by whom were all things made, we praise
  For ever, and tell out in sweetest lays
      An endless Alleluia.

9 Almighty Christ, to Thee our voices sing
  Glory for evermore; to Thee we bring
      An endless Alleluia.

Brightly gleams our banner.

T. J. Potter, 1860. Alt.　　　　"ST. THERESA."　　　　A. S. Sullivan.

1. Bright - ly gleams our ban - ner, Point - ing to the sky, Wav - ing on Christ's
2. Je - sus, Lord and Mas - ter, At Thy sa - cred feet, Here with hearts re -
3. All our days di - rect us, In the way we go; Crown us still vic -
4. Then with saints and an - gels May we join a - bove, Of - f'ring pray'rs and

sol - diers To their home on high. Marching thro' the des-ert, Glad - ly thus we pray,
joic - ing, See Thy chil-dren meet. Oft - en have we left Thee, Oft - en gone a - stray;
to - rious, O - ver ev - 'ry foe: Bid Thine an-gels shield us When the storm-clouds low'r;
prais - es At Thy throne of love. When the toil is o - ver, Then come rest and peace,

Refrain.

Still with hearts u - nit - ed, Sing-ing on our way.
Keep us, might-y Sav - iour, In the nar - row way.
Par - don, Lord, and save us In the last dread hour.
Je - sus in His beau - ty Songs that nev-er cease.

Brightly gleams our ban - ner,

Point-ing to the sky, Waving on Christ's sol - diers To their home on high. A - men.

264

On our way rejoicing.

J. S. B. Monsell, 1863.　　　　　"ST. ALBAN."　　　　Fr. F. J. Haydn (1732—1809).
Arr. J. B. Dykes.

1. On our way re - joic - ing, As we home-ward move, Heark-en to our prais - es,
2. If with hon - est - heart - ed Love for God and man, Day by day Thou find us
3. On our way re - joic - ing Glad-ly let us go; Con-quer'd hath our Lead - er,
4. Un - to God the Fa - ther Joy - ful songs we sing; Un - to God the Sav - iour

O Thou God of love! Is there grief or sad - ness, Firm our trust shall be;
Do - ing what we can; Thou who giv'st the seed - time Wilt give large in - crease,
Vanquish'd is our foe! Christ with-out, our safe - ty; Christ with - in, our joy;
Thankful hearts we bring; Un - to God the Spir - it Bow we and a - dore,

Refrain.

Is our sky be - cloud - ed, Light shall come from Thee.
Crown the head with bless - ings, Fill the heart with peace.
Who, if we be faith - ful, Can our hope de - stroy?　On our way re - joic - ing,
On our way re - joic - ing Now and ev - er - more!

As we home-ward move, Heark-en to our prais - es, O Thou God of love! A - men.

Heavenly Father, send Thy blessing.

C. WORDSWORTH, 1863.   "BETHANY (SMART)."   H. SMART, 1867.

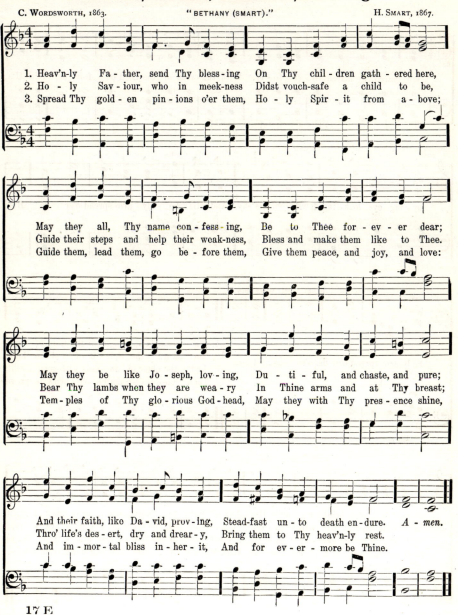

1. Heav'n-ly Fa - ther, send Thy bless-ing On Thy chil - dren gath - ered here,
2. Ho - ly Sav - iour, who in meek-ness Didst vouch-safe a child to be,
3. Spread Thy gold - en pin - ions o'er them, Ho - ly Spir - it from a - bove;

May they all, Thy name con - fess-ing, Be to Thee for - ev - er dear;
Guide their steps and help their weak-ness, Bless and make them like to Thee.
Guide them, lead them, go be - fore them, Give them peace, and joy, and love:

May they be like Jo - seph, lov - ing, Du - ti - ful, and chaste, and pure;
Bear Thy lambs when they are wea - ry In Thine arms and at Thy breast;
Tem - ples of Thy glo - rious God-head, May they with Thy pres - ence shine,

And their faith, like Da - vid, prov-ing, Stead-fast un - to death en - dure. A - men.
Thro' life's des - ert, dry and drear - y, Bring them to Thy heav'n-ly rest.
And im - mor - tal bliss in - her - it, And for ev - er - more be Thine.

266

We march, we march to victory.

G. Moultrie, 1867.   "MARCH TO VICTORY."   J. Barnby, 1869.

We march, we march to vic-to-ry, With the cross of the Lord be-fore us, With His

lov-ing eye look-ing down from the sky, And His ho-ly arm spread o'er us, His

FINE. *Last verse only.*

ho-ly arm spread o'er us. o'er us. A-men.

His arm

1. We   come in the might of the Lord of light,
2. Our   sword is the Spir-it of God on high,
3. And   the choir of an-gels with song a-waits
4. Then on-ward we march, our arms to prove,

With ar-mor bright to meet Him; And we put to... flight the.. ar-mies of night.
Our hel-met is His sal-va-tion, Our... ban-ner, the cross of... Cal-va-ry,
Our march to the gold-en Zi-on, For our Cap-tain has bro-ken the bra-zen gates,
With the ban-ner of Christ be-fore us, With His eye of... love look-ing down from a-bove,

We march, we march.—*Concluded.*

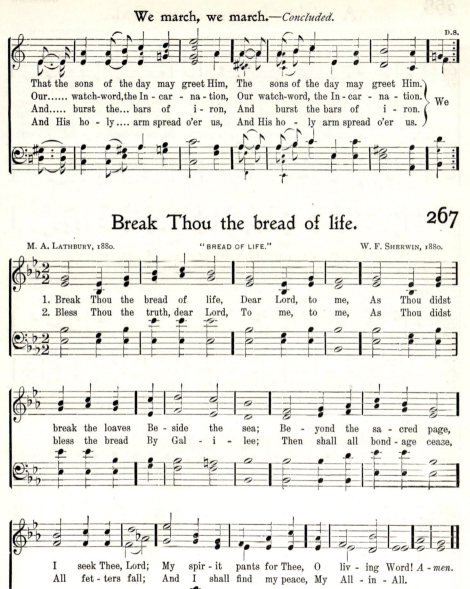

D.S.

That the sons of the day may greet Him, The sons of the day may greet Him,
Our...... watch-word, the In - car - na - tion, Our watch-word, the In - car - na - tion.
And..... burst the... bars of i - ron, And burst the bars of i - ron.
And His ho - ly .... arm spread o'er us, And His ho - ly arm spread o'er us.

We

Break Thou the bread of life.

267

M. A. LATHBURY, 1880.   "BREAD OF LIFE."   W. F. SHERWIN, 1880.

1. Break Thou the bread of life, Dear Lord, to me, As Thou didst
2. Bless Thou the truth, dear Lord, To me, to me, As Thou didst

break the loaves Be - side the sea; Be - yond the sa - cred page,
bless the bread By Gal - i - lee; Then shall all bond - age cease,

I seek Thee, Lord; My spir - it pants for Thee, O liv - ing Word! A - men.
All fet - ters fall; And I shall find my peace, My All - in - All.

268 A mighty fortress is our God.

MARTIN LUTHER, 1527.
Tr. E. H. HEDGE, 1852.   "EIN' FESTE BURG."   MARTIN LUTHER, 1529.
                                                              Arr. S. P. WARREN.

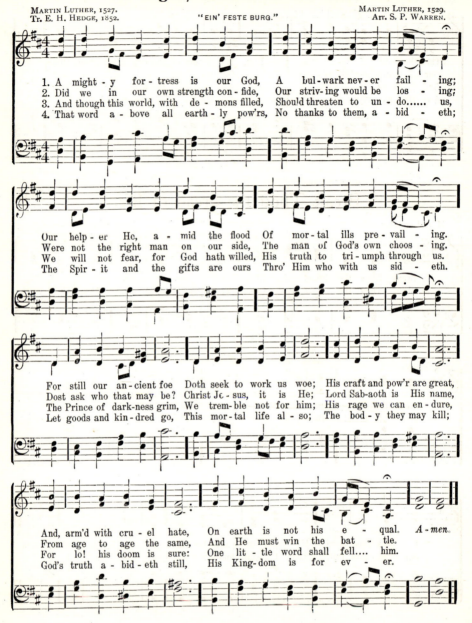

1. A might - y for - tress is our God, A bul-wark nev - er fail - ing;
2. Did we in our own strength con - fide, Our striv-ing would be los - ing;
3. And though this world, with de - mons filled, Should threaten to un - do...... us,
4. That word a - bove all earth - ly pow'rs, No thanks to them, a - bid - eth;

Our help - er He, a - mid the flood Of mor - tal ills pre - vail - ing.
Were not the right man on our side, The man of God's own choos - ing.
We will not fear, for God hath willed, His truth to tri - umph through us.
The Spir - it and the gifts are ours Thro' Him who with us sid - eth.

For still our an - cient foe Doth seek to work us woe; His craft and pow'r are great,
Dost ask who that may be? Christ Je - sus, it is He; Lord Sab-aoth is His name,
The Prince of dark-ness grim, We trem - ble not for him; His rage we can en - dure,
Let goods and kin - dred go, This mor - tal life al - so; The bod - y they may kill;

And, arm'd with cru - el hate, On earth is not his e - qual. A - men.
From age to age the same, And He must win the bat - tle.
For lo! his doom is sure: One lit - tle word shall fell.... him.
God's truth a - bid - eth still, His King-dom is for ev - er.

The beautiful bright sunshine.

ANON.   "SUNSHINE."   G. E. OLIVER.

1. The beau-ti-ful bright sun-shine, That smiles on all be-low,
2. The beau-ti-ful af-fec-tions That gath-er round our way,
3. But bright-er is the shin-ing, And ten-d'rer is the love,

The wav-ing trees, the cool, soft breeze, The rip-pling streams that flow,
The joys that rise from house-hold ties And deep-en day by day;
And pur-er still the joys which fill The un-seen home a-bove,—

Solo.

The shad-ows on the hill-sides, The ma-ny-tint-ed flow'rs,
The ten-der love that guards us When-ev-er dan-ger low'rs,
The home where all His chil-dren Shall sing with full-er pow'rs,

Chorus.

O God! how fair Thy lov-ing care Has made this earth of ours.   A-men.
O God! how fair Thy lov-ing care Has made this earth of ours.
"O God! how fair Thy lov-ing care Has made this heav'n of ours."

270

I ought to love my Saviour.

Anon.   "LOVING FRIEND."   J. R. FAIRLAMB, 1887.

1. I ought to love my Sav - iour; No earth - ly friend can be
2. He left His home in glo - ry To save my soul from death;
3. It is but ver - y lit - tle For Him that I can do;
4. And when I reach the man - sion He has pre - pared for me,

So lov - ing, kind, and faith - ful As He hath been to me.
And now in all life's dan - gers He still sus - tains my breath.
Then let me seek to serve Him My earth - ly jour - ney through;
'T will be my grate - ful pleas - ure My Sav - iour's face to see;

Be - fore my lips could ut - ter His sweet and pre - cious name,
I lay me down and slum - ber All through the hours of night,
And with - out sigh or mur - mur, To do His ho - ly will,
And 'mid the an - gels' mu - sic, Which then will greet my ear

Un - til the pres - ent mo - ment, His love hath been the same. A - men.
And wake a - gain in safe - ty To hail the morn - ing light.
And in my dai - ly du - ties, His wise commands ful - fil.
How ea - ger - ly I'll list - en My Sav - iour's voice to hear!

God be with you.

J. E. RANKIN, 1882. "FAREWELL." W. G. TOMER, 1882.

1. God be with you till we meet a - gain, By His counsels guide, up - hold you,
2. God be with you till we meet a - gain, 'Neath His wings protect-ing hide you,
3. God be with you till we meet a - gain, When life's per - ils thick con-found you,
4. God be with you till we. meet a - gain, Keep love's ban-ner float-ing o'er you,

With His sheep se - cure - ly fold you, God be with you till we meet a - gain.
Dai - ly man - na still di - vide you, God be with you till we meet a - gain.
Put His arms un - fail - ing round you, God be with you till we meet a - gain.
Smite death's threat'ning wave be-fore you, God be with you till we meet a - gain.

Refrain.

Till we meet,...... till we meet, Till we meet at Je - sus' feet;

Till we meet, till we meet, till we meet, Till we meet,

Till we meet,...... till we meet, God be with you till we meet a - gain. A-men.

Till we meet, till we meet, till we meet,

By permission.

PART II.

HYMNS FOR YOUNG CHILDREN.

272   Our God of love Who reigns above.

S. J. STONE.   "CONSTANT LOVE."   G. C. MARTIN.

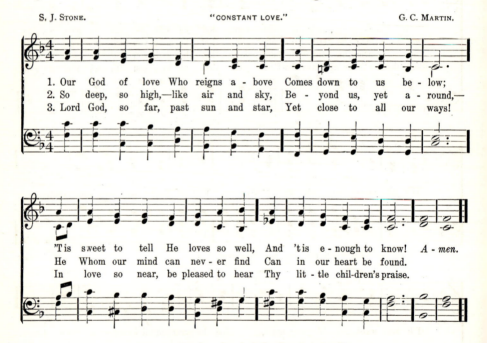

1. Our God of love Who reigns a - bove Comes down to us be - low;
2. So deep, so high,—like air and sky, Be - yond us, yet a - round,—
3. Lord God, so far, past sun and star, Yet close to all our ways!

'Tis sweet to tell He loves so well, And 'tis e - nough to know! A - men.
He Whom our mind can nev - er find Can in our heart be found.
In love so near, be pleased to hear Thy lit - tle chil-dren's praise.

4 Through all our way, and every day
Believed, beloved, adored,
Be this our grace to see Thy Face
In Jesus Christ our Lord.

I love to hear the story.

E. H. MILLER, 1867.   "KING OF GLORY."   CYRIL BOWDLER.

1. I love to hear the sto - ry Which an - gel - voic - es tell,
2. I'm glad my bless - ed Sav - iour Was once a child like me,
3. To sing His love and mer - cy, My sweet - est songs I'll raise;

REF.—I love to hear the sto - ry Which an - gel - voic - es tell,

How once the King of glo - ry Came down on earth to dwell.
To show how pure and ho - ly His lit - tle ones might be;
And though I can - not see Him, I know He hears my praise;

How once the King of glo - ry Came down on earth to dwell.

I am both weak and sin - ful, But this I sure - ly know,
And if I try to fol - low His foot - steps here be - low,
For He has kind - ly prom - ised That e - ven I may go

The Lord came down to save me, Be - cause He loved me so.
He nev - er will for - get me, Be - cause He loves me so.
To sing a - mong His an - gels, Be - cause He loves me so.

A-men.

274

There's a Friend for little children.

A. Midlane, 1860, Abr. "HESLINGTON." F. Peel, 1894.

1. There's a Friend for lit - tle chil - dren A - bove the bright blue sky,
2. There's a home for lit - tle chil - dren A - bove the bright blue sky,
3. There's a crown for lit - tle chil - dren A - bove the bright blue sky,
4. There's a song for lit - tle chil - dren A - bove the bright blue sky,

A Friend who nev - er chang - es, Whose love will nev - er die;
Where Je - sus reigns in glo - ry, A home of peace and joy;
And all who look for Je - sus Shall wear it by and by;
A song that will not wea - ry, Though sung con - tin - ual - ly;

Our earth - ly friends may fail us, And change with chang - ing years;
No home on earth is like it, Nor can with it com - pare;
A crown of bright - est glo - ry, Which He will then be - stow
A song which e - ven an - gels Can nev - er, nev - er sing;

This Friend is al - ways wor - thy Of that dear name He bears. A - men.
For ev - ery one is hap - py, Nor could be hap - pier, there.
On those who found His fa - vor And loved His name be - low.
They know not Christ as Sav - iour, But wor - ship Him as King.

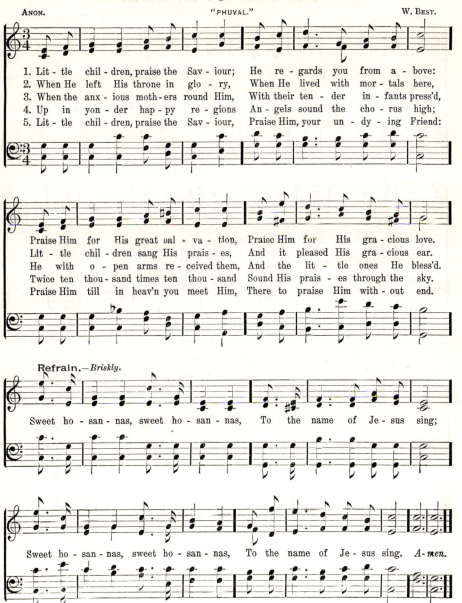

Little children, praise the Saviour.

ANON. "PHUVAL." W. BEST.

1. Lit - tle chil - dren, praise the Sav - iour; He re - gards you from a - bove:
2. When He left His throne in glo - ry, When He lived with mor - tals here,
3. When the anx - ious moth - ers round Him, With their ten - der in - fants press'd,
4. Up in yon - der hap - py re - gions An - gels sound the cho - rus high:
5. Lit - tle chil - dren, praise the Sav - iour, Praise Him, your un - dy - ing Friend:

Praise Him for His great sal - va - tion, Praise Him for His gra - cious love.
Lit - tle chil - dren sang His prais - es, And it pleased His gra - cious ear.
He with o - pen arms re - ceived them, And the lit - tle ones He bless'd.
Twice ten thou - sand times ten thou - sand Sound His prais - es through the sky.
Praise Him till in heav'n you meet Him, There to praise Him with - out end.

Refrain.—*Briskly.*

Sweet ho - san - nas, sweet ho - san - nas, To the name of Je - sus sing;

Sweet ho - san - nas, sweet ho - san - nas, To the name of Je - sus sing. *A-men.*

276

The fields are all white.

ANON.   "JUNIOR ENDEAVOR."   J. ADCOCK (1788—1860).

1. The fields are all white, And the reap-ers are few, We chil-dren are will-ing,
2. Our hands are so small, And our words are so weak, We can-not teach oth-ers,
3. We'll work by our pray'rs, By the off'rings we bring, By small self-de-ni-als;
4. Un-til, by and by, As the years pass at length, We too may be reap-ers,

But what can we do To work for our Lord in His har - - vest? A - men.
How then shall we seek To work for our Lord in His har - - vest?
The least lit-tle thing May work for our Lord in His har - - vest.
And go forth in strength To work for our Lord in His har - - vest.

SECOND TUNE.

"LITTLE REAPERS."   M. B. FOSTER, 1880.

TREBLES ONLY.

The fields are all white, And the reap-ers are few, We chil-dren are will-ing,

But what can we do To work for our Lord in His har - vest? A - men.

Can a little child, like me.

M. M. Dodge, 1876.   "DODGE."   Wm. K. Bassford, 1877.

1. Can a lit-tle child, like me, Thank the Fa-ther fit-ting-ly?
2. For the fruit up-on the tree, For the birds that sing of Thee,
3. For the sun-shine warm and bright, For the day and for the night;
4. For our com-rades and our plays, And our hap-py hol-i-days;

Yes, oh, yes! be good and true, Pa-tient, kind, in all you do:
For the earth in beau-ty drest, Fa-ther, moth-er and the rest;
For the les-sons of our youth— Hon-or, grat-i-tude and truth;
For the joy-ful work and true That a lit-tle child may do;

Love the Lord, and do your part; Learn to say with all your heart:—
For Thy pre-cious, lov-ing care, For Thy boun-ty ev-ery-where,—
For the love that met us here, For the home and for the cheer,—
For our lives but just be-gun; For the great gift of Thy Son,—

Refrain.

Father, we thank Thee! Father, we thank Thee! Father, in heaven, we thank Thee! A - men.

Copyright, 1877, by The Century Co.

278

Sadly bend the flowers.

ANON.   "SUNBEAMS."   A. RANDEGGER.

1. Sad - ly bend the flow - ers,   In the heav - y   rain: Af - ter beat-ing show-ers,
2. When a sud - den sor - row   Comes like cloud and night,   Wait for God's to-mor-row;

Sun-beams come a - gain.   Lit - tle birds are si - lent   All the dark night through;
All   will then be   bright.   On - ly wait and trust Him, Just a   lit - tle   while;

But when morn-ing dawn - eth,   Their songs are sweet and   new....   A - men.
Af - ter eve-ning tear - drops   Shall come the morn-ing   smile...

The morning bright.

Anon.

"SOHO."

J. Barnby, 1886.

1. The morn-ing bright, With ro-sy light, Has waked me up from sleep;
2. All through the day, I hum-bly pray, Be Thou my guard and guide,
3. O make Thy rest With-in my breast, Great Spir-it of all grace;

Fa-ther, I own Thy love a-lone Thy lit-tle one doth keep. A-men.
My sins for-give, And let me live, Blest Je-sus, near Thy side.
Make me like Thee, Then shall I be Pre-pared to see Thy face.

God who made the earth.

S. B. Rhodes.

"BEECHWOOD"

J. Booth (1852—).

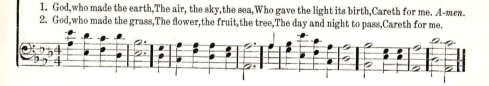

1. God, who made the earth, The air, the sky, the sea, Who gave the light its birth, Careth for me. A-men.
2. God, who made the grass, The flower, the fruit, the tree, The day and night to pass, Careth for me.

3 God, who made the sun,
   The moon, the stars, is He
Who, when life's clouds come on,
   Careth for me.

4 God, who made all things
   On earth, in air, in sea,
Who changing seasons brings,
   Careth for me.

Hosanna we sing, like the children dear.

G. S. HODGES, 1874. "HOSANNA WE SING." J. B. DYKES, 1875.

1. Ho - san - na we sing, like the chil - dren dear, In the old - en
2. Ho - san - na we sing, for He bends His ear, And re - joic - es the

days when the Lord lived here; He bless'd lit - tle children, and smiled on them,
hymns of His own to hear; We know that His heart will nev-er wax cold

While they chant-ed His praise in Je - ru - sa - lem. Al - le - lu - ia we
To the lambs that He feeds in His earth - ly fold. Al - le - lu - ia we

sing, like the chil - dren bright, With their harps of gold and their rai - ment white,
sing in the Church we love, Al - le - lu - ia re-sounds in the Church a - bove;

Hosanna we sing.—*Concluded.*

As they fol - low their Shep - herd with lov - ing eyes
To Thy lit - tle ones, Lord, may such grace be giv - en,

Through the beau - ti - ful val - leys of Par - a - - dise. *A - men.*
That we lose not our part in the song of heav'n.

Jesus loves me, this I know. 282

A. B. WARNER, 1859.   "NEWINGTON."   W. D. MACLAGAN, 1885.

1. Je - sus loves me, this I know, For the bi - ble tells me so:
2. Je - sus loves me, He who died Glo - ry's gate to o - pen wide,
3. Je - sus loves me, loves me still, Though I'm ver - y weak and ill;
4. Je - sus loves me; He will stay Close be - side me all the way,

Lit - tle ones to Him be - long; They are weak, but He is strong. *A - men.*
He will wash a - way my sin; Let His lit - tle one come in.
From His shin - ing throne on high He will watch me where I lie.
And, when suf-f'ring days are past, Take me to His home at last.

283

Jesus, tender Shepherd.

M. L. DUNCAN, 1839.   "ST. SYLVESTER."   J. B. DYKES, 1862.

1. Je - sus, ten - der Shep-herd, hear   me;   Bless Thy lit - tle Lamb to - night;
2. All this day Thy hand has   led   me,   And I thank Thee for Thy   care;
3. Let my sins be all for - giv - en;   Bless the friends I love so   well:

Thro' the dark-ness be Thou near   me;   Keep me safe till morn-ing light. A - men.
Thou hast cloth'd me warm'd and fed   me;   List - en to my eve-ning pray'r!
Take us all at last to heav - en,   Hap - py there with Thee to dwell.

SECOND TUNE.

"BROCKLESBURY."   A. C. BARNARD (1830—1869).

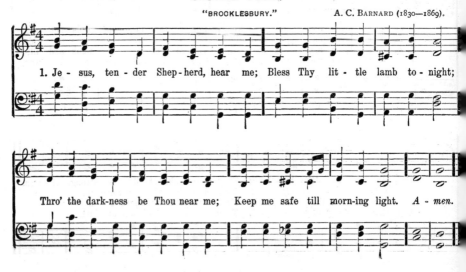

1. Je - sus, ten - der Shep-herd, hear me; Bless Thy lit - tle lamb to - night;

Thro' the dark-ness be Thou near me; Keep me safe till morn-ing light. A - men.

Jesus, meek and gentle.

G. R. PRYNNE, 1856. "ST. CONSTANTINE." W. H. MONK (1823—1889).

1. Je - sus, meek and gen - tle, Son of God Most High, Pit-ying, lov-ing Sav - iour,
2. Par - don our of - fenc - es, Loose our cap-tive chains, Break down ev-'ry i - dol
3. Give us ho - ly free - dom, Fill our hearts with love; Draw us, ho - ly Je - sus!

Omit for last verse | Last verse only

Hear Thy children's cry. Hear Thy children's cry. A-men.
Which our soul de - tains.
To the realms a - bove.

4 Lead us on our journey,
Be Thyself the Way
Through terrestrial darkness
To celestial day.

5 Jesus, meek and gentle,
Son of God Most High,
Pitying, loving Saviour,
Hear Thy children's cry.

SECOND TUNE.

"CASWALL." F. FILITZ, Ph.D. (1804—1860).

1. Je - sus, meek and gen - tle, Son of God Most High,

Pit - ying, lov - ing Sav - iour, Hear Thy chil - dren's cry. A - men.

285

The wise may bring their learning.

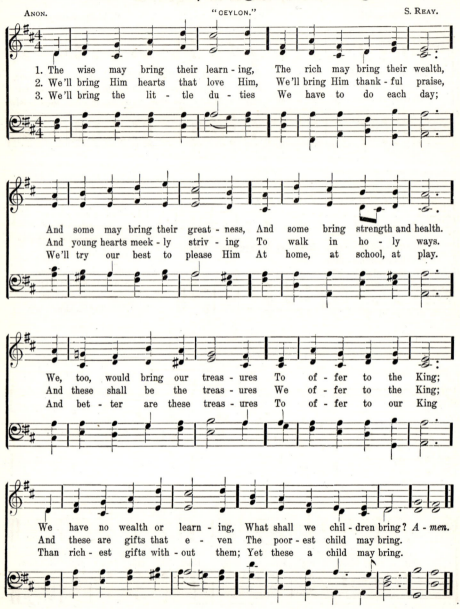

Anon.   "CEYLON."   S. Reay.

1. The wise may bring their learn - ing, The rich may bring their wealth,
2. We'll bring Him hearts that love Him, We'll bring Him thank - ful praise,
3. We'll bring the lit - tle du - ties We have to do each day;

And some may bring their great - ness, And some bring strength and health.
And young hearts meek - ly striv - ing To walk in ho - ly ways.
We'll try our best to please Him At home, at school, at play.

We, too, would bring our treas - ures To of - fer to the King;
And these shall be the treas - ures We of - fer to the King;
And bet - ter are these treas - ures To of - fer to our King

We have no wealth or learn - ing, What shall we chil - dren bring? A - men.
And these are gifts that e - ven The poor - est child may bring.
Than rich - est gifts with - out them; Yet these a child may bring.

If I come to Jesus.

F. J. Van Alstyne, 1868.   "WOODBROOK."   J. Adcock (1778—1860).

1. If I come to Je - sus, He will make me glad;
2. If I come to Je - sus, He will hear my pray'r;
3. If I come to Je - sus, He will take my hand,
4. There with hap - py chil - dren, Robed in snow - y white,

He will give me pleas - ure When my heart is sad.
He will love me dear - ly; He my sins did bear.
He will kind - ly lead me To a bet - ter land.
I shall see my Sav - iour In that world so bright.

Refrain.

If I come to Je - sus, Hap - py shall I be;

He is gen - tly call - ing Lit - tle ones like me. A - men.

287

Gracious Saviour, gentle shepherd.

J. E. Leeson, 1857. "REQUIEM." W. A. F. Schulthes, 1868.

1. Gra - cious Sav - iour, gen - tle shep - herd, Chil - dren all are dear to Thee;
2. Let Thy ho - ly word in - struct them; Fill their minds with heav'n - ly light;
3. Taught to lisp Thy ho - ly prais - es Which on earth Thy chil - dren sing,

Gath - ered with Thine arms, and car - ried In Thy bo - som, may they be;
Let Thy love and grace con - strain them, To ap - prove what - e'er is right;
With, both lips and hearts, un - feign - ed, Glad thank - of - f'rings may they bring;

Sweet - ly, fond - ly, safe - ly tend - ed, From all want and dan - ger free. *A - men.*
Let them feel Thy yoke is ea - sy, Let them prove Thy bur - den light.
Then with all Thy saints in glo - ry, Join to praise their Lord and King.

Org.

288

See, Israel's gentle shepherd stands.

P. Doddridge, 1740. "EVAN." W. H. Havergal, 1846.

1. See, Is - rael's gen - tle shep - herd stands, With all - en - gag - ing charms;
2. "Per - mit them to ap - proach," He cries, "Nor scorn their hum - ble name;
3. We bring them, Lord, in thank - ful hands, And yield them up to Thee;

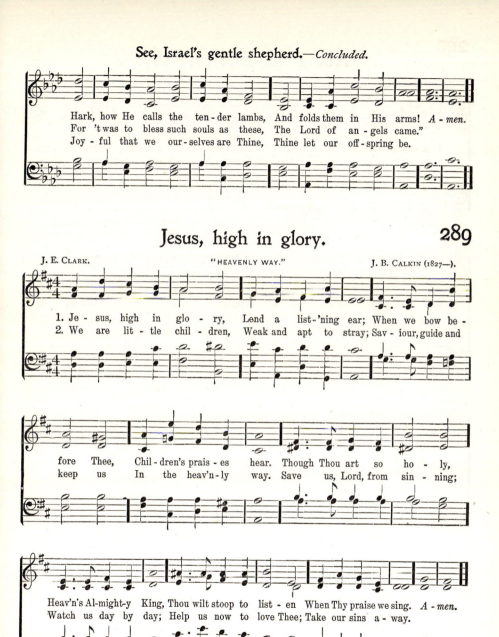

Hark, how He calls the ten - der lambs, And folds them in His arms! A - men.
For 'twas to bless such souls as these, The Lord of an - gels came."
Joy - ful that we our - selves are Thine, Thine let our off - spring be.

Jesus, high in glory. 289

J. E. CLARK.   "HEAVENLY WAY."   J. B. CALKIN (1827—).

1. Je - sus, high in glo - ry, Lend a list-'ning ear; When we bow be -
2. We are lit - tle chil - dren, Weak and apt to stray; Sav - iour, guide and

fore Thee, Chil - dren's prais - es hear. Though Thou art so ho - ly,
keep us In the heav'n - ly way. Save us, Lord, from sin - ning;

Heav'n's Al-might-y King, Thou wilt stoop to list - en When Thy praise we sing. A - men.
Watch us day by day; Help us now to love Thee; Take our sins a - way.

Above the clear blue sky.

J. Chandler, 1841.　　　　　"Children's Voices."　　　　　E. J. Hopkins, 1818—).

1. A - bove the clear blue sky, In Heav-en's bright a - bode, The an - gel -
2. But God from in - fant tongues On earth re - ceiv - eth praise, We then our

host on high Sing prais - es to their God. Al - le - lu - ia,
cheer-ful songs In sweet ac - cord will raise. Al - le - lu - ia,

They love to sing To God their King; Al - le - lu - ia...... A - men.
We too will sing To God our King; Al - le - lu - ia......

3 O blessèd Lord, Thy truth
　To us Thy babes impart,
And teach us in our youth
To know Thee as Thou art.
　　Alleluia,
　Then shall we sing
　To God our King;
　Alleluia.

4 O may Thy holy word
　Spread all the world around:
And all with one accord
Uplift the joyful sound.
　　Alleluia,
　All then shall sing
　To God their King;
　Alleluia.

I think when I read that sweet story of old.

J. LUKE, 1841.   "SWEET STORY."   English.

1. I........ think when I read that sweet sto - ry of old, When
2. I........ wish that His hands had been placed on my head, That His
3. Yet.... still to His foot - stool in pray'r I may go, And...

Je - sus was here a - mong men, How He called lit - tle chil - dren as
arm had been thrown a - round me, And that I..... might have seen His kind
ask for a share of His love; And if I..... thus... ear - nest - ly

lambs to His fold, I should like... to have been with them then. A - men.
look when He said, "Let the lit - tle ones... come un - to Me."
seek Him be - low, I shall see Him and.... hear Him a - bove,

4 In that beautiful place He has gone to prepare
For all who are washed and forgiven:
And many dear children shall be with Him there,
For of such is the kingdom of heaven.

5 But thousands and thousands who wander and fall,
Never heard of that heavenly home,
I wish they could know there is room for them all,
And that Jesus has bid them to come.

18 E*

292

There is a happy land.

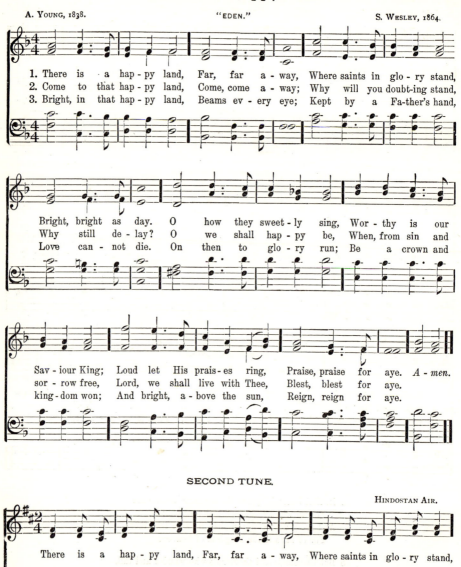

A. YOUNG, 1838.   "EDEN."   S. WESLEY, 1864.

1. There is a hap-py land, Far, far a-way, Where saints in glo-ry stand,
2. Come to that hap-py land, Come, come a-way; Why will you doubt-ing stand,
3. Bright, in that hap-py land, Beams ev-ery eye; Kept by a Fa-ther's hand,

Bright, bright as day. O how they sweet-ly sing, Wor-thy is our
Why still de-lay? O we shall hap-py be, When, from sin and
Love can-not die. On then to glo-ry run; Be a crown and

Sav-iour King; Loud let His prais-es ring, Praise, praise for aye. A - men.
sor-row free, Lord, we shall live with Thee, Blest, blest for aye.
king-dom won; And bright, a-bove the sun, Reign, reign for aye.

SECOND TUNE.

HINDOSTAN AIR.

There is a hap-py land, Far, far a-way, Where saints in glo-ry stand,

There is a happy land.—*Concluded.*

Bright, bright as day. O how they sweet - ly sing, Wor - thy is our

Sav - iour King; Loud let His prais - es ring, Praise, praise for aye. A - men.

O what can little hands do? 293

"FARIN," 1865.   "CHILD SERVICE."   H. E. BUTTON, 1870.

1. O what can lit - tle hands do To please the King of heaven? The lit - tle hands some
2. O what can lit - tle lips do To please the King of heaven? The lit - tle lips can
3. O what can lit - tle eyes do To please the King of heaven? The lit - tle eyes can
4. O what can lit - tle hearts do To please the King of heaven? The hearts, if God His

work may try To help the poor in mis - er - y— Such grace to mine be given. A - men.
praise and pray, And gen-tle words of kind-ness say—Such grace to mine be given.
up - ward look, Can learn to read God's ho-ly book: Such grace to mine be given.
Spir - it send, Can love and trust our Saviour Friend Such grace to mine be given.

Jesus, from Thy throne on high.

T. B. POLLOCK, 1875. Abr. "LITANY FOR CHILDREN." F. A. J. HERVEY (1846–).

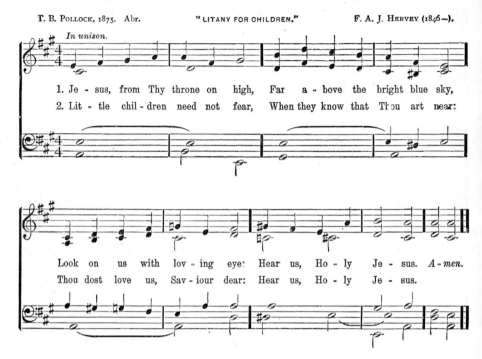

In unison.

1. Je - sus, from Thy throne on high, Far a - bove the bright blue sky,
2. Lit - tle chil - dren need not fear, When they know that Thou art near:

Look on us with lov - ing eye: Hear us, Ho - ly Je - sus. A - men.
Thou dost love us, Sav - iour dear: Hear us, Ho - ly Je - sus.

3 Little hearts may love Thee well
  Little lips Thy love may tell,
  Little hymns Thy praises swell:
    Hear us, Holy Jesus.

4 Little lives may be divine,
  Little deeds of love may shine,
  Little ones be wholly Thine:
    Hear us, Holy Jesus.

5 Jesus, once an infant small,
  Cradled in the oxen's stall,
  Though the God and Lord of all
    Hear us, Holy Jesus.

6 Once a child so good and fair,
  Feeling want, and toil, and care,
  All that we may have to bear:
    Hear us, Holy Jesus.

7 Jesus, Thou dost love us still,
  And it is Thy holy will
  That we should be safe from ill:
    Hear us, Holy Jesus.

8 Be Thou with us every day,
  In our work and in our play,
  When we learn and when we pray:
    Hear us, Holy Jesus.

Gentle Jesus, meek and mild.

C. WESLEY, 1742. "GLEBE FIELD." J. B. DYKES, 1874.

1. Gen - tle Je - sus, meek and mild, Look up - on a lit - tle child;
2. Fain I would to Thee be brought; Dear - est Lord, for - bid it not:

Pit - y my sim - plic - i - ty; Suf - fer me to come to Thee. *A-men.*
Give me, dear - est Lord, a place In the king - dom of Thy grace.

3 Lamb of God, I look to Thee,
  Thou shalt my Example be:
  Thou art gentle, meek, and mild,
  Thou wast once a little child.

4 Fain I would be as Thou art,
  Give me Thine obedient heart;
  Thou art pitiful and kind,
  Let me have Thy loving mind.

5 Let me, above all, fulfil
  God my Heavenly Father's will;
  Never His good Spirit grieve,
  Only to His glory live.

6 Thou didst live to God alone,
  Thou didst never seek Thine own,
  Thou Thyself didst never please;
  God was all Thy happiness.

7 Loving Jesus, gentle Lamb,
  In Thy gracious hands I am;
  Make me, Saviour, what Thou art,
  Live Thyself within my heart.

8 I shall then show forth Thy praise,
  Serve Thee all my happy days;
  Then the world shall always see
  Christ, the Holy Child, in me.

By cool Siloam's shady rill.

R. Heber, 1827.   "SABBATA." (SHARON.)   H. F. Hemy, 1865.

1. By cool Si - lo - am's sha - dy rill, How fair the lil - y grows;
2. Lo, such the child whose ear - ly feet The paths of peace have trod,
3. By cool Si - lo - am's sha - dy rill The lil - y must de - cay;
4. And soon, too soon the win - try hour Of man's ma - tur - er age

How sweet the breath, be - neath the hill, Of Shar - on's dew - y rose! A - men.
Whose se - cret heart, with in - fluence sweet, Is up - ward drawn to God.
The rose that blooms be - neath the hill Must short - ly fade a - way.
Will shake the soul with sor - row's pow'r, And storm - y pas - sion's rage.

5 O Thou, whose infant feet were found
    Within Thy Father's shrine,
  Whose years with changeless virtue crowned,
    Were all alike divine:

6 Dependent on Thy bounteous breath,
    We seek Thy grace alone,
  In childhood, manhood, age, and death,
    To keep us still Thine own.

Thou that once, by mother's knee.

F. J. Palgrave, 1867.   "GLASTONBURY."   J. B. Dykes, 1870.

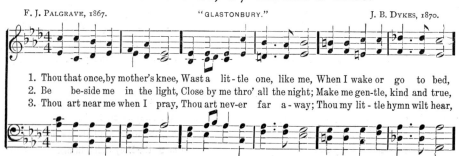

1. Thou that once, by mother's knee, Wast a lit - tle one, like me, When I wake or go to bed,
2. Be be - side me in the light, Close by me thro' all the night; Make me gen - tle, kind and true,
3. Thou art near me when I pray, Thou art nev - er far a - way; Thou my lit - tle hymn wilt hear,

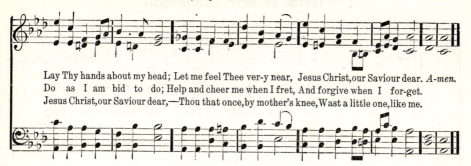

Lay Thy hands about my head; Let me feel Thee ver-y near, Jesus Christ, our Saviour dear. *A-men.*
Do as I am bid to do; Help and cheer me when I fret, And forgive when I for-get.
Jesus Christ, our Saviour dear,—Thou that once, by mother's knee, Wast a little one, like me.

God is in heaven. 298

A. GILBERT, 1809.   "PANCRATIUS."   H. H. WOODWARD, 1894.

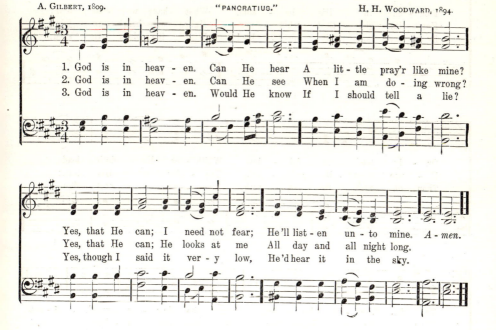

1. God is in heav-en. Can He hear A lit-tle pray'r like mine?
2. God is in heav-en. Can He see When I am do-ing wrong?
3. God is in heav-en. Would He know If I should tell a lie?

Yes, that He can; I need not fear; He'll list-en un-to mine. *A-men.*
Yes, that He can; He looks at me All day and all night long.
Yes, though I said it ver-y low, He'd hear it in the sky.

4 God is in heaven. Does He care,
   Or is He good to me?
  Yes; all I have to eat or wear;
   'T is God that gives it me.

5 God is in heaven. May I pray
   To go there when I die?
  Yes; love Him, seek Him, and one day
   He'll call me to the sky.

299

Jesus is our Shepherd.

H. Stowell, 1849. Abr. "ELLWOOD." G. A. Macfarren.

1. Je - sus is our Shep - herd, Wip - ing ev - ery tear;
2. Je - sus is our Shep - herd, Well we know His voice
3. Je - sus is our Shep - herd, For the sheep He bled;

Fold - ed in His bo - som, What have we to fear?
How its gen - tlest whis - per Makes our heart re - joice;
Ev - ery lamb is sprin - kled With the blood He shed;

On - ly let us fol - low Whith - er He doth lead
E - ven when He chid - eth, Ten - der is His tone:
Then on each He set - teth His own se - cret sign,—

To the thirst - y des - ert, Or the dew - y mead. A - men.
None but He shall guide us: We are His a - lone.
"They that have My Spir - it, These," saith He, "are Mine."

Gloria in Excelsis.

OLD CHANT.

1 Glory *be* to | God on | high ‖ and on *earth* | peace good | will · towards | men.
2 We praise Thee, we bless *Thee,* we | wor-ship | Thee ‖ we glorify Thee, we give *Thanks* to | Thee
   for | Thy great | glory.

3 O Lord *God* | Heaven- · ly | King ‖ *God* the | Fa-ther | Al- — | mighty.
4 O Lord, the only begotten *Son* | Je-sus | Christ ‖ O Lord God, Lamb of *God* | Son — | of the |
   Father,

5 That takest a*way* the | sins · of the | world ‖ have *mercy* up- | on — | us.
6 Thou that takest a*way* the | sins · of the | world ‖ have *mercy* up- | on — | us.
7 Thou that takest a*way* the | sins · of the | world ‖ re- | ceive our | prayer.
8 Thou that sittest at the right *hand* of | God the | Father ‖ have *mercy* up- | on — | us.

A - men.

9 For Thou *only* | art — | holy ‖ *Thou* | on-ly | art the | Lord.
10 Thou only, O *Christ* with the | Ho-ly | Ghost ‖ art most *high* in the | glory · of | God the | Father.

Te Deum Laudamus.

H. Lawes (1596—1662).

1 We *praise* | Thee O | God ‖ we ac*knowl*edge | Thee to | be the | Lord.
2 All the *earth* doth | wor-ship | Thee ‖ *the* | Fa-ther | ev-er- | lasting.
3 To Thee all *Angels* | cry a- | loud ‖ the *Heavens* and | all the | Powers there- | in
4 To Thee Cherub*im* and | Ser-a- | phim ‖ *con*- | tin-ual- | ly do | cry,
5 *Holy* | Ho-ly | Ho-ly ‖ *Lord* | God of | Sab-a- | oth;
6 Heaven and earth are *full* of the | Maj-es- | ty ‖ *of* | Thy — | Glo- — | ry.
7 The glorious *company* | of · the A- | postles ‖ *praise* | — — | — — | Thee.
8 The goodly *fellow*ship | of the | Prophets ‖ *praise* | — — | — — | Thee.
9 The *noble* | army · of | Martyrs ‖ *praise* | — — | — — | Thee.
10 The holy *Church* throughout | all the | world ‖ *doth* | — ac- | knowl-edge | Thee:
11 *The* | Fa- — | ther ‖ *of* an | in- · finite | Maj-es- | ty;
12 *Thine* a- | dor- · able, | true ‖ *and* | on- — | — ly | Son;
13 ✱ *Also the* | Holy | Ghost ‖ *the* | com- — | fort- — | er.
14 *Thou* art the | King of | Glory ‖ O | — — | — — | Christ.
15 Thou art the *ever*- | last-ing | Son ‖ *of* | — the | Fa- — | ther.

✱ Last half of Chant.

R. Cooke (1768—1814).

16 When Thou tookest upon *Thee* to de- | liv-er | man ‖ Thou didst humble *Thyself* to be | born — | of a | Virgin.
17 When Thou hadst over*come* the | sharpness · of | death ‖ Thou didst open the *King*dom of | Heaven · to | all be- | lievers.
18 Thou sittest at the *right* | hand of | God ‖ *in* | the | Glo-ry | of the | Father.
19 We be*lieve* that | Thou shalt | come ‖ *to* | be — | our — | Judge.
20 We therefore *pray* Thee | help Thy | servants ‖ whom Thou hast re*deem*ed | with Thy | pre-cious | blood.
21 Make them to be *numbered* | with Thy | Saints ‖ *in* | glo-ry | ev-er- | lasting.
22 O *Lord* | save Thy | people ‖ *and* | bless Thine | her-it- | age.
23 *Gov*- | — ern | them ‖ *and* | lift them | up for- | ever.

Return to chant in B♭ at the top of page

24 *Day* | by — | day ‖ *we* | mag-ni- | fy — | Thee;
25 *And* we | worship · Thy | Name ‖ *ever* | world with- | out — | end.
26 *Vouch*- | safe O | Lord ‖ to keep *us* this | day with- | out — | sin.
27 O *Lord* · have | mercy · up- | on us ‖ *have* | mercy · up- | on — | us.
28 O Lord, let Thy *mercy* | be up- | on us ‖ *as* our | trust — | is in | Thee
29 O Lord, in *Thee* | have I | trusted ‖ *let* me | nev-er | be con- | founded.

Dominus Regit Me. *(Ps. xxiii.)* 302

ANON.

1 The *Lord* | is my | shepherd ‖ *I* | shall — | not — ⁞ want.
2 He maketh me to lie *down* in | green — | pastures ‖ He leadeth *me* be- | side the | still — | waters.
3 *He* re- | storeth · my | soul ‖ He leadeth me in the paths of righteous*ness* | for His | name's — | sake.
4 Yea though I walk through the valley of the shadow of *death* I will | fear no | evil ‖ for Thou art
   with me; Thy *rod* and Thy ⁞ staff they | com-fort | me.
5 Thou preparest a table before me in the *presence* | of mine | enemies ‖ Thou anointest my head with
   oil my | cup — | run-neth | over.
6 Surely goodness and mercy shall follow me all the *days* | of my | life ‖ and I will dwell in the *house* |
   of the | Lord for- | ever.

Glory be to the *Father* | and · to the | Son ‖ *and* | to the | Ho-ly | Ghost;
As it was in the beginning, is *now* and | ev-er | shall be ‖ *world* without | end. — | A- — | men.

Gloria Patri. 303

H. W. GREATOREX.

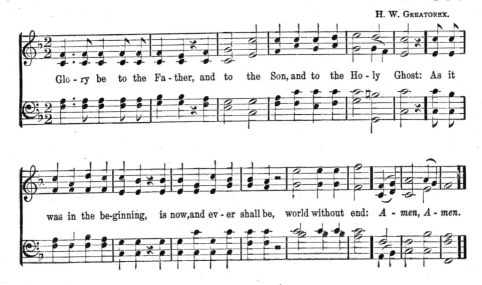

Glo - ry be to the Fa - ther, and to the Son, and to the Ho - ly Ghost: As it
was in the be-ginning, is now, and ev - er shall be, world without end: A - men, A - men.

304 The Beatitudes. *(Matthew v. 3–12.)*

J. TURLE (1802.—1882).

S. P. WARREN, 1872.

1 Bless*ed* are the | poor in | spirit ‖ *for* | theirs · is the | kingdom · of | heaven.

2 Bless*ed* are | they that | mourn ‖ *for* | they — | shall be | comforted.

3 Bless*ed* | are the | meek ‖ *for* | they · shall in- | herit · the | earth.

4 Bless*ed* are they which do hunger and *thirst* after | right-eous- | ness ‖ *for* | they — | shall be | filled.

5 Bless*ed* are the | mer- ci- | ful ‖ *for* | they · shall ob- | tain — | mercy.

6 Bless*ed* are the | pure in | heart ‖ *for* | they shall | see — | God.

7 Bless*ed* are the | peace- — | makers ‖ for they shall be *call*ed the | children | of — | God.

8 Bless*ed* are they which are persecut*ed* for | righteous- · ness' | sake ‖ *for* | theirs · is the | kingdom ·
  of | heaven.

9 Bless*ed* are ye, when men shall revile *you* and | perse- · cute | you ‖ and shall say all manner of evil
  against you | false-ly | for my | sake.

10 Rejoice and be exceeding glad, for great is *your* re- | ward in | heaven ‖ for so persecuted *they* the |
  prophets · which | were be- | fore you.

   Glory be to the *Father* | and · to the | Son ‖ *and* | to the | Ho-ly | Ghost;

   As it was in the beginning, is *now* and | ev-er | shall be ‖ *world* without | end.— | A - — | men.

305 On the Presentation of the Alms.

ANON.

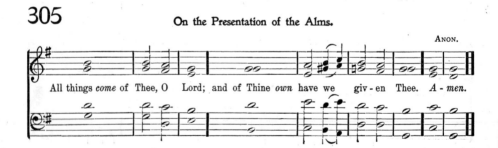

All things *come* of Thee, O   Lord; and of Thine *own* have we   giv - en Thee.   A - men.

Responsive

Services

NEW YORK
THE CENTURY CO.
1924

PRINTED IN U. S. A.

Responsive Services

INDEX

Responsive Services

SELECTION 1

Psalms VIII, XCIII, CXI

O LORD our Lord, how excellent is thy name in all the earth! who hast set thy glory above the heavens.

Out of the mouth of babes and sucklings hast thou ordained strength because of thine enemies, that thou mightest still the enemy and the avenger.

When I consider thy heavens, the work of thy fingers, the moon and the stars, which thou hast ordained; what is man, that thou art mindful of him? and the son of man, that thou visitest him?

For thou hast made him a little lower than the angels, and hast crowned him with glory and honour.

Thou madest him to have dominion over the works of thy hands;

Thou hast put all things under his feet:

All sheep and oxen, yea, and the beasts of the field; the fowl of the air, and the fish of the sea, and whatsoever passeth through the paths of the seas.

O LORD our Lord, how excellent is thy name in all the earth!

The LORD reigneth, he is clothed with majesty;

The LORD is clothed with strength, wherewith he hath girded himself:

The world also is stablished, that it cannot be moved.

Thy throne is established of old: thou art from everlasting.

The floods have lifted up, O LORD, the floods have lifted up their voice; the floods lift up their waves.

The LORD on high is mightier than the noise of many waters, yea, than the mighty waves of the sea.

Thy testimonies are very sure:

Holiness becometh thine house, O LORD, for ever.

Praise ye the LORD.

I will praise the LORD with my whole heart, in the assembly of the upright, and in the congregation.

The works of the LORD are great, sought out of all them that have pleasure therein.

His work is honourable and glorious: and his righteousness endureth for ever.

He hath made his wonderful works to be remembered: the LORD is gracious and full of compassion.

He hath given meat unto them that fear him: he will ever be mindful of his covenant.

He hath shewed his people the power of his works, that he may give them the heritage of the heathen.

The works of his hands are verity and judgment;

All his commandments are sure.

They stand fast for ever and ever, and are done in truth and uprightness.

He sent redemption unto his people:

He hath commanded his covenant for ever: holy and reverend is his name.

The fear of the LORD is the beginning of wisdom: a good understanding have all they that do his commandments:

His praise endureth for ever.

SELECTION 2

Psalms LXXXVII, CXXV, CXXVI, CXXII

HIS foundation is in the holy mountains. The LORD loveth the gates of Zion more than all the dwellings of Jacob.

Glorious things are spoken of thee, O city of God.

I will make mention of Rahab and Babylon to them that know me: behold Philistia, and Tyre, with Ethiopia; this man was born there.

And of Zion it shall be said, This and that man was born in her: and the Highest himself shall establish her.

The LORD shall count, when he writeth up the people, that this man was born there.

As well the singers as the players on instruments shall be there: all my springs are in thee.

They that trust in the LORD shall be as Mount Zion, which cannot be removed, but abideth for ever.

As the mountains are round about Jerusalem, so the LORD is round about his people from henceforth even for ever.

For the rod of the wicked shall not rest upon the lot of the righteous; lest the righteous put forth their hands unto iniquity.

Do good, O LORD, unto those that be good, and to them that are upright in their hearts.

As for such as turn aside unto their crooked ways, the LORD shall lead them forth with the workers of iniquity:

But peace shall be upon Israel.

When the LORD turned again the captivity of Zion, we were like them that dream.

Then was our mouth filled with laughter, and our tongue with singing:

Then said they among the heathen, The LORD hath done great things for them.

The LORD hath done great things for us; whereof we are glad.

Turn again our captivity, O LORD, as the streams in the south. They that sow in tears shall reap in joy.

He that goeth forth and weepeth, bearing precious seed, shall doubtless come again with rejoicing, bringing his sheaves with him.

I was glad when they said unto me, Let us go into the house of the LORD.

Our feet shall stand within thy gates, O Jerusalem.

Jerusalem is builded as a city that is compact together: whither the tribes go up, the tribes of the LORD, unto the testimony of Israel, to give thanks unto the name of the LORD.

For there are set thrones of judgment, the thrones of the house of David.

Pray for the peace of Jerusalem: they shall prosper that love thee.

Peace be within thy walls, and prosperity within thy palaces.

For my brethren and companions' sakes, I will now say, Peace be within thee.

Because of the house of the LORD our God I will seek thy good.

SELECTION 3

Psalms XLII, XLIII, LXXXIV

AS the hart panteth after the water brooks, so panteth my soul after thee, O God.

My soul thirsteth for God, for the living God: when shall I come and appear before God?

My tears have been my meat day and night, while they continually say unto me, Where is thy God?

When I remember these things, I pour out my soul in me: for I had gone with the multitude, I went with them to the house of God, with the voice of joy and praise, with a multitude that kept holyday.

Why art thou cast down, O my soul? and why art thou disquieted in me?

Hope thou in God: for I shall yet praise him for the help of his countenance.

O my God, my soul is cast down within me:

Therefore will I remember thee from the land of Jordan, and of the Hermonites, from the hill Mizar.

Deep calleth unto deep at the noise of thy waterspouts:

All thy waves and thy billows are gone over me.

Yet the LORD will command his lovingkindness in the daytime,

And in the night his song shall be with me, and my prayer unto the God of my life.

I will say unto God my rock, Why hast thou forgotten me? why go I mourning because of the oppression of the enemy?

As with a sword in my bones, mine enemies reproach me; while they say daily unto me, Where is thy God?

Why art thou cast down, O my soul? and why art thou disquieted within me?

Hope thou in God: for I shall yet praise him, who is the health of my countenance, and my God.

Judge me, O God, and plead my cause against an ungodly nation: O deliver me from the deceitful and unjust man.

For thou art the God of my strength: why dost thou cast me off? why go I mourning because of the oppression of the enemy?

O send out thy light and thy truth: let them lead me;

Let them bring me unto thy holy hill, and to thy tabernacles.

Then will I go unto the altar of God, unto God my exceeding joy:

Yea, upon the harp will I praise thee, O God my God.

Why art thou cast down, O my soul? and why art thou disquieted within me?

Hope in God: for I shall yet praise him, who is the health of my countenance, and my God.

How amiable are thy tabernacles, O LORD of hosts!

My soul longeth, yea, even fainteth for the courts of the LORD: my heart and my flesh crieth out for the living God.

Yea, the sparrow hath found a house, and the swallow a nest for herself, where she may lay her young,

Even thine altars, O LORD of hosts, my King, and my God.

Blessed are they that dwell in thy house: they will be still praising thee.

Blessed is the man whose strength is in thee; in whose heart are the ways of them.

Who passing through the valley of Baca make it a well; the rain also filleth the pools.

They go from strength to strength, every one of them in Zion appeareth before God.

O LORD God of hosts, hear my prayer: give ear, O God of Jacob.

Behold, O God our shield, and look upon the face of thine anointed.

For a day in thy courts is better than a thousand.

I had rather be a doorkeeper in the house of my God, than to dwell in the tents of wickedness.

For the LORD God is a sun and shield: the LORD will give grace and glory: no good thing will he withhold from them that walk uprightly.

O LORD of hosts, blessed is the man that trusteth in thee.

SELECTION 4

Psalms XXIX, XXIV, CL

GIVE unto the LORD, O ye mighty, give unto the LORD glory and strength.

Give unto the LORD the glory due unto his name; worship the LORD in the beauty of holiness.

The voice of the LORD is upon the waters: the God of glory thundereth: the LORD is upon many waters.

The voice of the LORD is powerful; the voice of the LORD is full of majesty.

The voice of the LORD breaketh the cedars; yea, the LORD breaketh the cedars of Lebanon.

He maketh them also to skip like a calf; Lebanon and Sirion like a young unicorn.

The voice of the LORD divideth the flames of fire.

The voice of the LORD shaketh the wilderness; the LORD shaketh the wilderness of Kadesh.

The voice of the LORD maketh the hinds to calve, and discovereth the forests: and in his temple doth every one speak of his glory.

The LORD sitteth upon the flood; yea, the LORD sitteth King for ever.

The LORD will give strength unto his people;

The LORD will bless his people with peace.

The earth is the LORD'S, and the fulness thereof; the world, and they that dwell therein.

For he hath founded it upon the seas, and established it upon the floods.

Who shall ascend into the hill of the LORD? or who shall stand in his holy place?

He that hath clean hands, and a pure heart; who hath not lifted up his soul unto vanity, nor sworn deceitfully.

He shall receive the blessing from the LORD, and righteousness from the God of his salvation.

This is the generation of them that seek him, that seek thy face, O Jacob.

Lift up your heads, O ye gates; and be ye lifted up, ye everlasting doors;

And the King of glory shall come in.

Who is this King of glory?

The LORD strong and mighty, the LORD mighty in battle.

Lift up your heads, O ye gates; even lift them up, ye everlasting doors;

And the King of glory shall come in.

Who is this King of glory?

The LORD of hosts, he is the King of glory.

Praise ye the LORD. Praise God in his sanctuary:

Praise him in the firmament of his power.

Praise him for his mighty acts: praise him according to his excellent greatness.

Praise him with the sound of the trumpet: praise him with the psaltery and harp.

Praise him with the timbrel and dance: praise him with stringed instruments and organs.

Praise him upon the loud cymbals: praise him upon the high sounding cymbals.

Let every thing that hath breath praise the LORD.

Praise ye the LORD.

SELECTION 5

Psalms C, LXV, LXVII

MAKE a joyful noise unto the LORD, all ye lands.

Serve the LORD with gladness: come before his presence with singing.

Know ye that the LORD he is God: it is he that hath made us, and not we ourselves;

We are his people, and the sheep of his pasture.

Enter into his gates with thanksgiving, and into his courts with praise: be thankful unto him, and bless his name.

For the LORD is good; his mercy is everlasting; and his truth endureth to all generations.

Praise waiteth for thee, O God, in Zion:

And unto thee shall the vow be performed.

O thou that hearest prayer, unto thee shall all flesh come.

Iniquities prevail against me: as for our transgressions, thou shalt purge them away.

Blessed is the man whom thou choosest, and causest to approach unto thee, that he may dwell in thy courts:

We shall be satisfied with the goodness of thy house, even of thy holy temple.

By terrible things in righteousness wilt thou answer us, O God of our salvation;

Who art the confidence of all the ends of the earth, and of them that are afar off upon the sea:

Which by his strength setteth fast the mountains; being girded with power:

Which stilleth the noise of the seas, the noise of their waves, and the tumult of the people.

They also that dwell in the uttermost parts are afraid at thy tokens:

Thou makest the outgoings of the morning and evening to rejoice.

Thou visitest the earth, and waterest it: thou greatly enrichest it with the river of God, which is full of water:

Thou preparest them corn, when thou hast so provided for it.

Thou waterest the ridges thereof abundantly: thou settlest the furrows thereof: thou makest it soft with showers: thou blessest the springing thereof.

Thou crownest the year with thy goodness; and thy paths drop fatness.

They drop upon the pastures of the wilderness: and the little hills rejoice on every side.

The pastures are clothed with flocks; the valleys also are covered over with corn; they shout for joy, they also sing.

God be merciful unto us, and bless us; and cause his face to shine upon us; that thy way may be known upon earth, thy saving health among all nations.

Let the people praise thee, O God; let all the people praise thee.

O let the nations be glad and sing for joy: for thou shalt judge the people righteously, and govern the nations upon earth.

Let the people praise thee, O God; let all the people praise thee.

Then shall the earth yield her increase; and God, even our own God, shall bless us.

God shall bless us; and all the ends of the earth shall fear him.

SELECTION 6

Psalms XCVII, XCVIII, XCIX

THE LORD reigneth; let the earth rejoice; let the multitude of isles be glad thereof.

Clouds and darkness are round about him: righteousness and judgment are the habitation of his throne.

A fire goeth before him, and burneth up his enemies round about.

His lightnings enlightened the world: the earth saw, and trembled.

The hills melted like wax at the presence of the LORD, at the presence of the Lord of the whole earth.

The heavens declare his righteousness, and all the people see his glory.

Confounded be all they that serve graven images, that boast themselves of idols:

Worship him, all ye gods.

Zion heard, and was glad; and the daughters of Judah rejoiced because of thy judgments, O LORD.

For thou, LORD, art high above all the earth: thou art exalted far above all gods.

Ye that love the LORD, hate evil: he preserveth the souls of his saints;

He delivereth them out of the hand of the wicked.

Light is sown for the righteous, and gladness for the upright in heart.

Rejoice in the LORD, ye righteous; and give thanks at the remembrance of his holiness.

O sing unto the LORD a new song; for he hath done marvellous things:

His right hand, and his holy arm, hath gotten him the victory.

The LORD hath made known his salvation:

His righteousness hath he openly shewed in the sight of the heathen.

He hath remembered his mercy and his truth toward the house of Israel:

All the ends of the earth have seen the salvation of our God.

Make a joyful noise unto the LORD, all the earth:

Make a loud noise, and rejoice, and sing praise.

Sing unto the LORD with the harp; with the harp, and the voice of a psalm.

With trumpets and sound of cornet make a joyful noise before the LORD, the King.

Let the sea roar, and the fulness thereof; the world, and they that dwell therein.

Let the floods clap their hands: let the hills be joyful together before the LORD;

For he cometh to judge the earth:

With righteousness shall he judge the world, and the people with equity.

The LORD reigneth; let the people tremble:

He sitteth between the cherubim; let the earth be moved.

The LORD is great in Zion; and he is high above all the people.

Let them praise thy great and terrible name; for it is holy.

The king's strength also loveth judgment; thou dost establish equity, thou executest judgment and righteousness in Jacob.

Exalt ye the LORD our God, and worship at his footstool; for he is holy.

Moses and Aaron among his priests, and Samuel among them that call upon his name; they called upon the LORD, and he answered them.

He spake unto them in the cloudy pillar: they kept his testimonies, and the ordinance that he gave them.

Thou answeredst them, O LORD our God: thou wast a God that forgavest them, though thou tookest vengeance of their inventions.

Exalt the LORD our God, and worship at his holy hill; for the LORD our God is holy.

SELECTION 7

Psalms XCV, XCVI, CXLIX

O COME, let us sing unto the LORD:

Let us make a joyful noise to the Rock of our salvation.

Let us come before his presence with thanksgiving, and make a joyful noise unto him with psalms.

For the LORD is a great God, and a great King above all gods.

In his hand are the deep places of the earth: the strength of the hills is his also.

The sea is his, and he made it: and his hands formed the dry land.

O come, let us worship and bow down: let us kneel before the LORD our maker.

For he is our God; and we are the people of his pasture, and the sheep of his hand.

To day if ye will hear his voice, harden not your heart, as in the provocation, and as in the day of temptation in the wilderness:

When your fathers tempted me, proved me, and saw my work.

Forty years long was I grieved with this generation, and said, It is a people that do err in their heart, and they have not known my ways:

Unto whom I sware in my wrath that they should not enter into my rest.

O sing unto the LORD a new song: sing unto the LORD, all the earth.

Sing unto the LORD, bless his name; shew forth his salvation from day to day.

Declare his glory among the heathen, his wonders among all people.

For the LORD is great, and greatly to be praised: he is to be feared above all gods.

For all the gods of the nations are idols: but the LORD made the heavens.

Honour and majesty are before him; strength and beauty are in his sanctuary.

Give unto the LORD, O ye kindreds of the people, give unto the LORD glory and strength.

Give unto the LORD the glory due unto his name: bring an offering, and come into his courts.

O worship the LORD in the beauty of holiness: fear before him, all the earth.

Say among the heathen that the LORD reigneth: the world also shall be established that it shall not be moved: he shall judge the people righteously.

Let the heavens rejoice, and let the earth be glad; let the sea roar, and the fulness thereof.

Let the field be joyful, and all that is therein: then shall all the trees of the wood rejoice before the LORD:

For he cometh, for he cometh to judge the earth:

He shall judge the world with righteousness, and the people with his truth.

Praise ye the LORD.

Sing unto the LORD a new song, and his praise in the congregation of saints.

Let Israel rejoice in him that made him:

Let the children of Zion be joyful in their King.

Let them praise his name in the dance:

Let them sing praises unto him with the timbrel and harp.

For the LORD taketh pleasure in his people:

He will beautify the meek with salvation.

Let the saints be joyful in glory: let them sing aloud upon their beds.

Let the high praises of God be in their mouth. Praise ye the LORD.

SELECTION 8

Psalms CXLVII, CXLVIII

PRAISE ye the LORD: for it is good to sing praises unto our God;

For it is pleasant; and praise is comely.

The LORD doth build up Jerusalem: he gathereth together the outcasts of Israel.

He healeth the broken in heart, and bindeth up their wounds.

He telleth the number of the stars; he calleth them all by their names.

Great is our Lord, and of great power: his understanding is infinite.

The LORD lifteth up the meek:

He casteth the wicked down to the ground.

Sing unto the LORD with thanksgiving;

Sing praise upon the harp unto our God:

Who covereth the heaven with clouds, who prepareth rain for the earth, who maketh grass to grow upon the mountains.

He giveth to the beast his food, and to the young ravens which cry.

He delighteth not in the strength of the horse: he taketh not pleasure in the legs of a man.

The LORD taketh pleasure in them that fear him, in those that hope in his mercy.

Praise the LORD, O Jerusalem; praise thy God, O Zion.

For he hath strengthened the bars of thy gates; he hath blessed thy children within thee.

He maketh peace in thy borders, and filleth thee with the finest of the wheat.

He sendeth forth his commandment upon earth: his word runneth very swiftly.

He giveth snow like wool: he scattereth the hoar frost like ashes.

He casteth forth his ice like morsels: who can stand before his cold?

He sendeth out his word, and melteth them:

He causeth his wind to blow, and the waters flow.

He sheweth his word unto Jacob, his statutes and his judgments unto Israel.

He hath not dealt so with any nation: and as for his judgments, they have not known them. Praise ye the LORD.

Praise ye the LORD. Praise ye the LORD from the heavens: praise him in the heights.

Praise ye him, all his angels: praise ye him, all his hosts.

Praise ye him, sun and moon: praise him, all ye stars of light.

Praise him, ye heavens of heavens, and ye waters that be above the heavens.

Let them praise the name of the LORD: for he commanded, and they were created.

He hath also stablished them for ever and ever: he hath made a decree which shall not pass.

Praise the LORD from the earth, ye dragons, and all deeps:

Fire, and hail; snow, and vapour; stormy wind fulfilling his word:

Mountains, and all hills; fruitful trees, and all cedars:

Beasts, and all cattle; creeping things, and flying fowl:

Kings of the earth, and all people; princes, and all judges of the earth:

Both young men, and maidens; old men, and children:

Let them praise the name of the LORD: for his name alone is excellent;

His glory is above the earth and heaven.

He also exalteth the horn of his people, the praise of all his saints; even of the children of Israel, a people near unto him.

Praise ye the LORD.

SELECTION 9

Psalms CXII, CXIII, CXXXV

PRAISE ye the LORD. Blessed is the man that feareth the LORD, that delighteth greatly in his commandments.

His seed shall be mighty upon earth: the generation of the upright shall be blessed.

Wealth and riches shall be in his house: and his righteousness endureth for ever.

Unto the upright there ariseth light in the darkness: he is gracious, and full of compassion, and righteous.

A good man sheweth favour, and lendeth: he will guide his affairs with discretion.

Surely he shall not be moved for ever: the righteous shall be in everlasting remembrance.

He shall not be afraid of evil tidings:

His heart is fixed, trusting in the LORD.

Praise ye the LORD. Praise, O ye servants of the LORD, praise the name of the LORD.

Blessed be the name of the LORD from this time forth and for evermore.

From the rising of the sun unto the going down of the same the LORD's name is to be praised.

The LORD is high above all nations, and his glory above the heavens.

Who is like unto the LORD our God, who dwelleth on high,

Who humbleth himself to behold the things that are in heaven, and in the earth!

Praise ye the LORD. Praise ye the name of the LORD;

Praise him, O ye servants of the LORD.

Ye that stand in the house of the LORD, in the courts of the house of our God, praise the LORD;

For the LORD is good: sing praises unto his name; for it is pleasant.

For the LORD hath chosen Jacob unto himself, and Israel for his peculiar treasure.

For I know that the LORD is great, and that our Lord is above all gods.

Whatsoever the LORD pleased, that did he in heaven, and in earth, in the seas, and all deep places.

He causeth the vapours to ascend from the ends of the earth; he maketh lightnings for the rain; he bringeth the wind out of his treasuries.

Who smote the firstborn of Egypt, both of man and beast.

Who sent tokens and wonders into the midst of thee, O Egypt, upon Pharaoh, and upon all his servants.

Who smote great nations, and slew mighty kings; Sihon king of the Amorites, and Og king of Bashan, and all the kingdoms of Canaan:

And gave their land for a heritage, a heritage unto Israel his people.

Thy name, O LORD, endureth for ever; and thy memorial, O LORD, throughout all generations.

For the LORD will judge his people, and he will repent himself concerning his servants.

The idols of the heathen are silver and gold, the work of men's hands.

They have mouths, but they speak not; eyes have they, but they see not;

They have ears, but they hear not; neither is there any breath in their mouths.

They that make them are like unto them: so is every one that trusteth in them.

Bless the LORD, O house of Israel: bless the LORD, O house of Aaron:

Bless the LORD, O house of Levi: ye that fear the LORD, bless the LORD.

Blessed be the LORD out of Zion, which dwelleth at Jerusalem.

Praise ye the LORD.

SELECTION 10

Psalms CXXXVI, XXXIV, CXXXIV

O GIVE thanks unto the LORD; for he is good:

For his mercy endureth for ever.

O give thanks unto the God of gods: for his mercy endureth for ever.

O give thanks to the Lord of lords: for his mercy endureth for ever.

To him who alone doeth great wonders: for his mercy endureth for ever.

To him that by wisdom made the heavens: for his mercy endureth for ever.

To him that stretched out the earth above the waters: for his mercy endureth for ever:

To him that made great lights: for his mercy endureth for ever:

The sun to rule by day: for his mercy endureth for ever:

The moon and stars to rule by night: for his mercy endureth for ever.

Who remembered us in our low estate: for his mercy endureth for ever:

And hath redeemed us from our enemies: for his mercy endureth for ever.

Who giveth food to all flesh: for his mercy endureth for ever.

O give thanks unto the God of heaven: for his mercy endureth for ever.

I will bless the LORD at all times:

His praise shall continually be in my mouth.

My soul shall make her boast in the LORD: the humble shall hear thereof, and be glad.

O magnify the LORD with me, and let us exalt his name together.

I sought the LORD, and he heard me, and delivered me from all my fears.

They looked unto him, and were lightened: and their faces were not ashamed.

This poor man cried, and the LORD heard him, and saved him out of all his troubles.

The angel of the LORD encampeth round about them that fear him, and delivereth them.

O taste and see that the LORD is good: blessed is the man that trusteth in him.

O fear the LORD, ye his saints: for there is no want to them that fear him.

The young lions do lack, and suffer hunger:

But they that seek the LORD shall not want any good thing.

Come, ye children, hearken unto me:

I will teach you the fear of the LORD.

What man is he that desireth life, and loveth many days, that he may see good?

Keep thy tongue from evil, and thy lips from speaking guile: depart from evil, and do good; seek peace, and pursue it.

The eyes of the LORD are upon the righteous, and his ears are open unto their cry.

The face of the LORD is against them that do evil, to cut off the remembrance of them from the earth.

The righteous cry, and the LORD heareth, and delivereth them out of all their troubles.

The LORD is nigh unto them that are of a broken heart; and saveth such as be of a contrite spirit.

Many are the afflictions of the righteous: but the LORD delivereth him out of them all.

He keepeth all his bones: not one of them is broken.

Evil shall slay the wicked: and they that hate the righteous shall be desolate.

The LORD redeemeth the soul of his servants: and none of them that trust in him shall be desolate.

Behold, bless ye the LORD, all ye servants of the LORD,

Which by night stand in the house of the LORD.

Lift up your hands in the sanctuary, and bless the LORD.

The LORD that made heaven and earth bless thee out of Zion.

SELECTION 11

Psalms XLVI, XLVII, XLVIII

GOD is our refuge and strength, a very present help in trouble.

Therefore will not we fear, though the earth be removed, and though the mountains be carried into the midst of the sea ;

Though the waters thereof roar and be troubled,

Though the mountains shake with the swelling thereof.

There is a river, the streams whereof shall make glad the city of God, the holy place of the tabernacles of the Most High.

God is in the midst of her ; she shall not be moved : God shall help her, and that right early.

The heathen raged, the kingdoms were moved : he uttered his voice, the earth melted.

The LORD of hosts is with us; the God of Jacob is our refuge.

Come, behold the works of the LORD, what desolations he hath made in the earth.

He maketh wars to cease unto the end of the earth ; he breaketh the bow, and cutteth the spear in sunder ; he burneth the chariot in the fire.

Be still, and know that I am God: I will be exalted among the heathen, I will be exalted in the earth.

The LORD of hosts is with us; the God of Jacob is our refuge.

O clap your hands, all ye people; shout unto God with the voice of triumph.

For the LORD most high is terrible; he is a great King over all the earth.

He shall subdue the people under us, and the nations under our feet.

He shall choose our inheritance for us, the excellency of Jacob whom he loved.

God is gone up with a shout, the LORD with the sound of a trumpet.

Sing praises to God, sing praises: sing praises unto our King, sing praises.

For God is the King of all the earth: sing ye praises with understanding.

God reigneth over the heathen: God sitteth upon the throne of his holiness.

The princes of the people are gathered together, even the people of the God of Abraham:

For the shields of the earth belong unto God: he is greatly exalted.

Great is the LORD, and greatly to be praised,

In the city of our God, in the mountain of his holiness.

Beautiful for situation, the joy of the whole earth, is mount Zion, on the sides of the north, the city of the great King.

God is known in her palaces for a refuge.

For, lo, the kings were assembled, they passed by together.

They saw it, and so they marvelled; they were troubled, and hasted away.

Fear took hold upon them there, and pain, as of a woman in travail.

Thou breakest the ships of Tarshish with an east wind.

As we have heard, so have we seen in the city of the LORD of hosts, in the city of our God:

God will establish it for ever.

We have thought of thy lovingkindness, O God, in the midst of thy temple.

According to thy name, O God, so is thy praise unto the ends of the earth: thy right hand is full of righteousness.

Let mount Zion rejoice,

Let the daughters of Judah be glad, because of thy judgments.

Walk about Zion, and go round about her: tell the towers thereof.

Mark ye well her bulwarks, consider her palaces; that ye may tell it to the generation following.

For this God is our God for ever and ever:

He will be our guide even unto death.

SELECTION 12

Psalms CXLV, CXLVI

I WILL extol thee, my God, O King; and I will bless thy name for ever and ever.

Every day will I bless thee; and I will praise thy name for ever and ever.

Great is the LORD, and greatly to be praised; and his greatness is unsearchable.

One generation shall praise thy works to another, and shall declare thy mighty acts.

I will speak of the glorious honour of thy majesty, and of thy wondrous works.

And men shall speak of the might of thy terrible acts: and I will declare thy greatness.

They shall abundantly utter the memory of thy great goodness,

And shall sing of thy righteousness.

The LORD is gracious, and full of compassion; slow to anger, and of great mercy.

The LORD is good to all: and his tender mercies are over all his works.

All thy works shall praise thee, O LORD; and thy saints shall bless thee.

They shall speak of the glory of thy kingdom, and talk of thy power;

To make known to the sons of men his mighty acts, and the glorious majesty of his kingdom.

Thy kingdom is an everlasting kingdom, and thy dominion endureth throughout all generations.

The LORD upholdeth all that fall,

And raiseth up all those that be bowed down.

The eyes of all wait upon thee; and thou givest them their meat in due season.

Thou openest thine hand, and satisfiest the desire of every living thing.

The LORD is righteous in all his ways, and holy in all his works.

The LORD is nigh unto all them that call upon him, to all that call upon him in truth.

He will fulfil the desire of them that fear him: he also will hear their cry, and will save them.

The LORD preserveth all them that love him: but all the wicked will he destroy.

My mouth shall speak the praise of the LORD:

And let all flesh bless his holy name for ever and ever.

Praise ye the LORD. Praise the LORD, O my soul.

While I live will I praise the LORD: I will sing praises unto my God while I have any being.

Put not your trust in princes, nor in the son of man, in whom there is no help.

His breath goeth forth, he returneth to his earth; in that very day his thoughts perish.

Happy is he that hath the God of Jacob for his help,

Whose hope is in the LORD his God:

Which made heaven, and earth, the sea, and all that therein is: which keepeth truth for ever:

Which executeth judgment for the oppressed: which giveth food to the hungry.

The LORD looseth the prisoners: the LORD openeth the eyes of the blind:

The LORD raiseth them that are bowed down: the LORD loveth the righteous:

The LORD preserveth the strangers; he relieveth the fatherless and widow:

But the way of the wicked he turneth upside down.

The LORD shall reign for ever, even thy God, O Zion, unto all generations.

Praise ye the LORD.

SELECTION 13

Psalm LXVIII

SING unto God, sing praises to his name:

Extol him that rideth upon the heavens by his name JEHOVAH, and rejoice before him.

A father of the fatherless, and a judge of the widows, is God in his holy habitation.

God setteth the solitary in families: he bringeth out those which are bound with chains: but the rebellious dwell in a dry land.

O God, when thou wentest forth before thy people, when thou didst march through the wilderness; the earth shook, the heavens also dropped at the presence of God:

Even Sinai itself was moved at the presence of God, the God of Israel.

Thou, O God, didst send a plentiful rain, whereby thou didst confirm thine inheritance, when it was weary.

Thy congregation hath dwelt therein: thou, O God, hast prepared of thy goodness for the poor.

The Lord gave the word: great was the company of those that published it.

Kings of armies did flee apace: and she that tarried at home divided the spoil.

Though ye have lain among the pots, yet shall ye be as the wings of a dove covered with silver, and her feathers with yellow gold.

When the Almighty scattered kings in it, it was white as snow in Salmon.

The hill of God is as the hill of Bashan;

A high hill as the hill of Bashan.

Why leap ye, ye high hills? this is the hill which God desireth to dwell in;

Yea, the LORD will dwell in it for ever.

The chariots of God are twenty thousand, even thousands of angels:

The Lord is among them, as in Sinai, in the holy place.

Thou hast ascended on high, thou hast led captivity captive: thou hast received gifts for men;

Yea, for the rebellious also, that the LORD God might dwell among them.

Blessed be the Lord, who daily loadeth us with benefits, even the God of our salvation.

He that is our God is the God of salvation; and unto GOD the Lord belong the issues from death.

Thy God hath commanded thy strength: strengthen, O God, that which thou hast wrought for us.

Because of thy temple at Jerusalem shall kings bring presents unto thee.

Rebuke the company of spearmen, the multitude of the bulls, with the calves of the people, till every one submit himself with pieces of silver:

Scatter thou the people that delight in war.

Princes shall come out of Egypt;

Ethiopia shall soon stretch out her hands unto God.

Sing unto God, ye kingdoms of the earth;

O sing praises unto the Lord;

To him that rideth upon the heavens of heavens, which were of old; lo, he doth send out his voice, and that a mighty voice.

Ascribe ye strength unto God: his excellency is over Israel, and his strength is in the clouds.

O God, thou art terrible out of thy holy places:

The God of Israel is he that giveth strength and power unto his people. Blessed be God.

SELECTION 14

Psalms LXVI, CXXXVIII

MAKE a joyful noise unto God, all ye lands:

Sing forth the honour of his name: make his praise glorious.

Say unto God, How terrible art thou in thy works! through the greatness of thy power shall thine enemies submit themselves unto thee.

All the earth shall worship thee, and shall sing unto thee; they shall sing to thy name.

Come and see the works of God: he is terrible in his doing toward the children of men.

He turned the sea into dry land: they went through the flood on foot: there did we rejoice in him.

He ruleth by his power for ever; his eyes behold the nations:

Let not the rebellious exalt themselves.

O bless our God, ye people, and make the voice of his praise to be heard:

Which holdeth our soul in life, and suffereth not our feet to be moved.

For thou, O God, hast proved us: thou hast tried us, as silver is tried.

Thou broughtest us into the net; thou laidst affliction upon our loins.

Thou hast caused men to ride over our heads; we went through fire and through water:

But thou broughtest us out into a wealthy place.

I will go into thy house with burnt offerings: I will pay thee my vows, which my lips have uttered, and my mouth hath spoken, when I was in trouble,

I will offer unto thee burnt sacrifices of fatlings, with the incense of rams: I will offer bullocks with goats.

Come and hear, all ye that fear God, and I will declare what he hath done for my soul.

I cried unto him with my mouth, and he was extolled with my tongue.

If I regard iniquity in my heart, the Lord will not hear me: but verily God hath heard me; he hath attended to the voice of my prayer.

Blessed be God, which hath not turned away my prayer, nor his mercy from me.

I will praise thee with my whole heart:

Before the gods will I sing praise unto thee.

I will worship toward thy holy temple, and praise thy name for thy lovingkindness and for thy truth: for thou hast magnified thy word above all thy name.

In the day when I cried thou answeredst me, and strengthenedst me with strength in my soul.

All the kings of the earth shall praise thee, O Lord, when they hear the words of thy mouth.

Yea, they shall sing in the ways of the Lord: for great is the glory of the Lord.

Though the Lord be high, yet hath he respect unto the lowly:

But the proud he knoweth afar off.

Though I walk in the midst of trouble, thou wilt revive me:

Thou shalt stretch forth thine hand against the wrath of mine enemies, and thy right hand shall save me.

The Lord will perfect that which concerneth me:

Thy mercy, O Lord, endureth for ever: forsake not the works of thine own hands.

SELECTION 15

Psalms CXVII, CXVIII

O PRAISE the Lord, all ye nations:

Praise him, all ye people.

For his merciful kindness is great toward us: and the truth of the Lord endureth for ever.

Praise ye the Lord.

O give thanks unto the Lord; for he is good: because his mercy endureth for ever.

Let Israel now say, that his mercy endureth for ever.

Let the house of Aaron now say, that his mercy endureth for ever.

Let them now that fear the LORD say, that his mercy endureth for ever.

I called upon the LORD in distress:

The LORD answered me, and set me in a large place.

The LORD is on my side; I will not fear: what can man do unto me?

The LORD taketh my part with them that help me: therefore shall I see my desire upon them that hate me.

It is better to trust in the LORD than to put confidence in man.

It is better to trust in the LORD than to put confidence in princes.

The LORD is my strength and song, and is become my salvation.

The voice of rejoicing and salvation is in the tabernacles of the righteous:

The right hand of the LORD doeth valiantly.

The right hand of the LORD is exalted: the right hand of the LORD doeth valiantly.

I shall not die, but live, and declare the works of the LORD.

The LORD hath chastened me sore: but he hath not given me over unto death.

Open to me the gates of righteousness: I will go into them, and I will praise the LORD:

This gate of the LORD, into which the righteous shall enter. I will praise thee: for thou hast heard me, and art become my salvation.

The stone which the builders refused is become the head stone of the corner.

This is the LORD's doing; it is marvellous in our eyes.

This is the day which the LORD hath made; we will rejoice and be glad in it.

Save now, I beseech thee, O LORD: O LORD, I beseech thee, send now prosperity.

Blessed be he that cometh in the name of the LORD: we have blessed you out of the house of the LORD.

God is the LORD, which hath shewed us light: bind the sacrifice with cords, even unto the horns of the altar.

Thou art my God, and I will praise thee: thou art my God, I will exalt thee.

O give thanks unto the LORD; for he is good: for his mercy endureth for ever.

SELECTION 16

Psalm CIV

BLESS the LORD, O my soul. O LORD my God, thou art very great;

Thou art clothed with honour and majesty:

Who coverest thyself with light as with a garment:

Who stretchest out the heavens like a curtain:

Who layeth the beams of his chambers in the waters:

Who maketh the clouds his chariot: who walketh upon the wings of the wind:

Who maketh his angels spirits; his ministers a flaming fire:

Who laid the foundations of the earth, that it should not be removed for ever.

Thou coveredst it with the deep as with a garment: the waters stood above the mountains.

At thy rebuke they fled; at the voice of thy thunder they hasted away.

They go up by the mountains; they go down by the valleys unto the place which thou hast founded for them.

Thou hast set a bound that they may not pass over; that they turn not again to cover the earth.

He sendeth the springs into the valleys, which run among the hills.

They give drink to every beast of the field: the wild asses quench their thirst.

By them shall the fowls of the heaven have their habitation, which sing among the branches.

He watereth the hills from his chambers: the earth is satisfied with the fruit of thy works.

He causeth the grass to grow for the cattle, and herb for the service of man: that he may bring forth food out of the earth;

And wine that maketh glad the heart of man, and oil to make his face to shine, and bread which strengtheneth man's heart.

The trees of the LORD are full of sap; the cedars of Lebanon, which he hath planted;

Where the birds make their nests: as for the stork, the fir trees are her house.

The high hills are a refuge for the wild goats;

And the rocks for the conies.

He appointed the moon for seasons: the sun knoweth his going down.

Thou makest darkness, and it is night: wherein all the beasts of the forest do creep forth: the young lions roar after their prey, and seek their meat from God.

The sun ariseth, they gather themselves together, and lay them down in their dens.

Man goeth forth unto his work and to his labour until the evening.

O LORD, how manifold are thy works! in wisdom hast thou made them all:

The earth is full of thy riches.

So is this great and wide sea, wherein are things creeping innumerable, both small and great beasts.

There go the ships: there is that leviathan, whom thou hast made to play therein.

These wait all upon thee; that thou mayest give them their meat in due season.

That thou givest them they gather: thou openest thine hand, they are filled with good.

Thou hidest thy face, they are troubled: thou takest away their breath, they die, and return to their dust.

Thou sendest forth thy spirit, they are created: and thou renewest the face of the earth.

The glory of the LORD shall endure for ever: the LORD shall rejoice in his works.

He looketh on the earth, and it trembleth: he toucheth the hills, and they smoke.

I will sing unto the LORD as long as I live: I will sing praise to my God while I have my being.

My meditation of him shall be sweet: I will be glad in the LORD.

SELECTION 17

Psalm LXXXIX

I WILL sing of the mercies of the LORD for ever:

With my mouth will I make known thy faithfulness to all generations.

For I have said, Mercy shall be built up for ever:

Thy faithfulness shalt thou establish in the very heavens.

I have made a covenant with my chosen, I have sworn unto David my servant,

Thy seed will I establish for ever, and build up thy throne to all generations.

And the heavens shall praise thy wonders, O LORD: thy faithfulness also in the congregation of the saints.

For who in the heaven can be compared unto the LORD? who among the sons of the mighty can be likened unto the LORD?

God is greatly to be feared in the assembly of the saints, and to be had in reverence of all them that are about him.

O LORD God of hosts, who is a strong LORD like unto thee? or to thy faithfulness round about thee?

Thou rulest the raging of the sea: when the waves thereof arise, thou stillest them.

Thou hast broken Rahab in pieces, as one that is slain; thou hast scattered thine enemies with thy strong arm.

The heavens are thine, the earth also is thine: as for the world and the fulness thereof, thou hast founded them.

The north and the south thou hast created them: Tabor and Hermon shall rejoice in thy name.

Thou hast a mighty arm: strong is thy hand, and high is thy right hand.

Justice and judgment are the habitation of thy throne: mercy and truth shall go before thy face.

Blessed is the people that know the joyful sound: they shall walk, O LORD, in the light of thy countenance.

In thy name shall they rejoice all the day: and in thy righteousness shall they be exalted.

For thou art the glory of their strength: and in thy favour our horn shall be exalted.

For the LORD is our defence; and the Holy One of Israel is our King.

Then thou spakest in vision to thy Holy One, and saidst, I have laid help upon one that is mighty;

I have exalted one chosen out of the people.

I have found David my servant; with my holy oil have I anointed him:

With whom my hand shall be established: mine arm also shall strengthen him.

The enemy shall not exact upon him; nor the son of wickedness afflict him.

And I will beat down his foes before his face, and plague them that hate him.

But my faithfulness and my mercy shall be with him: and in my name shall his horn be exalted.

I will set his hand also in the sea, and his right hand in the rivers.

He shall cry unto me, Thou art my Father, my God, and the Rock of my salvation.

Also I will make him my firstborn, higher than the kings of the earth.

My mercy will I keep for him for evermore, and my covenant shall stand fast with him.

His seed also will I make to endure for ever, and his throne as the days of heaven.

If his children forsake my law, and walk not in my judgments; if they break my statutes, and keep not my commandments;

Then will I visit their transgression with the rod, and their iniquity with stripes.

Nevertheless my lovingkindness will I not utterly take from him, nor suffer my faithfulness to fail.

My covenant will I not break, nor alter the thing that is gone out of my lips.

Once have I sworn by my holiness that I will not lie unto David.

His seed shall endure for ever, and his throne as the sun before me.

It shall be established for ever as the moon, and as a faithful witness in heaven.

Blessed be the LORD for evermore. Amen, and Amen.

SELECTION 18

Psalms CXXXII, LXXX

LORD, remember David, and all his afflictions: how he sware unto the LORD, and vowed unto the mighty God of Jacob;

Surely I will not come into the tabernacle of my house, nor go up into my bed;

I will not give sleep to mine eyes, or slumber to mine eyelids,

Until I find out a place for the LORD, a habitation for the mighty God of Jacob.

Lo, we heard of it at Ephratah: we found it in the fields of the wood.

We will go into his tabernacles: we will worship at his footstool.

Arise, O LORD, into thy rest; thou, and the ark of thy strength.

Let thy priests be clothed with righteousness; and let thy saints shout for joy.

For thy servant David's sake turn not away the face of thine anointed.

The LORD hath sworn in truth unto David; he will not turn from it; Of the fruit of thy body will I set upon thy throne.

If thy children will keep my covenant and my testimony that I shall teach them, their children shall also sit upon thy throne for evermore.

For the LORD hath chosen Zion; he hath desired it for his habitation.

This is my rest for ever: here will I dwell; for I have desired it.

I will abundantly bless her provision: I will satisfy her poor with bread.

I will also clothe her priests with salvation:

And her saints shall shout aloud for joy.

There will I make the horn of David to bud: I have ordained a lamp for mine anointed.

His enemies will I clothe with shame: but upon himself shall his crown flourish.

Give ear, O Shepherd of Israel, thou that leadest Joseph like a flock;

Thou that dwellest between the cherubim, shine forth.

Before Ephraim and Benjamin and Manasseh stir up thy strength, and come and save us.

Turn us again, O God, and cause thy face to shine; and we shall be saved.

O LORD God of hosts, how long wilt thou be angry against the prayer of thy people?

Thou feedest them with the bread of tears; and givest them tears to drink in great measure.

Thou makest us a strife unto our neighbours: and our enemies laugh among themselves.

Turn us again, O God of hosts, and cause thy face to shine; and we shall be saved.

Thou hast brought a vine out of Egypt: thou hast cast out the heathen, and planted it.

Thou preparedst room before it, and didst cause it to take deep root, and it filled the land.

The hills were covered with the shadow of it, and the boughs thereof were like the goodly cedars.

She sent out her boughs unto the sea, and her branches unto the river.

Why hast thou then broken down her hedges, so that all they which pass by the way do pluck her?

The boar out of the wood doth waste it, and the wild beast of the field doth devour it.

Return, we beseech thee, O God of hosts: look down from heaven, and behold, and visit this vine;

And the vineyard which thy right hand hath planted, and the branch that thou madest strong for thyself.

It is burned with fire, it is cut down:

They perish at the rebuke of thy countenance.

Let thy hand be upon the man of thy right hand,

Upon the son of man whom thou madest strong for thyself.

So will not we go back from thee: quicken us, and we will call upon thy name.

Turn us again, O LORD God of hosts, cause thy face to shine; and we shall be saved.

SELECTION 19

Psalms XX, LXXII

THE LORD hear thee in the day of trouble; the name of the God of Jacob defend thee;

Send thee help from the sanctuary, and strengthen thee out of Zion;

Remember all thy offerings, and accept thy burnt sacrifice;

Grant thee according to thine own heart, and fulfil all thy counsel.

We will rejoice in thy salvation, and in the name of our God we will set up our banners:

The LORD fulfil all thy petitions.

Now know I that the LORD saveth his anointed;

He will hear him from his holy heaven with the saving strength of his right hand.

Some trust in chariots, and some in horses:

But we will remember the name of the LORD our God.

They are brought down and fallen: but we are risen, and stand upright.

Save, LORD: let the king hear us when we call.

Give the king thy judgments, O God, and thy righteousness unto the king's son.

He shall judge thy people with righteousness, and thy poor with judgment.

The mountains shall bring peace to the people, and the little hills, by righteousness.

He shall judge the poor of the people, he shall save the children of the needy, and shall break in pieces the oppressor.

They shall fear thee as long as the sun and moon endure, throughout all generations.

He shall come down like rain upon the mown grass: as showers that water the earth.

In his days shall the righteous flourish;

And abundance of peace so long as the moon endureth.

He shall have dominion also from sea to sea, and from the river unto the ends of the earth.

They that dwell in the wilderness shall bow before him; and his enemies shall lick the dust.

The kings of Tarshish and of the isles shall bring presents: the kings of Sheba and Seba shall offer gifts.

Yea, all kings shall fall down before him: all nations shall serve him.

For he shall deliver the needy when he crieth; the poor also, and him that hath no helper.

He shall spare the poor and needy, and shall save the souls of the needy.

He shall redeem their soul from deceit and violence:

And precious shall their blood be in his sight.

And he shall live, and to him shall be given of the gold of Sheba:

Prayer also shall be made for him continually; and daily shall he be praised.

There shall be a handful of corn in the earth upon the top of the mountains;

The fruit thereof shall shake like Lebanon; and they of the city shall flourish like grass of the earth.

His name shall endure for ever: his name shall be continued as long as the sun:

And men shall be blessed in him: all nations shall call him blessed.

Blessed be the LORD God, the God of Israel, who only doeth wondrous things.

And blessed be his glorious name for ever: and let the whole earth be filled with his glory. Amen, and Amen.

SELECTION 20

Psalms II, CX, XXI

WHY do the heathen rage, and the people imagine a vain thing?

The kings of the earth set themselves, and the rulers take counsel together,

against the LORD, and against his Anointed, saying, Let us break their bands asunder, and cast away their cords from us.

He that sitteth in the heavens shall laugh: the Lord shall have them in derision.

Then shall he speak unto them in his wrath, and vex them in his sore displeasure. Yet have I set my King upon my holy hill of Zion.

I will declare the decree: the LORD hath said unto me, Thou art my Son; this day have I begotten thee.

Ask of me, and I shall give thee the heathen for thine inheritance, and the uttermost parts of the earth for thy possession.

Thou shalt break them with a rod of iron;

Thou shalt dash them in pieces like a potter's vessel.

Be wise now therefore, O ye kings: be instructed, ye judges of the earth.

Serve the LORD with fear, and rejoice with trembling.

Kiss the Son, lest he be angry, and ye perish from the way, when his wrath is kindled but a little.

Blessed are all they that put their trust in him.

The LORD said unto my Lord, Sit thou at my right hand, until I make thine enemies thy footstool.

The LORD shall send the rod of thy strength out of Zion: rule thou in the midst of thine enemies.

Thy people shall be willing in the day of thy power, in the beauties of holiness from the womb of the morning: thou hast the dew of thy youth.

The LORD hath sworn, and will not repent, Thou art a priest for ever after the order of Melchizedek.

The Lord at thy right hand shall strike through kings in the day of his wrath.

He shall judge among the heathen, he shall fill the places with the dead bodies;

He shall wound the heads over many countries.

He shall drink of the brook in the way: therefore shall he lift up the head.

The king shall joy in thy strength, O LORD; and in thy salvation how greatly shall he rejoice!

Thou hast given him his heart's desire, and hast not withholden the request of his lips.

For thou preventest him with the blessings of goodness: thou settest a crown of pure gold on his head.

He asked life of thee, and thou gavest it him, even length of days for ever and ever.

His glory is great in thy salvation:

Honour and majesty hast thou laid upon him.

For thou hast made him most blessed for ever: thou hast made him exceeding glad with thy countenance.

For the king trusteth in the LORD, and through the mercy of the Most High he shall not be moved.

Thine hand shall find out all thine enemies:

Thy right hand shall find out those that hate thee.

Thou shalt make them as a fiery oven in the time of thine anger: the LORD shall swallow them up in his wrath, and the fire shall devour them.

Their fruit shalt thou destroy from the earth, and their seed from among the children of men.

For they intended evil against thee: they imagined a mischievous device, which they are not able to perform.

Therefore shalt thou make them turn their back, when thou shalt make ready thine arrows upon thy strings against the face of them.

Be thou exalted, LORD, in thine own strength:

So will we sing and praise thy power.

SELECTION 21

Psalms CXV, CXVI

NOT unto us, O LORD, not unto us, but unto thy name give glory,

For thy mercy, and for thy truth's sake.

Wherefore should the heathen say, Where is now their God?

But our God is in the heavens: he hath done whatsoever he hath pleased.

Their idols are silver and gold, the work of men's hands.

They have mouths, but they speak not: eyes have they, but they see not:

They have ears, but they hear not: noses have they, but they smell not:

They have hands, but they handle not: feet have they, but they walk not: neither speak they through their throat.

They that make them are like unto them;

So is every one that trusteth in them.

O Israel, trust thou in the LORD: he is their help and their shield.

O house of Aaron, trust in the LORD: he is their help and their shield.

Ye that fear the LORD, trust in the LORD:

He is their help and their shield.

The LORD hath been mindful of us: he will bless us;

He will bless the house of Israel; he will bless the house of Aaron.

He will bless them that fear the LORD, both small and great.

The LORD shall increase you more and more, you and your children.

Ye are blessed of the LORD which made heaven and earth.

The heaven, even the heavens, are the LORD'S: but the earth hath he given to the children of men.

The dead praise not the LORD, neither any that go down into silence.

But we will bless the LORD from this time forth and for evermore. Praise the LORD.

I love the LORD, because he hath heard my voice and my supplications.

Because he hath inclined his ear unto me, therefore will I call upon him as long as I live.

The sorrows of death compassed me, and the pains of hell gat hold upon me: I found trouble and sorrow.

Then called I upon the name of the LORD; O LORD, I beseech thee, deliver my soul.

Gracious is the LORD, and righteous; yea, our God is merciful.

The LORD preserveth the simple: I was brought low, and he helped me.

Return unto thy rest, O my soul; for the LORD hath dealt bountifully with thee.

For thou hast delivered my soul from death, mine eyes from tears, and my feet from falling.

I will walk before the LORD in the land of the living.

I believed, therefore have I spoken: I was greatly afflicted: I said in my haste, All men are liars.

What shall I render unto the LORD for all his benefits toward me?

I will take the cup of salvation, and call upon the name of the LORD: I will pay my vows unto the LORD now in the presence of all his people.

Precious in the sight of the LORD is the death of his saints.

O LORD, truly I am thy servant; I am thy servant, and the son of thine handmaid: thou hast loosed my bonds.

I will offer to thee the sacrifice of thanksgiving, and will call upon the name of the LORD.

I will pay my vows unto the LORD now in the presence of all his people, in the courts of the LORD'S house, in the midst of thee, O Jerusalem. Praise ye the LORD.

SELECTION 22

Psalms LXXXVI, LXXXV

BOW down thine ear, O LORD, hear me: for I am poor and needy.

Preserve my soul; for I am holy: O thou my God, save thy servant that trusteth in thee.

Be merciful unto me, O Lord: for I cry unto thee daily.

Rejoice the soul of thy servant: for unto thee, O Lord, do I lift up my soul.

For thou, Lord, art good, and ready to forgive;

And plenteous in mercy unto all them that call upon thee.

Give ear, O LORD, unto my prayer; and attend to the voice of my supplications.

In the day of my trouble I will call upon thee: for thou wilt answer me.

Among the gods there is none like unto thee, O Lord;

Neither are there any works like unto thy works.

All nations whom thou hast made shall come and worship before thee, O Lord; and shall glorify thy name.

For thou art great, and doest wondrous things: thou art God alone.

Teach me thy way, O LORD; I will walk in thy truth:

Unite my heart to fear thy name.

I will praise thee, O Lord my God, with all my heart: and I will glorify thy name for evermore.

For great is thy mercy toward me: and thou hast delivered my soul from the lowest hell.

O God, the proud are risen against me, and the assemblies of violent men have sought after my soul; and have not set thee before them.

But thou, O Lord, art a God full of compassion, and gracious, longsuffering, and plenteous in mercy and truth.

O turn unto me, and have mercy upon me;

Give thy strength unto thy servant, and save the son of thine handmaid.

Shew me a token for good; that they which hate me may see it, and be ashamed:

Because thou, LORD, hast holpen me, and comforted me.

LORD, thou hast been favourable unto thy land: thou hast brought back the captivity of Jacob.

Thou hast forgiven the iniquity of thy people; thou hast covered all their sin.

Thou hast taken away all thy wrath:

Thou hast turned thyself from the fierceness of thine anger.

Turn us, O God of our salvation, and cause thine anger toward us to cease.

Wilt thou be angry with us for ever? wilt thou draw out thine anger to all generations?

Wilt thou not revive us again: that thy people may rejoice in thee?

Shew us thy mercy, O LORD, and grant us thy salvation.

I will hear what God the LORD will speak: for he will speak peace unto his people, and to his saints: but let them not turn again to folly.

Surely his salvation is nigh them that fear him; that glory may dwell in our land.

Mercy and truth are met together; righteousness and peace have kissed each other.

Truth shall spring out of the earth; and righteousness shall look down from heaven.

Yea, the LORD shall give that which is good; and our land shall yield her increase.

Righteousness shall go before him; and shall set us in the way of his steps.

SELECTION 23

Psalm CIII

BLESS the LORD, O my soul;

And all that is within me, bless his holy name.

Bless the LORD, O my soul, and forget not all his benefits:

Who forgiveth all thine iniquities; who healeth all thy diseases;

Who redeemeth thy life from destruction; who crowneth thee with lovingkindness and tender mercies;

Who satisfieth thy mouth with good things; so that thy youth is renewed like the eagle's.

The LORD executeth righteousness and judgment for all that are oppressed.

He made known his ways unto Moses, his acts unto the children of Israel.

The LORD is merciful and gracious, slow to anger, and plenteous in mercy.

He will not always chide; neither will he keep his anger for ever.

He hath not dealt with us after our sins;

Nor rewarded us according to our iniquities.

For as the heaven is high above the earth, so great is his mercy toward them that fear him.

As far as the east is from the west, so far hath he removed our transgressions from us.

Like as a father pitieth his children, so the LORD pitieth them that fear him.

For he knoweth our frame; he remembereth that we are dust.

As for man, his days are as grass: as a flower of the field, so he flourisheth.

For the wind passeth over it, and it is gone; and the place thereof shall know it no more.

But the mercy of the LORD is from everlasting to everlasting upon them that fear him, and his righteousness unto children's children;

To such as keep his covenant, and to those that remember his commandments to do them.

The LORD hath prepared his throne in the heavens;

And his kingdom ruleth over all.

Bless the LORD, ye his angels, that excel in strength, that do his commandments, hearkening unto the voice of his word.

Bless ye the LORD, all ye his hosts; ye ministers of his, that do his pleasure.

Bless the LORD, all his works in all places of his dominion:

Bless the LORD, O my soul.

SELECTION 24

Psalms CXXI, XXVII, XXIII

I WILL lift up mine eyes unto the hills, from whence cometh my help.

My help cometh from the LORD, which made heaven and earth.

He will not suffer thy foot to be moved: he that keepeth thee will not slumber.

Behold, he that keepeth Israel shall neither slumber nor sleep.

The LORD is thy keeper: the LORD is thy shade upon thy right hand.

The sun shall not smite thee by day, nor the moon by night.

The LORD shall preserve thee from all evil: he shall preserve thy soul.

The LORD shall preserve thy going out and thy coming in from this time forth, and even for evermore.

The LORD is my light and my salvation; whom shall I fear?

The LORD is the strength of my life; of whom shall I be afraid?

When the wicked, even mine enemies and my foes, came upon me to eat up my flesh, they stumbled and fell.

Though a host should encamp against me, my heart shall not fear: though war should rise against me, in this will I be confident.

One thing have I desired of the LORD, that will I seek after; that I may dwell in the house of the LORD all the days of my life,

To behold the beauty of the LORD, and to inquire in his temple.

For in the time of trouble he shall hide me in his pavilion:

In the secret of his tabernacle shall he hide me; he shall set me up upon a rock.

And now shall mine head be lifted up above mine enemies round about me: therefore will I offer in his tabernacle sacrifices of joy;

I will sing, yea, I will sing praises unto the LORD.

Hear, O LORD, when I cry with my voice: have mercy also upon me, and answer me.

When thou saidst, Seek ye my face; my heart said unto thee, Thy face, LORD, will I seek.

Hide not thy face far from me; put not thy servant away in anger: thou hast been my help; leave me not, neither forsake me, O God of my salvation.

When my father and my mother forsake me, then the LORD will take me up.

Teach me thy way, O LORD, and lead me in a plain path, because of mine enemies.

Deliver me not over unto the will of mine enemies: for false witnesses are risen up against me, and such as breathe out cruelty.

I had fainted, unless I had believed to see the goodness of the LORD in the land of the living.

Wait on the LORD: be of good courage, and he shall strengthen thine heart: wait, I say, on the LORD.

The LORD is my shepherd; I shall not want. He maketh me to lie down in green pastures: he leadeth me beside the still waters.

He restoreth my soul: he leadeth me in the paths of righteousness for his name's sake.

Yea, though I walk through the valley of the shadow of death, I will fear no evil:

For thou art with me; thy rod and thy staff they comfort me.

Thou preparest a table before me in the presence of mine enemies:

Thou anointest my head with oil; my cup runneth over.

Surely goodness and mercy shall follow me all the days of my life:

And I will dwell in the house of the LORD for ever.

SELECTION 25

Psalm CXXXIX

O LORD, thou hast searched me, and known me.

Thou knowest my downsitting and mine uprising; thou understandest my thought afar off.

Thou compassest my path and my lying down, and art acquainted with all my ways.

For there is not a word in my tongue, but, lo, O LORD, thou knowest it altogether.

Thou hast beset me behind and before, and laid thine hand upon me.

Such knowledge is too wonderful for me: it is high, I cannot attain unto it.

Whither shall I go from thy Spirit? or whither shall I flee from thy presence?

If I ascend up into heaven, thou art there: if I make my bed in hell, behold, thou art there.

If I take the wings of the morning, and dwell in the uttermost parts of the sea;

Even there shall thy hand lead me, and thy right hand shall hold me.

If I say, Surely the darkness shall cover me; even the night shall be light about me.

Yea, the darkness hideth not from thee; but the night shineth as the day: the darkness and the light are both alike to thee.

For thou hast possessed my reins: thou hast covered me in my mother's womb.

I will praise thee; for I am fearfully and wonderfully made: marvellous are thy works; and that my soul knoweth right well.

My substance was not hid from thee, when I was made in secret, and curiously wrought in the lowest parts of the earth.

Thine eyes did see my substance, yet being unperfect; and in thy book all my members were written, which in continuance were fashioned, when as yet there was none of them.

How precious also are thy thoughts unto me, O God! how great is the sum of them!

If I should count them, they are more in number than the sand: when I awake, I am still with thee.

Surely thou wilt slay the wicked, O God: depart from me therefore, ye bloody men.

For they speak against thee wickedly, and thine enemies take thy name in vain.

Do not I hate them, O LORD, that hate thee? and am not I grieved with those that rise up against thee?

I hate them with perfect hatred: I count them mine enemies.

Search me, O God, and know my heart: try me, and know my thoughts:

And see if there be any wicked way in me, and lead me in the way everlasting.

SELECTION 26

Psalms XXXIII, CVIII

REJOICE in the LORD, O ye righteous: for praise is comely for the upright.

Praise the LORD with harp: sing unto him with the psaltery and an instrument of ten strings.

Sing unto him a new song; play skilfully with a loud noise.

For the word of the LORD is right; and all his works are done in truth.

He loveth righteousness and judgment:

The earth is full of the goodness of the LORD.

By the word of the LORD were the heavens made; and all the host of them by the breath of his mouth.

He gathereth the waters of the sea together as a heap: he layeth up the depth in storehouses.

Let all the earth fear the LORD: let all the inhabitants of the world stand in awe of him.

For he spake, and it was done; he commanded, and it stood fast.

The LORD bringeth the counsel of the heathen to nought: he maketh the devices of the people of none effect.

The counsel of the LORD standeth for ever, the thoughts of his heart to all generations.

Blessed is the nation whose God is the LORD;

And the people whom he hath chosen for his own inheritance.

The LORD looketh from heaven; he beholdeth all the sons of men: from the place of his habitation he looketh upon all the inhabitants of the earth.

He fashioneth their hearts alike; he considereth all their works.

There is no king saved by the multitude of a host: a mighty man is not delivered by much strength.

A horse is a vain thing for safety: neither shall he deliver any by his great strength.

Behold, the eye of the LORD is upon them that fear him, upon them that hope in his mercy; to deliver their soul from death, and to keep them alive in famine.

Our soul waiteth for the LORD: he is our help and our shield.

For our heart shall rejoice in him, because we have trusted in his holy name.

Let thy mercy, O LORD, be upon us, according as we hope in thee.

O God, my heart is fixed; I will sing and give praise, even with my glory.

Awake, psaltery and harp: I myself will awake early.

I will praise thee, O LORD, among the people: and I will sing praises unto thee among the nations.

For thy mercy is great above the heavens: and thy truth reacheth unto the clouds.

Be thou exalted, O God, above the heavens:

And thy glory above all the earth.

SELECTION 27

Psalm CVII.

O GIVE thanks unto the LORD, for he is good:

For his mercy endureth for ever.

Let the redeemed of the LORD say so, whom he hath redeemed from the hand of the enemy;

And gathered them out of the lands, from the east, and from the west, from the north, and from the south.

They wandered in the wilderness in a solitary way; they found no city to dwell in.

Hungry and thirsty, their soul fainted in them.

Then they cried unto the LORD in their trouble, and he delivered them out of their distresses.

And he led them forth by the right way, that they might go to a city of habitation.

Oh that men would praise the LORD for his goodness, and for his wonderful works to the children of men!

For he satisfieth the longing soul, and filleth the hungry soul with goodness.

Such as sit in darkness and in the shadow of death, being bound in affliction and iron; because they rebelled against the words of God, and contemned the counsel of the Most High:

Therefore he brought down their heart with labour; they fell down, and there was none to help.

Then they cried unto the LORD in their trouble, and he saved them out of their distresses.

He brought them out of darkness and the shadow of death, and brake their bands in sunder.

Oh that men would praise the LORD for his goodness, and for his wonderful works to the children of men!

For he hath broken the gates of brass, and cut the bars of iron in sunder.

Fools, because of their transgression, and because of their iniquities, are afflicted.

Their soul abhorreth all manner of meat; and they draw near unto the gates of death.

Then they cry unto the LORD in their trouble, and he saveth them out of their distresses.

He sent his word, and healed them, and delivered them from their destructions.

Oh that men would praise the LORD for his goodness, and for his wonderful works to the children of men!

And let them sacrifice the sacrifices of thanksgiving, and declare his works with rejoicing.

They that go down to the sea in ships, that do business in great waters; these see the works of the LORD, and his wonders in the deep.

For he commandeth, and raiseth the stormy wind, which lifteth up the waves thereof.

They mount up to the heaven, they go down again to the depths: their soul is melted because of trouble.

They reel to and fro, and stagger like a drunken man, and are at their wit's end.

Then they cry unto the LORD in their trouble, and he bringeth them out of their distresses.

He maketh the storm a calm, so that the waves thereof are still. Then are they glad because they be quiet; so he bringeth them unto their desired haven.

Oh that men would praise the LORD for his goodness, and for his wonderful works to the children of men!

Let them exalt him also in the congregation of the people, and praise him in the assembly of the elders.

He turneth rivers into a wilderness, and the watersprings into dry ground;

A fruitful land into barrenness, for the wickedness of them that dwell therein.

He turneth the wilderness into a standing water, and dry ground into watersprings.

And there he maketh the hungry to dwell, that they may prepare a city for habitation; and sow the fields, and plant vineyards, which may yield fruits of increase.

He blesseth them also, so that they are multiplied greatly; and suffereth not their cattle to decrease.

Again, they are minished and brought low through oppression, affliction, and sorrow.

He poureth contempt upon princes, and causeth them to wander in the wilderness, where there is no way.

Yet setteth he the poor on high from affliction, and maketh him families like a flock.

The righteous shall see it, and rejoice: and all iniquity shall stop her mouth.

Whoso is wise, and will observe these things, even they shall understand the lovingkindness of the LORD.

SELECTION 28

Psalms XCII, CXXIII, CXLII

IT is a good thing to give thanks unto the LORD, and to sing praises unto thy name, O Most High:

To shew forth thy lovingkindness in the morning, and thy faithfulness every night,

Upon an instrument of ten strings, and upon the psaltery; upon the harp with a solemn sound.

For thou, LORD, hast made me glad through thy work: I will triumph in the works of thy hands.

O LORD, how great are thy works! and thy thoughts are very deep.

A brutish man knoweth not; neither doth a fool understand this.

When the wicked spring as the grass, and when all the workers of iniquity do flourish; it is that they shall be destroyed for ever:

But thou, LORD, art most high for evermore.

For, lo, thine enemies, O LORD, for, lo, thine enemies shall perish;

All the workers of iniquity shall be scattered.

But my horn shalt thou exalt like the horn of a unicorn: I shall be anointed with fresh oil.

Mine eye also shall see my desire on mine enemies, and mine ears shall hear my desire of the wicked that rise up against me.

The righteous shall flourish like the palm tree: he shall grow like a cedar in Lebanon.

Those that be planted in the house of the LORD shall flourish in the courts of our God.

They shall still bring forth fruit in old age; they shall be fat and flourishing;

To shew that the LORD is upright: he is my rock, and there is no unrighteousness in him.

Unto thee lift I up mine eyes, O thou that dwellest in the heavens.

Behold, as the eyes of servants look unto the hand of their masters, and as the eyes of a maiden unto the hand of her mistress; so our eyes wait upon the LORD our God, until that he have mercy upon us.

Have mercy upon us, O LORD, have mercy upon us: for we are exceedingly filled with contempt.

Our soul is exceedingly filled with the scorning of those that are at ease, and with the contempt of the proud.

I cried unto the LORD with my voice; with my voice unto the LORD did I make my supplication.

I poured out my complaint before him; I shewed before him my trouble.

When my spirit was overwhelmed within me, then thou knewest my path.

In the way wherein I walked have they privily laid a snare for me.

I looked on my right hand, and beheld, but there was no man that would know me:

Refuge failed me; no man cared for my soul.

I cried unto thee, O LORD: I said, Thou art my refuge and my portion in the land of the living.

Attend unto my cry; for I am brought very low: deliver me from my persecutors; for they are stronger than I.

Bring my soul out of prison, that I may praise thy name:

The righteous shall compass me about; for thou shalt deal bountifully with me.

SELECTION 29

Psalm LXXIII

TRULY God is good to Israel, even to such as are of a clean heart.

But as for me, my feet were almost gone; my steps had well nigh slipped.

For I was envious at the foolish, when I saw the prosperity of the wicked.

For there are no bands in their death: but their strength is firm.

They are not in trouble as other men; neither are they plagued like other men.

Therefore pride compasseth them about as a chain; violence covereth them as a garment.

Their eyes stand out with fatness: they have more than heart could wish.

They are corrupt, and speak wickedly concerning oppression: they speak loftily.

They set their mouth against the heavens, and their tongue walketh through the earth.

Therefore his people return hither: and waters of a full cup are wrung out to them.

And they say, How doth God know? and is there knowledge in the Most High?

Behold, these are the ungodly, who prosper in the world; they increase in riches.

Verily I have cleansed my heart in vain, and washed my hands in innocency.

For all the day long have I been plagued, and chastened every morning.

If I say, I will speak thus; behold, I should offend against the generation of thy children.

When I thought to know this, it was too painful for me;

Until I went into the sanctuary of God; then understood I their end.

Surely thou didst set them in slippery places: thou castedst them down into destruction.

How are they brought into desolation, as in a moment! they are utterly consumed with terrors.

As a dream when one awaketh; so, O Lord, when thou awakest, thou shalt despise their image.

Thus my heart was grieved, and I was pricked in my reins.

So foolish was I, and ignorant: I was as a beast before thee.

Nevertheless I am continually with thee: thou hast holden me by my right hand.

Thou shalt guide me with thy counsel, and afterward receive me to glory.

Whom have I in heaven but thee? and there is none upon earth that I desire besides thee.

My flesh and my heart faileth: but God is the strength of my heart, and my portion for ever.

SELECTION 30

Psalms I, XV, XXVI

BLESSED is the man that walketh not in the counsel of the ungodly, nor standeth in the way of sinners, nor sitteth in the seat of the scornful.

But his delight is in the law of the LORD; and in his law doth he meditate day and night.

And he shall be like a tree planted by the rivers of water, that bringeth forth his fruit in his season;

His leaf also shall not wither; and whatsoever he doeth shall prosper.

The ungodly are not so: but are like the chaff which the wind driveth away.

Therefore the ungodly shall not stand in the judgment, nor sinners in the congregation of the righteous.

For the LORD knoweth the way of the righteous:

But the way of the ungodly shall perish.

LORD, who shall abide in thy tabernacle? who shall dwell in thy holy hill?

He that walketh uprightly, and worketh righteousness, and speaketh the truth in his heart.

He that backbiteth not with his tongue, nor doeth evil to his neighbour, nor taketh up a reproach against his neighbour.

In whose eyes a vile person is contemned; but he honoureth them that fear the LORD.

He that sweareth to his own hurt, and changeth not. He that putteth not out his money to usury, nor taketh reward against the innocent.

He that doeth these things shall never be moved.

Judge me, O LORD; for I have walked in mine integrity:

I have trusted also in the LORD; therefore I shall not slide.

Examine me, O LORD, and prove me; try my reins and my heart.

For thy lovingkindness is before mine eyes: and I have walked in thy truth.

I have not sat with vain persons, neither will I go in with dissemblers.

I have hated the congregation of evil doers; and will not sit with the wicked.

I will wash mine hands in innocency: so will I compass thine altar, O LORD:

That I may publish with the voice of thanksgiving, and tell of all thy wondrous works.

LORD, I have loved the habitation of thy house, and the place where thine honour dwelleth.

Gather not my soul with sinners, nor my life with bloody men:

In whose hands is mischief, and their right hand is full of bribes.

But as for me, I will walk in mine integrity: redeem me, and be merciful unto me.

My foot standeth in an even place:

In the congregations will I bless the LORD.

SELECTION 31

Psalm xxxvii

FRET not thyself because of evil doers, neither be thou envious against the workers of iniquity.

For they shall soon be cut down like the grass, and wither as the green herb.

Trust in the LORD, and do good; so shalt thou dwell in the land, and verily thou shalt be fed.

Delight thyself also in the LORD; and he shall give thee the desires of thine heart.

Commit thy way unto the LORD; trust also in him; and he shall bring it to pass.

And he shall bring forth thy righteousness as the light, and thy judgment as the noonday.

Rest in the LORD, and wait patiently for him:

Fret not thyself because of him who prospereth in his way, because of the man who bringeth wicked devices to pass.

Cease from anger, and forsake wrath: fret not thyself in any wise to do evil.

For evil doers shall be cut off: but those that wait upon the LORD, they shall inherit the earth.

For yet a little while, and the wicked shall not be: yea, thou shalt diligently consider his place, and it shall not be.

But the meek shall inherit the earth; and shall delight themselves in the abundance of peace.

The wicked plotteth against the just, and gnasheth upon him with his teeth.

The Lord shall laugh at him: for he seeth that his day is coming.

The wicked have drawn out the sword, and have bent their bow, to cast down the poor and needy, and to slay such as be of upright conversation.

Their sword shall enter into their own heart, and their bows shall be broken.

A little that a righteous man hath is better than the riches of many wicked.

For the arms of the wicked shall be broken: but the LORD upholdeth the righteous.

The LORD knoweth the days of the upright: and their inheritance shall be for ever.

They shall not be ashamed in the evil time: and in the days of famine they shall be satisfied.

But the wicked shall perish, and the enemies of the LORD shall be as the fat of lambs:

They shall consume; into smoke shall they consume away.

The wicked borroweth, and payeth not again: but the righteous sheweth mercy, and giveth.

For such as be blessed of him shall inherit the earth; and they that be cursed of him shall be cut off.

The steps of a good man are ordered by the LORD: and he delighteth in his way.

Though he fall, he shall not be utterly cast down: for the LORD upholdeth him with his hand.

I have been young, and now am old; yet have I not seen the righteous forsaken, nor his seed begging bread.

He is ever merciful, and lendeth; and his seed is blessed.

Depart from evil, and do good; and dwell for evermore.

For the LORD loveth judgment, and forsaketh not his saints;

They are preserved for ever: but the seed of the wicked shall be cut off.

The righteous shall inherit the land, and dwell therein for ever.

The mouth of the righteous speaketh wisdom, and his tongue talketh of judgment.

The law of his God is in his heart; none of his steps shall slide.

The wicked watcheth the righteous, and seeketh to slay him.

The LORD will not leave him in his hand, nor condemn him when he is judged.

Wait on the LORD, and keep his way, and he shall exalt thee to inherit the land:

When the wicked are cut off, thou shalt see it.

I have seen the wicked in great power, and spreading himself like a green bay tree.

Yet he passed away, and, lo, he was not: yea, I sought him, but he could not be found.

Mark the perfect man, and behold the upright: for the end of that man is peace.

But the transgressors shall be destroyed together: the end of the wicked shall be cut off.

But the salvation of the righteous is of the LORD: he is their strength in the time of trouble.

And the LORD shall help them, and deliver them: he shall deliver them from the wicked, and save them, because they trust in him.

SELECTION 32

Psalms LXXXI, L

SING aloud unto God our strength: make a joyful noise unto the God of Jacob.

Take a psalm, and bring hither the timbrel, the pleasant harp with the psaltery.

Blow up the trumpet in the new moon, in the time appointed, on our solemn feast day.

For this was a statute for Israel, and a law of the God of Jacob.

This he ordained in Joseph for a testimony, when he went out through the land of Egypt: where I heard a language that I understood not.

I removed his shoulder from the burden: his hands were delivered from the pots.

Thou calledst in trouble, and I delivered thee;

I answered thee in the secret place of thunder: I proved thee at the waters of Meribah.

Hear, O my people, and I will testify unto thee:

O Israel, if thou wilt hearken unto me; there shall no strange god be in thee; neither shalt thou worship any strange god.

I am the LORD thy God, which brought thee out of the land of Egypt:

Open thy mouth wide, and I will fill it.

But my people would not hearken to my voice; and Israel would none of me.

So I gave them up unto their own hearts' lust: and they walked in their own counsels.

Oh that my people had hearkened unto me, and Israel had walked in my ways!

I should soon have subdued their enemies, and turned my hand against their adversaries.

The haters of the LORD should have submitted themselves unto him: but their time should have endured for ever.

He should have fed them also with the finest of the wheat: and with honey out of the rock should I have satisfied thee.

The mighty God, even the LORD, hath spoken, and called the earth from the rising of the sun unto the going down thereof.

Out of Zion, the perfection of beauty, God hath shined.

Our God shall come, and shall not keep silence: a fire shall devour before him, and it shall be very tempestuous round about him.

He shall call to the heavens from above, and to the earth, that he may judge his people.

Gather my saints together unto me; those that have made a covenant with me by sacrifice.

And the heavens shall declare his righteousness: for God is judge himself.

Hear, O my people, and I will speak; O Israel, and I will testify against thee:

I am God, even thy God.

I will not reprove thee for thy sacrifices or thy burnt offerings, to have been continually before me.

I will take no bullock out of thy house nor he goats out of thy folds:

For every beast of the forest is mine, and the cattle upon a thousand hills.

I know all the fowls of the mountains: and the wild beasts of the field are mine.

If I were hungry, I would not tell thee; for the world is mine, and the fulness thereof.

Will I eat the flesh of bulls, or drink the blood of goats?

Offer unto God thanksgiving; and pay thy vows unto the Most High: and call upon me in the day of trouble:

I will deliver thee, and thou shalt glorify me.

SELECTION 33

Psalms XIX, CXIX

THE heavens declare the glory of God; and the firmament sheweth his handywork.

Day unto day uttereth speech, and night unto night sheweth knowledge.

There is no speech nor language, where their voice is not heard.

Their line is gone out through all the earth, and their words to the end of the world.

In them hath he set a tabernacle for the sun, which is as a bridegroom coming out of his chamber, and rejoiceth as a strong man to run a race.

His going forth is from the end of the heaven, and his circuit unto the ends of it: and there is nothing hid from the heat thereof.

The law of the LORD is perfect, converting the soul:

The testimony of the LORD is sure, making wise the simple.

The statutes of the LORD are right, rejoicing the heart:

The commandment of the LORD is pure, enlightening the eyes.

The fear of the LORD is clean, enduring for ever: the judgments of the LORD are true and righteous altogether.

More to be desired are they than gold, yea, than much fine gold: sweeter also than honey and the honeycomb.

Moreover by them is thy servant warned:

And in keeping of them there is great reward.

Who can understand his errors? cleanse thou me from secret faults.

Keep back thy servant also from presumptuous sins; let them not have dominion over me:

Then shall I be upright, and I shall be innocent from the great transgression.

Let the words of my mouth, and the meditation of my heart, be acceptable in thy sight, O LORD, my strength, and my redeemer.

For ever, O LORD, thy word is settled in heaven.

Thy faithfulness is unto all generations: thou hast established the earth, and it abideth.

They continue this day according to thine ordinances: for all are thy servants.

Unless thy law had been my delights, I should then have perished in mine affliction.

I will never forget thy precepts: for with them thou hast quickened me.

I am thine, save me; for I have sought thy precepts.

The wicked have waited for me to destroy me: but I will consider thy testimonies.

I have seen an end of all perfection: but thy commandment is exceeding broad.

Thy word is a lamp unto my feet, and a light unto my path.

I have sworn, and I will perform it, that I will keep thy righteous judgments.

I am afflicted very much: quicken me, O LORD, according unto thy word.

Accept, I beseech thee, the freewill offerings of my mouth, O LORD, and teach me thy judgments.

My soul is continually in my hand: yet do I not forget thy law.

The wicked have laid a snare for me: yet I erred not from thy precepts.

Thy testimonies have I taken as a heritage for ever: for they are the rejoicing of my heart.

I have inclined mine heart to perform thy statutes always, even unto the end.

SELECTION 34

Psalm CXIX

BLESSED are the undefiled in the way, who walk in the law of the LORD.

Blessed are they that keep his testimonies, and that seek him with the whole heart.

They also do no iniquity: they walk in his ways.

Thou hast commanded us to keep thy precepts diligently.

O that my ways were directed to keep thy statutes!

Then shall I not be ashamed, when I have respect unto all thy commandments.

I will praise thee with uprightness of heart, when I shall have learned thy righteous judgments.

I will keep thy statutes: O forsake me not utterly.

Wherewithal shall a young man cleanse his way? by taking heed thereto according to thy word.

With my whole heart have I sought thee: O let me not wander from thy commandments.

Thy word have I hid in mine heart, that I might not sin against thee.

Blessed art thou, O LORD: teach me thy statutes.

With my lips have I declared all the judgments of thy mouth.

I have rejoiced in the way of thy testimonies, as much as in all riches.

I will meditate in thy precepts, and have respect unto thy ways.

I will delight myself in thy statutes: I will not forget thy word.

Teach me, O LORD, the way of thy statutes; and I shall keep it unto the end.

Give me understanding, and I shall keep thy law; yea, I shall observe it with my whole heart.

Make me to go in the path of thy commandments; for therein do I delight.

Incline my heart unto thy testimonies, and not to covetousness.

Turn away mine eyes from beholding vanity; and quicken thou me in thy way.

Stablish thy word unto thy servant, who is devoted to thy fear.

Turn away my reproach which I fear: for thy judgments are good.

Behold, I have longed after thy precepts: quicken me in thy righteousness.

Let thy mercies come also unto me, O LORD, even thy salvation, according to thy word.

So shall I have wherewith to answer him that reproacheth me: for I trust in thy word.

And take not the word of truth utterly out of my mouth; for I have hoped in thy judgments.

So shall I keep thy law continually for ever and ever.

And I will walk at liberty: for I seek thy precepts.

I will speak of thy testimonies also before kings, and will not be ashamed.

And I will delight myself in thy commandments, which I have loved.

My hands also will I lift up unto thy commandments, which I have loved; and I will meditate in thy statutes.

SELECTION 35

Psalms XII, X, XIV

HELP, LORD; for the godly man ceaseth; for the faithful fail from among the children of men.

They speak vanity every one with his neighbour: with flattering lips and with a double heart do they speak.

The LORD shall cut off all flattering lips, and the tongue that speaketh proud things:

Who have said, With our tongue will we prevail; our lips are our own: who is lord over us?

For the oppression of the poor, for the sighing of the needy, now will I arise, saith the LORD; I will set him in safety from him that puffeth at him.

The words of the LORD are pure words: as silver tried in a furnace of earth, purified seven times.

Thou shalt keep them, O LORD, thou shalt preserve them from this generation for ever.

The wicked walk on every side, when the vilest men are exalted.

Why standest thou afar off, O LORD? why hidest thou thyself in times of trouble?

The wicked in his pride doth persecute the poor: let them be taken in the devices that they have imagined.

For the wicked boasteth of his heart's desire, and blesseth the covetous, whom the LORD abhorreth.

The wicked, through the pride of his countenance, will not seek after God: God is not in all his thoughts.

His ways are always grievous; thy judgments are far above out of his sight: as for all his enemies, he puffeth at them.

He hath said in his heart, I shall not be moved: for I shall never be in adversity.

His mouth is full of cursing and deceit and fraud: under his tongue is mischief and vanity.

He sitteth in the lurking places of the villages: in the secret places doth he murder the innocent: his eyes are privily set against the poor.

He lieth in wait secretly as a lion in his den: he lieth in wait to catch the poor: he doth catch the poor, when he draweth him into his net.

He croucheth, and humbleth himself, that the poor may fall by his strong ones.

He hath said in his heart, God hath forgotten: he hideth his face; he will never see it.

Arise, O LORD; O God, lift up thine hand: forget not the humble.

Wherefore doth the wicked contemn God? he hath said in his heart, Thou wilt not require it.

Thou hast seen it; for thou beholdest mischief and spite, to requite it with thy hand: the poor committeth himself unto thee; thou art the helper of the fatherless.

LORD, thou hast heard the desire of the humble; thou wilt prepare their heart, thou wilt cause thine ear to hear:

To judge the fatherless and the oppressed, that the man of the earth may no more oppress.

The fool hath said in his heart, There is no God. They are corrupt, they have done abominable works, there is none that doeth good.

The LORD looked down from heaven upon the children of men, to see if there were any that did understand, and seek God.

They are all gone aside, they are all together become filthy: there is none that doeth good, no, not one.

Have all the workers of iniquity no knowledge? who eat up my people as they eat bread, and call not upon the LORD.

There were they in great fear: for God is in the generation of the righteous.

Ye have shamed the counsel of the poor, because the LORD is his refuge.

Oh that the salvation of Israel were come out of Zion!

When the LORD bringeth back the captivity of his people, Jacob shall rejoice, and Israel shall be glad.

SELECTION 36

Psalms LI, CXXX

HAVE mercy upon me, O God, according to thy lovingkindness:

According unto the multitude of thy tender mercies blot out my transgressions.

Wash me thoroughly from mine iniquity, and cleanse me from my sin.

For I acknowledge my transgressions: and my sin is ever before me.

Against thee, thee only, have I sinned, and done this evil in thy sight:

That thou mightest be justified when thou speakest, and be clear when thou judgest.

Behold, I was shapen in iniquity; and in sin did my mother conceive me.

Behold, thou desirest truth in the inward parts: and in the hidden part thou shalt make me to know wisdom.

Purge me with hyssop, and I shall be clean:

Wash me, and I shall be whiter than snow.

Make me to hear joy and gladness; that the bones which thou hast broken may rejoice.

Hide thy face from my sins, and blot out all mine iniquities.

Create in me a clean heart, O God; and renew a right spirit within me.

Cast me not away from thy presence; and take not thy Holy Spirit from me.

Restore unto me the joy of thy salvation; and uphold me with thy free Spirit.

Then will I teach transgressors thy ways; and sinners shall be converted unto thee.

Deliver me from bloodguiltiness, O God, thou God of my salvation:

And my tongue shall sing aloud of thy righteousness.

O Lord, open thou my lips;

And my mouth shall shew forth thy praise.

For thou desirest not sacrifice; else would I give it: thou delightest not in burnt offering.

The sacrifices of God are a broken spirit: a broken and a contrite heart, O God, thou wilt not despise.

Do good in thy good pleasure unto Zion: build thou the walls of Jerusalem.

Then shalt thou be pleased with the sacrifices of righteousness, with burnt offering and whole burnt offering: then shall they offer bullocks upon thine altar.

Out of the depths have I cried unto thee, O LORD.

Lord, hear my voice: let thine ears be attentive to the voice of my supplications.

If thou, LORD, shouldest mark iniquities, O Lord, who shall stand?

But there is forgiveness with thee, that thou mayest be feared.

I wait for the LORD, my soul doth wait, and in his word do I hope.

My soul waiteth for the Lord more than they that watch for the morning: I say,

more than they that watch for the morning.

Let Israel hope in the LORD: for with the LORD there is mercy, and with him is plenteous redemption.

And he shall redeem Israel from all his iniquities.

SELECTION 37

Psalms XIII, VI, XXVIII

HOW long wilt thou forget me, O LORD? for ever? how long wilt thou hide thy face from me?

How long shall I take counsel in my soul, having sorrow in my heart daily? how long shall mine enemy be exalted over me?

Consider and hear me, O LORD my God: lighten mine eyes, lest I sleep the sleep of death;

Lest mine enemy say, I have prevailed against him; and those that trouble me rejoice when I am moved.

But I have trusted in thy mercy; my heart shall rejoice in thy salvation.

I will sing unto the LORD, because he hath dealt bountifully with me.

O LORD, rebuke me not in thine anger, neither chasten me in thy hot displeasure.

Have mercy upon me, O LORD; for I am weak: O LORD, heal me; for my bones are vexed.

My soul is also sore vexed: but thou, O LORD, how long?

Return, O LORD, deliver my soul: oh save me for thy mercies' sake.

For in death there is no remembrance of thee:

In the grave who shall give thee thanks?

I am weary with my groaning; all the night make I my bed to swim; I water my couch with my tears.

Mine eye is consumed because of grief; it waxeth old because of all mine enemies.

Depart from me, all ye workers of iniquity; for the LORD hath heard the voice of my weeping.

The LORD hath heard my supplication; the LORD will receive my prayer.

Unto thee will I cry, O LORD my rock; be not silent to me: lest, if thou be silent to me, I become like them that go down into the pit.

Hear the voice of my supplications, when I cry unto thee, when I lift up my hands toward thy holy oracle.

Draw me not away with the wicked, and with the workers of iniquity, which speak peace to their neighbours, but mischief is in their hearts.

Because they regard not the works of the LORD, nor the operation of his hands, he shall destroy them, and not build them up.

Blessed be the LORD, because he hath heard the voice of my supplications.

The LORD is my strength and my shield; my heart trusted in him, and I am helped:

Therefore my heart greatly rejoiceth; and with my song will I praise him.

The LORD is their strength, and he is the saving strength of his anointed.

Save thy people, and bless thine inheritance:

Feed them also, and lift them up for ever.

SELECTION 38

Psalms XXII, XXXI

MY God, my God, why hast thou forsaken me? why art thou so far from helping me, and from the words of my roaring?

O my God, I cry in the daytime, but thou hearest not; and in the night season, and am not silent.

But thou art holy, O thou that inhabitest the praises of Israel.

Our fathers trusted in thee: they trusted, and thou didst deliver them.

They cried unto thee, and were delivered:

They trusted in thee, and were not confounded.

But I am a worm, and no man; a reproach of men, and despised of the people. All they that see me laugh me to scorn:

They shoot out the lip, they shake the head, saying, he trusted on the LORD that he would deliver him: let him deliver him, seeing he delighted in him.

Many bulls have compassed me: strong bulls of Bashan have beset me round.

They gaped upon me with their mouths, as a ravening and a roaring lion.

I am poured out like water, and all my bones are out of joint: my heart is like wax; it is melted in the midst of my bowels.

My strength is dried up like a potsherd; and my tongue cleaveth to my jaws; and thou hast brought me into the dust of death.

For dogs have compassed me: the assembly of the wicked have inclosed me: they pierced my hands and my feet.

I may tell all my bones: they look and stare upon me.

They part my garments among them, and cast lots upon my vesture.

But be not thou far from me, O LORD: O my strength, haste thee to help me.

In thee, O LORD, do I put my trust; let me never be ashamed: deliver me in thy righteousness.

Bow down thine ear to me; deliver me speedily: be thou my strong rock, for a house of defence to save me.

For thou art my rock and my fortress; therefore for thy name's sake lead me, and guide me.

Pull me out of the net that they have laid privily for me: for thou art my strength.

Into thine hand I commit my spirit: thou hast redeemed me, O LORD God of truth.

I have hated them that regard lying vanities: but I trust in the LORD.

I was a reproach among all mine enemies, but especially among my neighbours, and a fear to mine acquaintance: they that did see me without fled from me.

I am forgotten as a dead man out of mind: I am like a broken vessel.

For I have heard the slander of many: fear was on every side: while they took counsel together against me, they devised to take away my life.

But I trusted in thee, O LORD: I said, Thou art my God.

My times are in thy hand: deliver me from the hand of mine enemies, and from them that persecute me.

Make thy face to shine upon thy servant: save me for thy mercies' sake.

Let me not be ashamed, O LORD; for I have called upon thee: let the wicked be ashamed, and let them be silent in the grave.

Let the lying lips be put to silence; which speak grievous things proudly and contemptuousiy against the righteous.

Oh how great is thy goodness, which thou hast laid up for them that fear thee;

Which thou hast wrought for them that trust in thee before the sons of men!

Thou shalt hide them in the secret of thy presence from the pride of man:

Thou shalt keep them secretly in a pavilion from the strife of tongues.

Blessed be the LORD: for he hath shewed me his marvellous kindness in a strong city.

For I said in my haste, I am cut off from before thine eyes: nevertheless thou heardest the voice of my supplications when I cried unto thee.

O love the LORD, all ye his saints: for the LORD preserveth the faithful, and plentifully rewardeth the proud doer.

Be of good courage, and he shall strengthen your heart, all ye that hope in the LORD.

SELECTION 39

Psalms LXI, LXII, LXIII

HEAR my cry, O God; attend unto my prayer. From the end of the earth will I cry unto thee, when my heart is overwhelmed:

Lead me to the rock that is higher than I.

For thou hast been a shelter for me, and a strong tower from the enemy.

I will abide in thy tabernacle for ever: I will trust in the covert of thy wings.

For thou, O God, hast heard my vows: thou hast given me the heritage of those that fear thy name.

Thou wilt prolong the king's life: and his years as many generations.

He shall abide before God for ever: O prepare mercy and truth, which may preserve him.

So will I sing praise unto thy name for ever, that I may daily perform my vows.

Truly my soul waiteth upon God: from him cometh my salvation.

He only is my rock and my salvation; he is my defence; I shall not be greatly moved.

How long will ye imagine mischief against a man? ye shall be slain all of you: as a bowing wall shall ye be, and as a tottering fence.

They only consult to cast him down from his excellency: they delight in lies: they bless with their mouth, but they curse inwardly.

My soul, wait thou only upon God; for my expectation is from him.

He only is my rock and my salvation: he is my defence; I shall not be moved.

In God is my salvation and my glory: the rock of my strength, and my refuge, is in God.

Trust in him at all times; ye people, pour out your heart before him: God is a refuge for us.

Surely men of low degree are vanity, and men of high degree are a lie:

To be laid in the balance, they are altogether lighter than vanity.

Trust not in oppression, and become not vain in robbery:

If riches increase, set not your heart upon them.

God hath spoken once; twice have I heard this; that power belongeth unto God.

Also unto thee, O Lord, belongeth mercy: for thou renderest to every man according to his work.

O God, thou art my God; early will I seek thee: my soul thirsteth for thee, my flesh longeth for thee in a dry and thirsty land, where no water is;

To see thy power and thy glory, so as I have seen thee in the sanctuary.

Because thy lovingkindness is better than life, my lips shall praise thee.

Thus will I bless thee while I live: I will lift up my hands in thy name.

My soul shall be satisfied as with marrow and fatness; and my mouth shall praise thee with joyful lips:

When I remember thee upon my bed, and meditate on thee in the night watches.

Because thou hast been my help, therefore in the shadow of thy wings will I rejoice.

My soul followeth hard after thee: thy right hand upholdeth me.

But those that seek my soul, to destroy it, shall go into the lower parts of the earth.

They shall fall by the sword: they shall be a portion for foxes.

But the king shall rejoice in God; every one that sweareth by him shall glory:

But the mouth of them that speak lies shall be stopped.

SELECTION 40

Psalms IV, V, LVII

HEAR me when I call, O God of my righteousness: thou hast enlarged me when I was in distress;

Have mercy upon me, and hear my prayer.

O ye sons of men, how long will ye turn my glory into shame?

How long will ye love vanity, and seek after leasing?

But know that the LORD hath set apart him that is godly for himself:

The LORD will hear when I call unto him.

Stand in awe, and sin not: commune with your own heart upon your bed, and be still.

Offer the sacrifices of righteousness, **and put your trust in the LORD.**

There be many that say, Who will shew us any good?

LORD, lift thou up the light of thy countenance upon us.

Thou hast put gladness in my heart, more than in the time that their corn and their wine increased.

I will both lay me down in peace, and sleep: for thou, LORD, only makest me dwell in safety.

Give ear to my words, O LORD; consider my meditation.

Hearken unto the voice of my cry, my King, and my God: for unto thee will I pray.

My voice shalt thou hear in the morning, O LORD;

In the morning will I direct my prayer unto thee, and will look up.

For thou art not a God that hath pleasure in wickedness: neither shall evil dwell with thee.

The foolish shall not stand in thy sight: thou hatest all workers of iniquity.

Thou shalt destroy them that speak leasing:

The LORD will abhor the bloody and deceitful man.

But as for me, I will come into thy house in the multitude of thy mercy:

And in thy fear will I worship toward thy holy temple.

Lead me, O LORD, in thy righteousness because of mine enemies; make thy way straight before my face.

For thou, LORD, wilt bless the righteous; with favour wilt thou compass him as with a shield.

Be merciful unto me, O God: for man would swallow me up; he fighting daily oppresseth me.

Mine enemies would daily swallow me up: for they be many that fight against me, O thou Most High.

What time I am afraid, I will trust in thee.

In God I will praise his word, in God I have put my trust; I will not fear what flesh can do unto me.

Every day they wrest my words:

All their thoughts are against me for evil.

They gather themselves together, they hide themselves, they mark my steps, when they wait for my soul.

Shall they escape by iniquity? in thine anger cast down the people, O God.

Thou tellest my wanderings: put thou my tears into thy bottle: are they not in thy book?

When I cry unto thee, then shall mine enemies turn back: this I know; for God is for me.

In God will I praise his word: in the LORD will I praise his word.

In God have I put my trust: I will not be afraid what man can do unto me.

Thy vows are upon me, O God: I will render praises unto thee.

For thou hast delivered my soul from death: wilt not thou deliver my feet from falling, that I may walk before God in the light of the living?

SELECTION 41

Psalm CII

HEAR my prayer, O LORD, and let my cry come unto thee.

Hide not thy face from me in the day when I am in trouble; incline thine ear

unto me: in the day when I call answer me speedily.

For my days are consumed like smoke,

And my bones are burned as a hearth.

My heart is smitten, and withered like grass; so that I forget to eat my bread.

By reason of the voice of my groaning my bones cleave to my skin.

I am like a pelican of the wilderness: I am like an owl of the desert.

I watch, and am as a sparrow alone upon the housetop.

Mine enemies reproach me all the day;

And they that are mad against me are sworn against me.

For I have eaten ashes like bread, and mingled my drink with weeping,

Because of thine indignation and thy wrath: for thou hast lifted me up, and cast me down.

My days are like a shadow that declineth; and I am withered like grass.

But thou, O LORD, shalt endure for ever; and thy remembrance unto all generations.

Thou shalt arise, and have mercy upon Zion: for the time to favour her, yea, the set time, is come.

For thy servants take pleasure in her stones, and favour the dust thereof.

So the heathen shall fear the name of the LORD,

And all the kings of the earth thy glory.

When the LORD shall build up Zion, he shall appear in his glory.

He will regard the prayer of the destitute, and not despise their prayer.

This shall be written for the generation to come:

And the people which shall be created shall praise the LORD.

For he hath looked down from the height of his sanctuary; from heaven did the LORD behold the earth;

To hear the groaning of the prisoner; to loose those that are appointed to death;

To declare the name of the LORD in Zion, and his praise in Jerusalem;

When the people are gathered together, and the kingdoms, to serve the LORD.

He weakened my strength in the way; he shortened my days.

I said, O my God, take me not away in the midst of my days: thy years are throughout all generations.

Of old hast thou laid the foundation of the earth:

And the heavens are the work of thy hands.

They shall perish, but thou shalt endure: yea, all of them shall wax old like a garment;

As a vesture shalt thou change them, and they shall be changed:

But thou art the same, and thy years shall have no end.

The children of thy servants shall continue, and their seed shall be established before thee.

SELECTION 42

Psalms XXV, XXXII

UNTO thee, O LORD, do I lift up my soul.

O my God, I trust in thee:

Let me not be ashamed, let not mine enemies triumph over me.

Yea, let none that wait on thee be ashamed: let them be ashamed which transgress without cause.

Shew me thy ways, O LORD; teach me thy paths.

Lead me in thy truth and teach me: for thou art the God of my salvation; on thee do I wait all the day.

Remember, O LORD, thy tender mercies and thy lovingkindnesses; for they have been ever of old.

Remember not the sins of my youth, nor my transgressions: according to thy mercy remember thou me for thy goodness' sake, O LORD.

Good and upright is the LORD: therefore will he teach sinners in the way.

The meek will he guide in judgment: and the meek will he teach his way.

All the paths of the LORD are mercy and truth unto such as keep his covenant and his testimonies.

For thy name's sake, O LORD, pardon mine iniquity; for it is great.

What man is he that feareth the LORD? him shall he teach in the way that he shall choose.

His soul shall dwell at ease; and his seed shall inherit the earth.

The secret of the LORD is with them that fear him; and he will shew them his covenant.

Mine eyes are ever toward the LORD; for he shall pluck my feet out of the net.

Turn thee unto me, and have mercy upon me; for I am desolate and afflicted.

The troubles of my heart are enlarged:

O bring thou me out of my distresses.

Look upon mine affliction and my pain; and forgive all my sins.

Consider mine enemies; for they are many; and they hate me with cruel hatred.

O keep my soul, and deliver me: let me not be ashamed; for I put my trust in thee.

Let integrity and uprightness preserve me; for I wait on thee.

> Redeem Israel, O God, out of all his troubles.

Blessed is he whose transgression is forgiven, whose sin is covered.

> Blessed is the man unto whom the LORD imputeth not iniquity, and in whose spirit there is no guile.

When I kept silence, my bones waxed old through my roaring all the day long.

> For day and night thy hand was heavy upon me: my moisture is turned into the drought of summer.

I acknowledged my sin unto thee, and mine iniquity have I not hid.

> I said, I will confess my transgressions unto the LORD; and thou forgavest the iniquity of my sin.

For this shall every one that is godly pray unto thee in a time when thou mayest be found:

> Surely in the floods of great waters they shall not come nigh unto him.

Thou art my hiding place; thou shalt preserve me from trouble;

> Thou shalt compass me about with songs of deliverance.

I will instruct thee and teach thee in the way which thou shalt go:

> I will guide thee with mine eye.

Be ye not as the horse, or as the mule, which have no understanding:

> Whose mouth must be held in with bit and bridle, lest they come near unto thee.

Many sorrows shall be to the wicked: but he that trusteth in the LORD, mercy shall compass him about.

> Be glad in the LORD, and rejoice, ye righteous: and shout for joy, all ye that are upright in heart.

SELECTION 43

Psalms XVI, XVII

PRESERVE me, O God: for in thee do I put my trust. O my soul, thou hast said unto the LORD, Thou art my Lord:

> My goodness extendeth not to thee; but to the saints that are in the earth, and to the excellent, in whom is all my delight.

Their sorrows shall be multiplied that hasten after another god:

> Their drink offerings of blood will I not offer, nor take up their names into my lips.

The LORD is the portion of mine inheritance and of my cup: thou maintainest my lot.

> The lines are fallen unto me in pleasant places; yea, I have a goodly heritage.

I will bless the LORD, who hath given me counsel: my reins also instruct me in the night seasons.

> I have set the LORD always before me: because he is at my right hand, I shall not be moved.

Therefore my heart is glad, and my glory rejoiceth: my flesh also shall rest in hope.

> For thou wilt not leave my soul in hell; neither wilt thou suffer thine Holy One to see corruption.

Thou wilt shew me the path of life: in thy presence is fulness of joy;

> At thy right hand there are pleasures for evermore.

Hear the right, O LORD, attend unto my cry; give ear unto my prayer, that goeth not out of feigned lips.

> Let my sentence come forth from thy presence; let thine eyes behold the things that are equal.

Thou hast proved mine heart; thou hast visited me in the night; thou hast tried me, and shalt find nothing:

I am purposed that my mouth shall not transgress.

Concerning the works of men, by the word of thy lips I have kept me from the paths of the destroyer.

Hold up my goings in thy paths, that my footsteps slip not.

I have called upon thee, for thou wilt hear me, O God: incline thine ear unto me, and hear my speech.

Shew thy marvellous lovingkindness, O thou that savest by thy right hand them which put their trust in thee from those that rise up against them.

Keep me as the apple of the eye; hide me under the shadow of thy wings, from the wicked that oppress me, from my deadly enemies, who compass me about.

They are inclosed in their own fat: with their mouth they speak proudly.

They have now compassed us in our steps: they have set their eyes bowing down to the earth; like as a lion that is greedy of his prey, and as it were a young lion lurking in secret places.

Arise, O Lord, disappoint him, cast him down: deliver my soul from the wicked, which is thy sword:

From men which are thy hand, O Lord, from men of the world, which have their portion in this life, and whose belly thou fillest with thy hid treasure: they are full of children, and leave the rest of their substance to their babes.

As for me, I will behold thy face in righteousness: I shall be satisfied, when I awake, with thy likeness.

SELECTION 44

Psalms XL, CXLIII

I WAITED patiently for the Lord; and he inclined unto me, and heard my cry.

He brought me up also out of a horrible pit, out of the miry clay, and set my feet upon a rock, and established my goings.

And he hath put a new song in my mouth, even praise unto our God: many shall see it, and fear, and shall trust in the Lord.

Blessed is that man that maketh the Lord his trust, and respecteth not the proud, nor such as turn aside to lies.

Many, O Lord my God, are thy wonderful works which thou hast done, and thy thoughts which are to us-ward:

They cannot be reckoned up in order unto thee: if I would declare and speak of them, they are more than can be numbered.

Sacrifice and offering thou didst not desire; mine ears hast thou opened:

Burnt offering and sin offering hast thou not required.

Then said I, Lo, I come: in the volume of the book it is written of me:

I delight to do thy will, O my God: yea, thy law is within my heart.

I have preached righteousness in the great congregation:

Lo, I have not refrained my lips, O Lord, thou knowest.

I have not hid thy righteousness within my heart; I have declared thy faithfulness and thy salvation:

I have not concealed thy lovingkindness and thy truth from the great congregation.

Withhold not thou thy tender mercies from me, O Lord:

Let thy lovingkindness and thy truth continually preserve me.

For innumerable evils have compassed me about: mine iniquities have taken hold upon me, so that I am not able to look up; they are more than the hairs of mine head: therefore my heart faileth me.

Be pleased, O LORD, to deliver me: O LORD, make haste to help me.

Let them be ashamed and confounded together that seek after my soul to destroy it;

Let them be driven backward and put to shame that wish me evil.

Let them be desolate for a reward of their shame that say unto me, Aha, aha.

Let all those that seek thee rejoice and be glad in thee: let such as love thy salvation say continually, The LORD be magnified.

But I am poor and needy; yet the Lord thinketh upon me:

Thou art my help and my deliverer; make no tarrying, O my God.

Hear my prayer, O LORD, give ear to my supplications: in thy faithfulness answer me, and in thy righteousness.

And enter not into judgment with thy servant: for in thy sight shall no man living be justified.

For the enemy hath persecuted my soul; he hath smitten my life down to the ground; he hath made me to dwell in darkness, as those that have been long dead.

Therefore is my spirit overwhelmed within me; my heart within me is desolate.

I remember the days of old; I meditate on all thy works; I muse on the work of thy hands.

I stretch forth my hands unto thee: my soul thirsteth after thee, as a thirsty land.

Hear me speedily, O LORD; my spirit faileth:

Hide not thy face from me, lest I be like unto them that go down into the pit.

Cause me to hear thy lovingkindness in the morning; for in thee do I trust:

Cause me to know the way wherein I should walk; for I lift up my soul unto thee.

Deliver me, O LORD, from mine enemies: I flee unto thee to hide me.

Teach me to do thy will; for thou art my God: thy Spirit is good; lead me into the land of uprightness.

Quicken me, O LORD, for thy name's sake:

For thy righteousness' sake bring my soul out of trouble.

SELECTION 45

Psalm XVIII

I WILL love thee, O LORD, my strength. The LORD is my rock, and my fortress, and my deliverer;

My God, my strength, in whom I will trust; my buckler, and the horn of my salvation, and my high tower.

I will call upon the LORD, who is worthy to be praised:

So shall I be saved from mine enemies.

The sorrows of death compassed me, and the floods of ungodly men made me afraid.

The sorrows of hell compassed me about: the snares of death prevented me.

In my distress I called upon the LORD, and cried unto my God:

He heard my voice out of his temple, and my cry came before him, even into his ears.

He delivered me from my strong enemy, and from them which hated me: for they were too strong for me.

They prevented me in the day of my calamity: but the LORD was my stay.

He brought me forth also into a large place; he delivered me, because he delighted in me.

The LORD rewarded me according to my righteousness; according to the cleanness of my hands hath he recompensed me.

For I have kept the ways of the LORD, and have not wickedly departed from my God.

For all his judgments were before me, and I did not put away his statutes from me.

I was also upright before him, and I kept myself from mine iniquity.

Therefore hath the LORD recompensed me according to my righteousness, according to the cleanness of my hands in his eyesight.

With the merciful thou wilt shew thyself merciful; with an upright man thou wilt shew thyself upright;

With the pure thou wilt shew thyself pure; and with the froward thou wilt shew thyself froward.

For thou wilt save the afflicted people;

But wilt bring down high looks.

For thou wilt light my candle:

The LORD my God will enlighten my darkness.

For by thee I have run through a troop;

And by my God have I leaped over a wall.

As for God, his way is perfect: the word of the LORD is tried:

He is a buckler to all those that trust in him.

For who is God save the LORD? or who is a rock save our God?

It is God that girdeth me with strength, and maketh my way perfect.

He maketh my feet like hinds' feet, and setteth me upon my high places.

He teacheth my hands to war, so that a bow of steel is broken by mine arms.

Thou hast also given me the shield of thy salvation: and thy right hand hath holden me up, and thy gentleness hath made me great.

The LORD liveth; and blessed be my Rock; and let the God of my salvation be exalted.

It is God that avengeth me, and subdueth the people under me.

He delivereth me from mine enemies: yea, thou liftest me up above those that rise up against me: thou hast delivered me from the violent man.

Therefore will I give thanks unto thee, O LORD, among the heathen, and sing praises unto thy name.

Great deliverance giveth he to his king; and sheweth mercy to his anointed, to David, and to his seed for evermore.

SELECTION 46

Psalms XXXVI, LXXI

THE transgression of the wicked saith within my heart, that there is no fear of God before his eyes.

For he flattereth himself in his own eyes, until his iniquity be found to be hateful.

The words of his mouth are iniquity and deceit: he hath left off to be wise, and to do good.

He deviseth mischief upon his bed; he setteth himself in a way that is not good; he abhorreth not evil.

Thy mercy, O LORD, is in the heavens; and thy faithfulness reacheth unto the clouds.

Thy righteousness is like the great mountains; thy judgments are a great deep: O LORD, thou preservest man and beast.

How excellent is thy lovingkindness, O God!

Therefore the children of men put their trust under the shadow of thy wings.

They shall be abundantly satisfied with the fatness of thy house;

And thou shalt make them drink of the river of thy pleasures.

For with thee is the fountain of life: in thy light shall we see light.

O continue thy lovingkindness unto them that know thee; and thy righteousness to the upright in heart.

In thee, O LORD, do I put my trust: let me never be put to confusion.

Deliver me in my righteousness, and cause me to escape: incline thine ear unto me, and save me.

Be thou my strong habitation, whereunto I may continually resort:

Thou hast given commandment to save me; for thou art my rock and my fortress.

Deliver me, O my God, out of the hand of the wicked,

Out of the hand of the unrighteous and cruel man.

For thou art my hope, O Lord GOD: thou art my trust from my youth.

Cast me not off in the time of old age; forsake me not when my strength faileth.

For mine enemies speak against me; and they that lay wait for my soul take counsel together, saying, God hath forsaken him: persecute and take him; for there is none to deliver him.

O God, be not far from me: O my God, make haste for my help.

Let them be confounded and consumed that are adversaries to my soul; let them be covered with reproach and dishonour that seek my hurt.

But I will hope continually, and will yet praise thee more and more.

My mouth shall shew forth thy righteousness and thy salvation all the day; for I know not the numbers thereof.

I will go in the strength of the Lord GOD: I will make mention of thy righteousness, even of thine only.

O God, thou hast taught me from my youth: and hitherto have I declared thy wondrous works.

Now also when I am old and gray-headed, O God, forsake me not; until I have shewed thy strength unto this generation, and thy power to every one that is to come.

Thy righteousness also, O God, is very high, who hast done great things: O God, who is like unto thee!

Thou, which hast shewed me great and sore troubles, shalt quicken me again, and shalt bring me up again from the depths of the earth.

Thou shalt increase my greatness, and comfort me on every side.

I will also praise thee with the psaltery, even thy truth, O my God: unto thee will I sing with the harp, O thou Holy One of Israel.

SELECTION 47

Psalms III, XXX, CXXIV

LORD, how are they increased that trouble me! many are they that rise up against me.

Many there be which say of my soul, There is no help for him in God.

But thou, O LORD, art a shield for me; my glory, and the lifter up of mine head.

I cried unto the LORD with my voice, and he heard me out of his holy hill.

I laid me down and slept; I awaked; for the LORD sustained me.

I will not be afraid of ten thousands of people, that have set themselves against me round about.

Arise, O LORD; save me, O my God: for thou hast smitten all mine enemies upon the cheek bone; thou hast broken the teeth of the ungodly.

Salvation belongeth unto the LORD: thy blessing is upon thy people.

I will extol thee, O LORD; for thou hast lifted me up, and hast not made my foes to rejoice over me.

O LORD my God, I cried unto thee, and thou hast healed me.

O LORD, thou hast brought up my soul from the grave: thou hast kept me alive, that I should not go down to the pit.

Sing unto the LORD, O ye saints of his, and give thanks at the remembrance of his holiness.

For his anger endureth but a moment; in his favour is life:

Weeping may endure for a night, but joy cometh in the morning.

And in my prosperity I said, I shall never be moved.

LORD, by thy favour thou hast made my mountain to stand strong: thou didst hide thy face, and I was troubled.

I cried to thee, O LORD; and unto the LORD I made supplication.

What profit is there in my blood, when I go down to the pit? Shall the dust praise thee? shall it declare thy truth?

Hear, O LORD, and have mercy upon me;

LORD, be thou my helper.

Thou hast turned for me my mourning into dancing:

Thou hast put off my sackcloth, and girded me with gladness;

To the end that my glory may sing praise to thee, and not be silent.

O LORD my God, I will give thanks unto thee for ever.

If it had not been the LORD who was on our side, now may Israel say; if it had not been the LORD who was on our side, when men rose up against us:

Then they had swallowed us up quick, when their wrath was kindled against us:

Then the waters had overwhelmed us, the stream had gone over our soul:

Then the proud waters had gone over our soul.

Blessed be the LORD, who hath not given us as a prey to their teeth. Our soul is escaped as a bird out of the snare of the fowlers:

The snare is broken, and we are escaped. Our help is in the name of the LORD, who made heaven and earth.

SELECTION 48

Psalms XLIX, XXXIX

HEAR this, all ye people; Give ear, all ye inhabitants of the world: both low and high, rich and poor, together.

My mouth shall speak of wisdom; and the meditation of my heart shall be of understanding.

I will incline mine ear to a parable: I will open my dark saying upon the harp.

Wherefore should I fear in the days of evil,

When the iniquity of my heels shall compass me about?

They that trust in their wealth, and boast themselves in the multitude of their riches; none of them can by any means redeem his brother, nor give to God a ransom for him:

(For the redemption of their soul is precious, and it ceaseth for ever:)

That he should still live for ever, and not see corruption.

For he seeth that wise men die, likewise the fool and the brutish person perish, and leave their wealth to others.

Their inward thought is, that their houses shall continue for ever, and their dwellingplaces to all generations;

They call their lands after their own names.

Nevertheless man being in honour abideth not: he is like the beasts that perish.

This their way is their folly: yet their posterity approve their sayings.

Like sheep they are laid in the grave; death shall feed on them; and the upright shall have dominion over them in the morning; and their beauty shall consume in the grave from their dwelling.

But God will redeem my soul from the power of the grave: for he shall receive me.

Be not thou afraid when one is made rich, when the glory of his house is increased; for when he dieth he shall carry nothing away: his glory shall not descend after him.

Though while he lived he blessed his soul, and men will praise thee, when thou doest well to thyself.

He shall go to the generation of his fathers; they shall never see light.

Man that is in honour, and understandeth not, is like the beasts that perish.

I said, I will take heed to my ways, that I sin not with my tongue: I will keep my mouth with a bridle, while the wicked is before me.

I was dumb with silence, I held my peace, even from good; and my sorrow was stirred.

My heart was hot within me; while I was musing the fire burned:

Then spake I with my tongue, LORD, make me to know mine end, and the measure of my days, what it is; that I may know how frail I am.

Behold, thou hast made my days as a handbreadth; and mine age is as nothing before thee:

Verily every man at his best state is altogether vanity.

Surely every man walketh in a vain shew: surely they are disquieted in vain:

He heapeth up riches, and knoweth not who shall gather them.

And now, Lord, what wait I for? my hope is in thee.

Deliver me from all my transgressions: make me not the reproach of the foolish.

I was dumb, I opened not my mouth; because thou didst it.

Remove thy stroke away from me: I am consumed by the blow of thine hand.

When thou with rebukes dost correct man for iniquity, thou makest his beauty to consume away like a moth:

Surely every man is vanity.

Hear my prayer, O LORD, and give ear unto my cry; hold not thy peace at my tears: for I am a stranger with thee, and a sojourner, as all my fathers were.

O spare me, that I may recover strength, before I go hence, and be no more.

SELECTION 49

Psalms XC, XCI

LORD, thou hast been our dwelling-place in all generations.

Before the mountains were brought forth, or ever thou hadst formed the earth and the world, even from everlasting to everlasting, thou art God.

Thou turnest man to destruction; and sayest, Return, ye children of men.

For a thousand years in thy sight are but as yesterday when it is past, and as a watch in the night.

Thou carriest them away as with a flood; they are as a sleep: in the morning they are like grass which groweth up.

In the morning it flourisheth, and groweth up; in the evening it is cut down, and withereth.

For we are consumed by thine anger, and by thy wrath are we troubled.

Thou hast set our iniquities before thee, our secret sins in the light of thy countenance.

For all our days are passed away in thy wrath: we spend our years as a tale that is told.

The days of our years are threescore years and ten; and if by reason of strength they be fourscore years, yet is their strength labour and sorrow; for it is soon cut off, and we fly away.

Who knoweth the power of thine anger? even according to thy fear, so is thy wrath.

So teach us to number our days, that we may apply our hearts unto wisdom.

Return, O LORD, how long? and let it repent thee concerning thy servants.

O satisfy us early with thy mercy; that we may rejoice and be glad all our days.

Make us glad according to the days wherein thou hast afflicted us, and the years wherein we have seen evil.

Let thy work appear unto thy servants, and thy glory unto their children.

And let the beauty of the LORD our God be upon us: and establish thou the work of our hands upon us;

Yea, the work of our hands establish thou it.

He that dwelleth in the secret place of the Most High shall abide under the shadow of the Almighty.

I will say of the LORD, He is my refuge and my fortress: my God; in him will I trust.

Surely he shall deliver thee from the snare of the fowler, and from the noisome pestilence.

He shall cover thee with his feathers, and under his wings shalt thou trust: his truth shall be thy shield and buckler.

Thou shalt not be afraid for the terror by night; nor for the arrow that flieth by day;

Nor for the pestilence that walketh in darkness; nor for the destruction that wasteth at noonday.

A thousand shall fall at thy side, and ten thousand at thy right hand; but it shall not come nigh thee.

Only with thine eyes shalt thou behold and see the reward of the wicked.

Because thou hast made the LORD, which is my refuge, even the Most High, thy habitation; there shall no evil befall thee, neither shall any plague come nigh thy dwelling.

For he shall give his angels charge over thee, to keep thee in all thy ways.

They shall bear thee up in their hands, lest thou dash thy foot against a stone.

Thou shalt tread upon the lion and adder: the young lion and the dragon shalt thou trample under feet.

Because he hath set his love upon me, therefore will I deliver him:

I will set him on high, because he hath known my name.

He shall call upon me, and I will answer him: I will be with him in trouble; I will deliver him, and honour him.

With long life will I satisfy him, and shew him my salvation.

SELECTION 50

THE BIRTH OF CHRIST

Isaiah

AND there shall come forth a rod out of the stem of Jesse,

And a Branch shall grow out of his roots:

And the Spirit of the LORD shall rest upon him, the spirit of wisdom and understanding,

The spirit of counsel and might, the spirit of knowledge and of the fear of the LORD;

And shall make him of quick understanding in the fear of the LORD:

And he shall not judge after the sight of his eyes, neither reprove after the hearing of his ears:

But with righteousness shall he judge the poor, and reprove with equity for the meek of the earth:

And he shall smite the earth with the rod of his mouth, and with the breath of his lips shall he slay the wicked.

And righteousness shall be the girdle of his loins,

And faithfulness the girdle of his reins.

The wolf also shall dwell with the lamb, and the leopard shall lie down with the kid; and the calf and the young lion and the fatling together;

And a little child shall lead them.

And the cow and the bear shall feed, their young ones shall lie down together: and the lion shall eat straw like the ox.

And the sucking child shall play on the hole of the asp, and the weaned child shall put his hand on the cockatrice' den.

They shall not hurt nor destroy in all my holy mountain:

For the earth shall be full of the knowledge of the LORD, as the waters cover the sea.

The voice of him that crieth in the wilderness, Prepare ye the way of the LORD,

Make straight in the desert a highway for our God.

Every valley shall be exalted, and every mountain and hill shall be made low:

And the crooked shall be made straight, and the rough places plain:

And the glory of the LORD shall be revealed, and all flesh shall see it together:

For the mouth of the LORD hath spoken it.

O Zion, that bringest good tidings, get thee up into the high mountain; O Jerusalem, that bringest good tidings, lift up thy voice with strength;

Lift it up, be not afraid; say unto the cities of Judah, Behold your God!

Behold, the Lord GOD will come with strong hand, and his arm shall rule for him:

Behold, his reward is with him, and his work before him.

He shall feed his flock like a shepherd:

He shall gather the lambs with his arm, and carry them in his bosom.

The people that walked in darkness have seen a great light:

They that dwell in the land of the shadow of death, upon them hath the light shined.

For unto us a child is born, unto us a son is given: and the government shall be upon his shoulder:

And his name shall be called Wonderful, Counsellor, The mighty God, The everlasting Father, The Prince of Peace.

Of the increase of his government and peace there shall be no end, upon the throne of David, and upon his kingdom, to order it, and to establish it with judgment and with justice from henceforth even for ever.

The zeal of the LORD of hosts will perform this.

The wilderness and the solitary place shall be glad for them;

And the desert shall rejoice, and blossom as the rose.

It shall blossom abundantly, and rejoice even with joy and singing: the glory of Lebanon shall be given unto it, the excellency of Carmel and Sharon;

They shall see the glory of the LORD, and the excellency of our God.

Strengthen ye the weak hands, and confirm the feeble knees. Say to them that are of a fearful heart, Be strong fear not:

Behold, your God will come with vengeance, even God with a recompense; he will come and save you.

Then the eyes of the blind shall be opened; and the ears of the deaf shall be unstopped.

Then shall the lame man leap as a hart, and the tongue of the dumb sing:

For in the wilderness shall waters break out, and streams in the desert.

And the parched ground shall become a pool, and the thirsty land springs of water: in the habitation of dragons, where each lay, shall be grass with reeds and rushes.

And a highway shall be there, and a way, and it shall be called The way of holiness; the unclean shall not pass over it; but it shall be for those:

The wayfaring men, though fools, shall not err therein.

No lion shall be there, nor any ravenous beast shall go up thereon, it shall not be found there;

But the redeemed shall walk there:

And the ransomed of the LORD shall return, and come to Zion with songs and everlasting joy upon their heads:

They shall obtain joy and gladness, and sorrow and sighing shall flee away.

SELECTION 51

THE DEATH OF CHRIST
Isaiah LIII

WHO hath believed our report?

And to whom is the arm of the LORD revealed?

For he shall grow up before him as a tender plant, and as a root out of a dry ground:

He hath no form nor comeliness; and when we shall see him, there is no beauty that we should desire him.

He is despised and rejected of men; a man of sorrows, and acquainted with grief:

And we hid as it were our faces from him; he was despised, and we esteemed him not.

Surely he hath borne our griefs, and carried our sorrows:

Yet we did esteem him stricken, smitten of God, and afflicted.

But he was wounded for our transgressions, he was bruised for our iniquities:

The chastisement of our peace was upon him; and with his stripes we are healed.

All we like sheep have gone astray; we have turned every one to his own way;

And the Lord hath laid on him the iniquity of us all.

He was oppressed, and he was afflicted, yet he opened not his mouth:

He is brought as a lamb to the slaughter, and as a sheep before her shearers is dumb, so he openeth not his mouth.

He was taken from prison and from judgment: and who shall declare his generation?

For he was cut off out of the land of the living: for the transgression of my people was he stricken.

And he made his grave with the wicked, and with the rich in his death;

Because he had done no violence, neither was any deceit in his mouth.

Yet it pleased the Lord to bruise him; he hath put him to grief:

When thou shalt make his soul an offering for sin, he shall see his seed, he shall prolong his days, and the pleasure of the Lord shall prosper in his hand.

He shall see of the travail of his soul, and shall be satisfied:

By his knowledge shall my righteous servant justify many; for he shall bear their iniquities.

Therefore will I divide him a portion with the great,

And he shall divide the spoil with the strong;

Because he hath poured out his soul unto death: and he was numbered with the transgressors;

And he bare the sin of many, and made intercession for the transgressors.

SELECTION 52

THE RESURRECTION OF CHRIST
Psalms

SING aloud unto God our strength:

Make a joyful noise unto the God of Jacob.

Take a psalm, and bring hither the timbrel, the pleasant harp with the psaltery.

Blow up the trumpet in the new moon, in the time appointed, on our solemn feast day.

I will extol thee, O Lord; for thou hast lifted me up, and hast not made my foes to rejoice over me.

O Lord my God, I cried unto thee, and thou hast healed me.

O Lord, thou hast brought up my soul from the grave:

Thou hast kept me alive, that I should not go down to the pit.

Sing unto the Lord, O ye saints of his,

And give thanks at the remembrance of his holiness.

For his anger endureth but a moment; in his favour is life:

Weeping may endure for a night, but joy cometh in the morning.

LORD, by thy favour thou hast made my mountain to stand strong: thou didst hide thy face, and I was troubled.

I cried to thee, O LORD; and unto the LORD I made supplication.

Thou hast turned for me my mourning into dancing:

Thou hast put off my sackcloth, and girded me with gladness;

To the end that my glory may sing praise to thee, and not be silent.

O LORD my God, I will give thanks unto thee for ever.

I have set the LORD always before me: because he is at my right hand, I shall not be moved.

Therefore my heart is glad, and my glory rejoiceth: my flesh also shall rest in hope.

For thou wilt not leave my soul in hell; neither wilt thou suffer thine Holy One to see corruption.

Thou wilt shew me the path of life: in thy presence is fulness of joy; at thy right hand there are pleasures for evermore.

Open to me the gates of righteousness:

I will go into them, and I will praise the LORD:

This gate of the LORD, into which the righteous shall enter.

I will praise thee: for thou hast heard me, and art become my salvation.

The stone which the builders refused is become the head stone of the corner.

This is the LORD'S doing; it is marvellous in our eyes.

This is the day which the LORD hath made;

We will rejoice and be glad in it.

Lift up your heads, O ye gates; and be ye lifted up, ye everlasting doors;

And the king of glory shall come in.

Who is this king of glory?

The LORD strong and mighty, the LORD mighty in battle.

Lift up your heads, O ye gates; even lift them up, ye everlasting doors;

And the King of glory shall come in.

Who is this King of glory?

The LORD of hosts, he is the King of glory.

He shall have dominion also from sea to sea, and from the river unto the ends of the earth.

Yea, all kings shall fall down before him; all nations shall serve him.

For he shall deliver the needy when he crieth; the poor also, and him that hath no helper.

He shall spare the poor and needy, and shall save the souls of the needy.

He shall redeem their soul from deceit and violence:

And precious shall their blood be in his sight.

And he shall live, and to him shall be given of the gold of Sheba:

Prayer also shall be made for him continually; and daily shall he be praised.

There shall be a handful of corn in the earth upon the top of the mountains;

The fruit thereof shall shake like Lebanon: and they of the city shall flourish like grass of the earth.

His name shall endure for ever: his name shall be continued as long as the sun:

And men shall be blessed in him: all nations shall call him blessed.

Blessed be the LORD God, the God of Israel, who only doeth wondrous things.

And blessed be his glorious name for ever: and let the whole earth be filled with his glory. Amen, and Amen.